HISTORY AND MEMORY

European Perspectives

European Perspectives

EUROPEAN PERSPECTIVES

A Series in Social Philosophy and Cultural Criticism

Lawrence D. Kritzman and
Richard Wolin, Editors

European Perspectives seeks to make available works of interdisciplinary interest by leading European thinkers. By presenting classic texts and outstanding contemporary works, the series hopes to shape the major intellectual controversies of our day and thereby to facilitate the tasks of historical understanding.

Julia Kristeva *Strangers to Ourselves*
Theodor W. Adorno *Notes to Literature,* vols. I and II
Richard Wolin *The Heidegger Controversy: A Critical Reader*
Antonio Gramsci *Prison Notebooks,* vol. I
Alain Finkielkraut *Remembering in Vain: The Klaus Barbie Trial and Crimes Against Humanity*
Pierre Vidal-Naquet *Assassins of Memory*

HISTORY AND MEMORY

JACQUES LE GOFF

Translated by Steven Rendall and Elizabeth Claman

Columbia University Press
New York

Columbia University Press wishes to express
its appreciation of assistance given by the
government of France through Le Ministère de la Culture
in the preparation of this translation.

Columbia University Press
New York Oxford

Library of Congress Cataloging-in-Publication Data

Le Goff, Jacques, 1949–
[Storia e memoria. English]
History and memory / Jacques Le Goff ; translated by Steven Rendall and Elizabeth Claman.
p. cm.—(European perspectives)
Includes bibliographical references and index.
ISBN 0-231-07590-1 PA ISBN 0-231-07591-X
1. History—Philosophy. 2. Memory (Philosophy) I. Title II. Series.
D16.9.L413 1992
901—dc20 92-19887
CIP

♾

Casebound editions of
Columbia University Press books
are Smyth-sewn and printed
on permanent and durable
acid-free paper.

Book design: Teresa Bonner
Printed in the United States of America
c 10 9 8 7 6 5 4 3 2 1
p 10 9 8 7 6 5 4 3 2 1

CONTENTS

PREFACE

I am pleased that my reflections on history and memory are being made available to the English-reading public. The essays in this book were written a decade ago, but apart from updating the bibliography, I have not attempted to revise them. If in fact historiography has undergone what some writers have called a crisis—I should prefer to call it a mutation—the changes that have occurred are still not definitive, or even clear.

In the essays that follow, I have discussed the "returns" in the sense of history: the return of narrative, the return of the event, the return of biography, the return of politics. These returns appear to develop in two quite different directions. For some historians, and this is both a renewal and an enrichment, the problem of narrative concerns the nature of historical writing rather than the conception of history itself. These historians have approached the event, biography, and politics with radically new conceptual frameworks that acknowledge the contributions made by new historical methods. The event is considered as the tip of an iceberg, biography does not oppose the individual and society but treats them as mutually illuminating, and politics does not deal with the old political history but with the new problematics of power. But at the same time, banal, reactionary modes of history—narrative, the history of events, biography, and political history—continue or stage comebacks. This shows, in my view, that the "fight for history" that Lucien Febvre talked about long ago is not yet over. History in general is never over, and historiography, which is part of history, is not over either.

The traditional history of ideas is tending to give way to a new intellectual history less focused on concepts and more concerned with institutions and with the social practice of ideas. The history of mentalities tends to draw on and gain precision from the history of values and the history of the Imaginary.

In 1989, on the occasion of the sixtieth anniversary of the founding of its journal, the *Annales* group published an article titled "A Critical Turning-point?" This article called on historians to foreswear lazy habits and to develop a new interdisciplinarity. If the social sciences in general are in crisis, and if historians are no longer able to converse with sociologists and ethnologists in the way they have become accustomed to doing for the past few decades, historians must nevertheless continue their dialogue with the social sciences even as the latter change.

Finally, it seems to me that the determination of certain historians not to confine themselves to European and Western historiographical traditions, along with the long-standing but little revitalized desire to move in the direction of comparative studies are more important than ever, and could bring about a profound change in the field of historiography in the coming years.

A twenty-first century historiography remains to be developed. I believe the relations between history as it occurs, history as historians write it, and the memory of men, women, peoples, and nations, will play a major role in the birth of this new historiography. That is why I will be delighted if the essays published in translation here can help the English-reading public participate in this transformation in a more informed and thoughtful way.

June 1992

The texts presented here first appeared in Italian translation in various volumes of the *Enciclopedia* published by Einaudi (Turin, 1977–82). They are the most important of a series of ten articles published in this encyclopedia. Their themes are: *past/present, antique/modern, memory,* and *history.* They were accompanied by articles on *progress/reaction, ages of myth, eschatology, decadence, calendar,* and *document/monument.* Einaudi later published these ten articles separately under the title *Storia e Memoria.*

Taken together, the four texts published here *(Past/Present, Antique/Modern, Memory, History)* form a general study of history. As encyclopedia articles, their first concern is to convey information. At one level, they are a history of history, or rather a history of historical procedures, historical mentalities, and the historian's craft. To lend depth, I have reflected on the relations between "objective" history as people experience it, whether they make it or undergo it, and the historical discipline—if one wants to avoid the word "science"—by which professional (and to a lesser degree, amateur) historians seek to master history as experienced, in order to conceive and explain it.

At the outset, I had to examine the relations between *history* and *memory.* Recent, naive trends seem virtually to identify history with memory, and even to give preference in some sense to memory, on the ground that it is more authentic, "truer" than history, which is presumed to be artificial and, above all, manipulative of memory. It is true that history involves a rearrangement of the past which is subject to the social, ideological, and political structures in which historians live and work. It is also true that history has been and still is, in some places, subject to conscious manipulation on the part of political regimes that oppose the truth. Nationalism and prejudices of all kinds have an impact on the way history is written, and the rapidly developing field of the history of history (a critical and highly evolved form of traditional historiography) is in part founded on the acknowledgment and study of these links between historical production and the context of its period as well as that of successive periods which modify its meaning. But the discipline of history, which has recognized these variations in historiography, must nonetheless seek to be objective and to remain based on the belief in historical "truth." Memory is the raw material of history. Whether mental, oral, or written, it is the living source from which historians draw. Because its workings are usually unconscious, it is in reality more dangerously subject to manipulation by time and by societies given to reflection than the discipline of history itself. Moreover, the discipline of history nourishes memory in turn, and enters into the great dialectical process of memory and forgetting experienced by individuals and societies. The historian must be there to render an account of these memories and of what is forgotten, to transform them into something that can be conceived, to make them knowable. To privilege memory excessively is to sink into the unconquerable flow of time.

I have also looked into the meaning for history of conceptual oppositions that are central to the historian's work. The opposition between *past* and *present* is fundamental, since the activity of memory and history is founded on this distinction, which appears in the history of collective knowledge, as it does—on other grounds and in other forms—in child psychology. The past/present opposition is essential, for historical work is carried out through a continual oscillation from one of its poles to the other. It is up to the historian to define the rules that govern this movement, to define conditions on which the "regressive" method supported by Marc Bloch is legitimate and fertile, and to maintain the distance and opacity that separate us from the past, even and especially if we agree with Croce that "history is always contemporary." We must also take care that chance illuminates rather than shackles us. The history of history in particular must be, as my friend Girolamo Arnaldi has put it, a "liberation from the past," and not the "burden of history" of which Hegel spoke.

This distinction between past and present, made both by common consciousness and by the historian, is seldom neutral. For some the past is a Golden Age, an exemplary time of innocence and virtue, an epoch of great ancestors; for others, it is barbarism, archaism, the lair of obsolete and outdated antiques, an epoch of physical and mental dwarfs. As for the present, it is, in corollary fashion, either the blessed age of progress, creativity, and civilization, or else a dangerous time of thoughtless innovations or a lamentable age of decline. Those who hold one or the other of these opinions are always able ultimately to find evidence for their views in history or in current events. Certainly, the Western world is coming out of a long phase dominated by the ideology of progress, which seems to have halted, in the seventeenth and eighteenth centuries, the dialectic of ancient and modern, but even in these centuries that lived and thought under the sign of progress there were traditionalists—"antirevolutionaries" or "reactionaries"—who challenged the reigning view. It seemed important to study this series of successive modernities, these recurring quarrels between ancients and moderns, that have punctuated the development of the historical mentality in the West.

I have, of course, conducted the study primarily in the domain of Western thought and historical production, which I know less poorly than those of other civilizations, and which have shown more sensitivity to the movement of history. But I have made an effort, using secondary sources, to give some attention to the attitudes of other societies toward history—including the so-called societies without history, which historians have long left to ethnologists and anthropologists. It was all the more important to go beyond Western civilization because the vicissitudes of our time have made us more sensitive to differences, to plurality, and to the Other.

In the vast fields that seem to me to lie open to historical science, and which are clearly linked to the evolution of the "objective" history of humanity, I distinguish two long-term, essential tasks, which are as yet hardly begun. The first is a comparative history, which alone would be able to give a relevant content to the apparently contradictory requirements of historical thought: the search for completeness on one hand, and the respect for singularities on the other; the determination of regularities on one hand, attention to the role of chance and rationality on the other: the articulation of concepts and histories. And beyond may loom, as Michel Foucault hoped, the still distant ambition to write a general history.

The reader must have guessed that if my primary concern in composing these texts was to provide information on the evolution of historical work and on the historian's craft, my own experiences, my background, and my choices also play a part in them. I have had the good luck to have worked and taught in the intellectual milieu that has probably contributed most to the renewal of history in our century, the one known as the "*Annales* School," associated with the journal founded in 1919 by Marc Bloch and Lucien Febvre, and directed by Fernand Braudel from 1956 to 1969. I have also had the privilege of being invited by Pierre Nora to prepare with him the three volumes of *Faire de l'histoire* (1974), which, with the cooperation of many historians in addition to those in the *Annales* group, has offered reference points and indicated possible avenues for enlarging the scope of history.

This is not the place to recall the details of this adventure or to take a position regarding the crisis in the social sciences, in history, and in the *Annales* School, which has been discussed from time to time with varying degrees of knowledge, sincerity, and competence. I shall respond to such views on another occasion, either personally, or with my *Annales* friends, who will be celebrating the sixtieth birthday of the journal in 1989. Here I shall simply say that the history to which these texts refer is what has been called "historical anthropology," in which history makes use of the methods of anthropology in order to reach the deepest levels of historical realities, whether these be material, mental, or political, while taking care to preserve the structured unity of humanity and of knowledge (see Burguière 1986:52–60).

It is nonetheless clear that the following texts bear the mark of the context in which they were written. Western historical thought has felt the full impact of the challenge to the idea of progress, an idea discredited by twentieth-century atrocities that have been brought to our attention by the media, a new source of historical documentation. From the Gulag to the torture chambers, from the Nazi extermination camps to apartheid and racism, from the horrors of war to those of famine, we have been forced to abandon our proud belief in a linear, continuous, and general progress, represented above all by spectacular advances in science and technology. A better knowledge of societies around the world, including the third world, and of their history, has led to the decline of the idea of a single model of development valid for all human societies.

In the less dramatic area of historical methodology, we have seen on the one hand what has been called the fragmentation of "history in small bits" (*histoire en miettes*) and, on the other, the return of traditional forms of history: a return of "narrative," of the "event," of "chronology," of "politics," of "biography." Here I shall simply say that if it is true that self-criticism and revisions are needed to make the historian's field more fertile, legitimate "returns" of this kind must not be like those of the émigrés who returned to France after the Revolution having "forgotten nothing and learned nothing." History needs changes and not reactions. In order to carry out the necessary changes and to resist those that would be regressive, historians have to call upon their lucidity, their vigilance, and their courage.

The front lines of history are still engaged in battle—despite the achievement of various kinds of consensus. A battle of ideas—about how best to "do history."

January 1988

Today, the concept of history seems to raise six kinds of questions:

1. What relationships are there between "lived history" (*histoire vécue*), that is, the "natural" if not "objective" history of human societies,

and the scientific effort to describe, think, and explain it? In other words, what is the relation between "lived history" and the science of history? The difference between these two senses of "history" has given rise to an ambiguous discipline: the philosophy of history. Since the beginning of the century, and especially for the past twenty years, a branch of historical science has been developing that studies its evolution within overall historical development: historiography or the history of history.

2. What relations does history entertain with time or duration, whether it is a matter of the "natural," cyclical time of climate and seasons or a matter of time as lived and naturally recorded by individuals and societies? On one hand, in order to domesticate natural time various societies and cultures have invented a basic instrument which is also an essential datum of history, the calendar; on the other, historians today are increasingly interested in the relations between history and memory.

3. The dialectic of history seems to be summed up in the opposition or dialogue between past and present (and/or between present and past). In general, this opposition is not neutral but subtends or expresses an evaluative system, as for example in the oppositional pairs ancient/modern and progress/reaction. From Antiquity to the eighteenth century, there developed around the concept of decadence a pessimistic vision of history that has been expressed in certain twentieth-century ideologies of history. In the Enlightenment, on the other hand, an optimistic vision of history based on the idea of progress was developed which entered a crisis in the second half of the twentieth century. Does history have a meaning? Is there a direction to history?

4. History is incapable of foreseeing and predicting the future. How then can it be situated with respect to a new "science," futurology? In reality, history ceases to be scientific when it seeks to answer questions about the beginning and the end of the history of the world and of humanity. As for origins, they are expressed in myth: the creation, the Golden Age, the mythical ages, or, in a scientific guise, the recent theory of the Big Bang. As for the end, history yields to religion (and in particular to the religions of salvation which have constructed a "knowledge of ultimate ends," eschatology) or to the utopias of progress, the chief one being Marxism, which juxtaposes an ideology of the meaning of history and an ideology of its goal (Communism, the classless society, internationalism). However, at the level of the historian's practice, a critique of the concept of origins is being developed, and the notion of genesis tends to replace the idea of origins.

5. As a result of his contacts with other social sciences, today's historian has a tendency to distinguish among different kinds of historical duration [*durée*]. There is a renaissance of interest in the event, but inversely, it is above all the perspective of "long duration" [*longue durée*] that interests historians. The latter leads certain historians, either in connection with the notion of structure, or through a dialogue with anthropology, to advance the hypothesis of an "almost immobile" history. But can there be an immobile history, and what are the relations between history and structuralism (or structuralisms)? Is there not also another, perhaps broader tendency to "reject history"?

6. The idea of history as human history has been replaced by the idea of history as a scientific study of humankind in society. But is there, can there ever be, a history of humankind? A history of climate has already developed; shouldn't there also be a history of nature?

1. Since its birth in Western societies—a birth traditionally located in Greek Antiquity (Herodotus, in the sixth century B.C. is supposed to be, if not the first historian, at least the "father of history"), but which actually goes back to a more distant past in the empires of the Near, Middle, and Far East—historical science has been defined in relation to a reality which is neither constructed nor observed (as in mathematics and the physical and biological sciences), but concerning which "investigations" and "testimonies" occur. That is the meaning of the Greek word *historia* and its Indo-European root *wid-weid* (to see). History thus began as a narrative told by someone who could say: "I have seen, I have heard it said." This aspect of history-as-narrative, of history-as-testimony has persisted throughout the development of historical science. Paradoxically, today we are seeing a critique of this kind of history motivated by the desire to substitute explanation for narration, but at the same time, we see the renaissance of history-as-testimony through the "return to the event" (Nora) that is connected with the new media, with the appearance of journalists among historians and with the development of "immediate history."

Nevertheless, since Antiquity, by collecting *written documents* and transforming them into testimony, historical science has gone beyond the fifty- to one-hundred-year span attained by historians who were ocular or auricular witnesses and by the oral transmission of the past. The establishment of libraries and archives has thus furnished the materials for history. *Scientific* methods of criticism have been elaborated, thereby conferring on history one of the characteristics that make it *scientific* in the technical sense. The first uncertain steps toward these methods were taken in the Middle Ages (Guenée), but they were developed primarily since the end of the seventeenth century by Du Cange, Mabillon, and the Benedictines of Saint-Maur, Muratori, and others. In fact, there is no such thing as history without *scholarship*. But just as the twentieth century has criticized the notion of historical fact (which is not a given object, because it is constructed by the historian), today it criticizes the notion of a document. The document is not objective, innocent raw material, but expresses past society's power over memory and over the future: the document is what remains (Foucault, Le Goff). At the same time, the range of documents has been broadened. Traditional history reduced it to texts and to the discoveries of an archeology too often separated from history. Today documents include the spoken word, the image, and gestures. *Oral archives* are being established, and *ethnotexts* collected. Even the archival storage of documents has been revolutionized by the use of computers. *Quantitative history*, from demography to economic and even cultural history, is linked to advances in statistical methods and information theory applied to the social sciences.

The distance between "historical reality" and historical science has allowed philosophers and historians from Antiquity to the present to propose systems of overall explanation for history (in the twentieth century, and in extremely different senses, Spengler, Weber, Croce, Gramsci, Toynbee, Aron, et al., may be mentioned). Most historians are more or less wary of the philosophy of history, but they are nonetheless turning away from the positivism that was dominant in German (Ranke) or French (Langlois and Seignobos) historiography at the turn of the century. Between ideology and pragmatism, we may locate the supporters of history-as-problem (Febvre).

To grasp the development of history and to make it the object of a genuine science, historians and philosophers since Antiquity have tried to find and define historical laws. The efforts that have gone farthest in this direction, and that resulted in the greatest failure, are the old Christian theories of Providentialism (Bossuet) on one hand, and on the other, vulgar Marxism. The latter persists—despite the fact that in Marx there is no mention of historical laws (contrary to what is the case in Lenin's writings)—in making historical materialism into a pseudoscience of historical determinism increasingly in conflict with the facts and with historical thought.

On the other hand, certain considerations allow us to set aside the possibility that history will return to pure narrative: the possibility of a rational interpretation of history, the recognition of certain regularities in the course of history (the basis for a *comparative* historical study of different societies and structures), and the elaboration of *models* that reject the existence of a single, unique model (the broadening of history to the whole world in all its complexity, the influence of ethnology, the sensitivity to differences and to the need to respect others all moving in this same direction).

Moreover, the conditions under which historians work explain why the problem of the historian's *objectivity* has been repeatedly raised. The recognition that the historical fact is constructed and that documents are not innocent has thrown a glaring light on the manipulations that manifest themselves at all levels of the construction of historical knowledge. But this observation must not result in a fundamental skepticism with regard to historical objectivity or in an abandonment of the notion of *truth* in history. On the contrary, the continual advances in unmasking and denouncing mystifications and falsifications allow us to be relatively optimistic in that regard.

Nevertheless, the historian's necessary horizon of objectivity should not be allowed to conceal the fact that history is *also* a social practice (de Certeau) and that if we have to reject positions which, in line with vulgar Marxism or an equally vulgar reaction, confuse historical science with politics, it is legitimate to observe that the interpretation of the history of the world hinges on a will to transform it (for example, in the Marxist revolutionary tradition, but also from other perspectives, such as those of the heirs of Tocqueville and Weber who closely associate historical analysis with political liberalism).

The criticism of the notion of historical fact has led, moreover, to the recognition of "historical realities" long unknown to historians. Alongside political, economic, social, and cultural history, a history of *representations* has grown up. The latter has taken diverse forms: a history of overall conceptions of society or a history of *ideologies*; a history of the mental structures common to members of a social category or a society in a particular period, or a history of *mentalities*; a history of intellectual productions linked not to texts, the spoken word, or gestures, but to images, or a history of the *imagination* [*imaginaire*] which allows us to treat the literary document and the artistic document as historical documents in their entirety, on the condition that we respect their specificity;

a history of the modes of conduct, practices, and rituals that refer to a hidden, underlying reality, or a history of the *Symbolic* which will perhaps lead someday to a *psychoanalytic* history whose scientific credentials seem not yet fully established. Finally, with the development of *historiography*, of the *history of history*, historical science itself has been situated within a historical perspective.

All these new areas of history represent an important broadening of the field. However, we must avoid two errors in this regard. Instead of subordinating the realities of the history of representations to other realities which are alone granted the status of first causes (material and economic realities), we must give up the false problematics of infrastructure and superstructure. But we must also avoid privileging the new realities, considering them in turn the driving force in history. An effective historical explanation must recognize the existence of the Symbolic within every historical reality (including economics), but also compare these historical representations with the realities they represent and which the historian apprehends by means of other documents and other methods. For example, we should compare political ideology with practice and with political events. Every history should be a *social history*.

Finally, the "unique" character of historical events, and the historian's need to mix narrative and explanation, have made history a literary genre, an art at the same time as a science. While this was true from Antiquity to the nineteenth century, from Thucydides to Michelet, it is less so today. The increasingly technical nature of historical science has made it more difficult for the historian also to be a writer. But there is still a *way of writing history* [*une écriture de l'histoire*] that cannot be reduced to the individual historian's style.

2. The basic material of history is time. For a long while, therefore, chronology has played an essential role as the armature and auxiliary of history. The main tool of chronology is the calendar, which goes back far beyond the historian's field, since it is the fundamental temporal framework within which societies function. The calendar shows the effort made by human societies to domesticate "natural" time, the natural movement of the moon or the sun, the cycle of the seasons, the alternation of day and night. But its most effective articulations, the hour and the week, are linked to culture and not to nature. The calendar is the product and the expression of history; it is linked to the mythical and religious origins of humanity (in festivals), to scientific and technological progress (as a measure of time), to economic, social, and cultural

evolution (times for work, times for leisure). It shows the effort made by human societies to transform the cyclical time of nature and myths, of the eternal return, into a linear time, punctuated by groups of years: *lustra*, Olympiads, centuries, eras, etc. Two important advances are intimately connected with history: the definition of the chronological starting point (the foundation of Rome, the birth of Christ, the Hegira, etc.) and the search for a *periodization*, the creation of equal, measurable units of time: the 24-hour day, the century, etc. Today, the application to history of the results of philosophy, science, and individual and collective experience tends to introduce, alongside these measurable categories of historical time, the notions of duration [*durée*], of lived time [*temps vécue*], of multiple and relative times, and of subjective or symbolic times. Historical time is rediscovering at a new, very sophisticated level the old time of memory, which is broader than history and supplies it with material.

3/4. The past/present opposition is essential to the acquisition of a consciousness of time. For the child, "understanding time" means freeing himself from the present (Piaget). But the time of history is not that of the psychologist or the linguist. All the same, an examination of temporality in psychology and linguistics confirms the fact that the present/past opposition is not a natural given but a construction. On the other hand, the recognition that the way the same past is perceived changes in different periods and that the historian is subject to the time in which he lives, has led to either skepticism regarding the possibility of knowing the past, or to an effort to eliminate any reference at all to the present (the illusion of romantic historians like Michelet—the "complete resurrection of the past"—or of positivist historians like Ranke—"what really happened"). In reality, the interest of the past is that it illuminates the present. The past is reached by starting out from the present (Bloch's regressive method). Until the Renaissance, and even up to the eighteenth century, occidental societies privileged the past; the time of origins and ancestors appeared to them to be a time of innocence and happiness. They imagined mythical ages, the Golden Age, the earthly paradise. The history of the world and of humanity seemed to be a long decline. This idea of decadence was taken up again to express the final phase in the history of societies and civilizations. It plays a role in a more or less cyclical view of history (Vico, Montesquieu, Gibbon, Spengler, Toynbee); it is generally the product of a reactionary philosophy of history, and a concept of little utility for historical science. In late seventeenth- and early eighteenth-century Europe, the "Quarrel of the Ancients and the Moderns," which began as a debate about science, literature, and art, showed a tendency to reverse the privilege accorded the past. "Ancient" became a synonym of "outdated," and "modern" a synonym of "progressive." In reality, the idea of progress triumphed in the Enlightenment, and developed all through the nineteenth and the early twentieth centuries, particularly with reference to scientific and technological advances. After the French Revolution, the ideology of progress confronted a reactionary tendency whose expression took mainly a political form, but was based on a "reactionary" interpretation of history. In the middle of the twentieth century, the failures of Marxism and the revelation of the reality of the Stalinist period and of the Gulag, the horrors of Fascism and especially of Nazism and the concentration camps, the death and destruction caused by the Second World War, the atomic bomb (the first "objective" historical incarnation of a possible apocalypse), and the discovery of cultures different from those of the West all led to a critique of the idea of progress (let us mention here Friedmann's *The Crisis of Progress*, 1936). The belief in a linear, continuous, irreversible progress, which develops according to the same model in all societies, is practically dead. History, which does not control the future, finds itself confronted by beliefs that are currently enjoying a great reawakening: prophecies, generally catastrophic visions of the end of the world, or, on the contrary, mystical revolutions like those invoked by millenarians, whether in sects within Western societies or in certain societies of the Third World. This is the return of eschatology.

But the natural sciences, and particularly biology, maintain a positive, even if attenuated, view of development as progress. Their perspectives can be applied to social sciences and to history. Thus genetics tends to renew the idea of evolution and progress, but to give a larger role to the event and to catastrophes (Thom). It is to history's advantage to substitute the dynamic idea of genesis for the passive idea of origins, which Marc Bloch criticized many years ago.

5. In the current renovation of historical science (which is accelerating, at least from the point of view of its diffusion; the principal impetus came from the journal *Annales*, founded by Bloch and Febvre in 1929), a major role is played by a new conception of historical time. According to this conception, history proceeds at different rates of speed, and the historian's task is above all to determine the rhythm of historical processes. It is not the superficial stratum, the rapid time of events, which is

most important, but rather the deeper level of the realities which change slowly (geography, material culture, mentalities; generally speaking, the *structures*). This is the level of "*longue durée*" (Braudel). The dialogue between historians of *longue durée* and other social sciences and with the physical and biological sciences—earlier, with economics and geography, and today with anthropology, demography, and biology—has led some historians to propose the idea of an "almost immobile" history (Braudel, Le Roy Ladurie). Some have even advanced the hypothesis that there is a completely immobile history. But *historical anthropology* begins on the contrary from the idea that movement and evolution are found in all the objects of all the social sciences because their common object is human societies (this is true not only in sociology and economics, but also in anthropology). As for history, it can only be a science of change and the explanation of change. History can have fruitful relations with various kinds of structuralisms on two conditions: a) that is does not forget that the structures it studies are dynamic; b) that it applies certain structuralist methods to the study of historical documents, to the analysis of *texts* (in the broad sense), and not to historical explanation proper. One may nevertheless wonder whether the vogue of structuralism is not connected with a certain rejection of history conceived as the dictatorship of the past, as a justification for "reproduction" (Bourdieu), as repressive power. But even on the extreme left it is recognized that it would be dangerous to make a "*tabula rasa* of the past" (Chesneaux). The "burden of history" in the "objective" sense of the term (Hegel) can and must be counterbalanced by historical science as a "means of liberation from the past" (Arnaldi).

6. In writing the history of their cities, their peoples, and their empires, the historians of Antiquity thought they were writing the history of humanity in general. Christian historians, Renaissance and Enlightenment historians (even though they recognized the diversity of "customs") thought they were writing the history of mankind. Modern historians observe that history is the science of the evolution of human societies. The evolution of the sciences has led us to ask whether there could not be a history different from that of man. A history of climate—the most changeable part of nature—has already been developed, but it is of interest to history only to the extent that it sheds light on certain phenomena in the history of human societies (changes in cultures, in the habitat, etc.). People are now thinking about a *history of nature* (Romano), but it would surely confirm the "cultural" (and hence historical)

conception of nature. Thus through the continual enlargement of its territory, history is still becoming coextensive with man.

While in its diverse forms (including the historical novel) history enjoys an unprecedented popularity in Western societies, and while third world nations are primarily preoccupied with giving themselves a history (which may, moreover, cause kinds of history to arise that are very different from those defined as such in Western countries), the paradox of historical science today is that if history has thus become an essential part of the need for individual and collective identity, it is precisely now that history is undergoing a crisis (of growth?). In its dialogue with other social sciences, in the considerable broadening of its problems, methods, and objects, historical science wonders whether it is not in the process of losing its way.

1986

HISTORY AND MEMORY

PAST/PRESENT

The distinction between past and present is an essential component of the concept of time. It is therefore fundamental to both historical consciousness and historical knowledge. Since the present cannot be limited to a single instant or point in time, the definition of the duration of the present constitutes an initial problem for the historian, whether it is acknowledged or not. The definition of the *contemporary* period in history curricula is a good test for this way of defining the historical present. For instance, it reveals the role played by the French Revolution in French national consciousness, because in France *contemporary* history begins officially in 1789. A variety of conscious and unconscious operations are presupposed at the collective level by this definition of the dividing point between past and present. Similar ideological dividing points are found among most peoples and nations. Thus Italy experienced two starting points for the "present" whose *telescoping* constitutes an important element of modern Italian historical consciousness: the Risorgimento and the demise of fascism. But this definition of the present—which is in fact a program, an ideological *project*—frequently runs into a much more complex historical obstacle. Gramsci wrote the following concerning the origin of the Risorgimento: "among Italians, the tradition of Roman and medieval universality limited the development of national (bourgeois) forces beyond the purely economic and municipal domain; that is, the "national" forces did not become a national "force" until after the French Revolution and the change in the position of the papacy in Europe." In this way the French Revolution (like the conversion of Constantine, the Hegira, or the Russian Revolution of 1917) first becomes a marker of the frontier between past and present, and later between a "before" and an "after." Gramsci's remark allows us to gauge the extent to which our relationship to the past, which Hegel called "the burden of history," is heavier for certain nations than for others (Le Goff 1974). But the *known* and *recognized* absence or brevity of the past can also create serious problems for the development of a collective mentality and identity—for instance, in young nations, particularly African ones (Assorodobraj). The United States provides a complex case in which the lack of a long history is combined with the varied and sometimes incompatible earlier heritages (especially European) accompanying the diverse ethnic components of the North American population, as well as with the overdetermination of relatively recent events in American history (the Revolutionary War, the Civil War, etc.) which are already part of a mythical past and are thus still actively present in the form of myths (Nora 1966).

Our habits concerning historical periodization thus lead us to privilege revolutions, wars, and changes in government—in other words, the history of *events*. This problem comes up again in the new relations between past and present that the so-called new history seeks to establish today. In addition, the official (i.e., academic) definition of *contemporary* history in countries such as France now requires us to speak of a *history of the present* in order to discuss the very recent past or the historical present (Nora 1974).

Although the past/present distinction that concerns us here exists in the collective consciousness, and more particularly in historical social consciousness, we must begin by commenting on the pertinence of this opposition, and by considering the past/present distinction from perspectives other than those of collective memory and history.

Let us note first that the perception and segmentation of time with respect to a before and an after, whether at the individual or the collective level, is not limited to the opposition between present and past. We must add a third dimension: the future. St. Augustine offered a profound formulation of this system composed of three temporal viewpoints when he said that we live only in the present, but this present has several dimensions: "the present of past things, the present of present things, and the present of future things."

Before considering the opposition between past and present in the framework of collective memory, it is also important to look at what it signifies in two other domains: psychology (especially child psychology) and linguistics.

The distinction between past and present in psychology

It would be a mistake to transpose the data of individual psychology into the domain of collective consciousness, and an even graver mistake to compare the child's acquisition of mastery over time to the evolution of conceptions of time through history. But reference to these domains can provide a certain number of clues (most of them metaphorical in nature) that can illuminate one aspect or another of the past/present opposition at the historical and collective levels.

For the child, "to understand time is to liberate oneself from the present: not only to anticipate the future in relation to the regularities unconsciously established in the past, but to deploy a series of states, each of which is different from the others, and whose connection can be established only by a gradual movement without fixation or stopping point" (Piaget 1946:274). To understand time "is essentially to demonstrate reversibility." In societies, the distinction between past and present (and future) also implies this ascent into memory and this liberation from the present, both of which in turn assume education, the constitution of a collective memory preceding and extending beyond the individual memory. The major difference is in fact that the child—despite the pressures of the external environment—personally constitutes in large measure his/her own memory, whereas the social, historical memory is shaped by tradition and education. But as an organized construct (see the section "Memory" below), the individual past parallels the collective past. "Through the play of these organizations, our temporal horizon develops far beyond the limits of our own lives. We treat the events provided by the history of our social group in the same way as we treat our own history. Moreover, these two histories tend to merge: the history of our childhood, for instance, is composed not only of our own first memories, but also of our parents' memories, and this part of our temporal perspective develops on the basis of both these components" (Fraisse, p. 170). Finally—and this is not automatically transferable to the domain of collective memory, but it clearly shows that human beings segment time in relation to a system with not two but three poles—the child progresses simultaneously in localizing the past and the future (Malrieu).

The pathology of individual attitudes toward time shows that "normal" behavior maintains an equilibrium between the consciousness of the past, the present and the future, but with a slight predominance of the orientation toward the future, whether the latter is feared or desired. The orientation toward the present, characteristic of very young children (who even "reconstitute the past in relation to the present," as Piaget has noted), of mentally defective or insane persons, as well as of former deportees whose personality has been disturbed, is encountered fairly commonly among old people and some persons with persecution complexes who fear the future. The classic example is Jean-Jacques Rousseau, who wrote in the *Confessions* that his "wild imagination," which led him "to foresee only a cruel future," made him take refuge in the present: "My heart is occupied by the present alone, which fills all its space and all its capacity." In other kinds of illness, the individual's anguish concerning time takes the form of a *flight toward the future* or a *refuge in the past*. The classic case of the latter, in literature, is Marcel Proust.

The opposition between the orientation toward the present and the orientation toward the past is fundamental to one of the central distinctions in Heymans and Le Senne's characterology; they posit the *primacy* of the former and the *secondariness* of the latter as basic structures of human character (Fraisse, p. 199).

The distinction between past and present in light of linguistics

The study of languages offers additional evidence whose value for our argument has to do both with the important role played in language by the distinction present/past/(future), especially in verbs, and with the fact that language is a phenomenon that is doubly dependent on collective history. Language—including its ways of expressing temporal relations—evolves through the ages, and it is closely linked to the recognition of national identity in the past. "The history of France," Michelet wrote, "begins with the French language."

Let us note first that the past/present/(future) distinction that seems so natural is far from universal in linguistics. Saussure pointed out long ago that "the distinction of tenses, which is so familiar to us, is alien to some languages: history does not recognize even the fundamental distinction between past present, and future. Proto-germanic does not have a specific form for the future. . . . Slavic languages regularly distinguish two aspects of the verb: the perfective represents an action as a whole, as a point, without reference to development; the imperfective shows it in process along a temporal line" (Saussure, see note). Modern linguistics adopts Saussure's insight: "the past/present/future distinction is not a universal characteristic" (J. Lyons). Some linguists insist on the construction of time in language, which goes far beyond the verb and concerns vocabulary, the sentence, and style. This leads some to refer to a "chronogenesis" (G. Guillaume). Here we encounter once more the fundamental idea of past and present seen as a construct, a logical organization, and not a simple given.

Joseph Vendryès has insisted on the inadequacy of the grammatical category of tense and the inconsistencies in the way languages make use of it. He notes for example that "it is a general tendency of language to use the present as a future[1] . . . . The past can also be expressed by using the present; in narratives, the so-called historical present is frequently used[2] . . . . Inversely, the past can serve to indicate the present[3] in French the past conditional can be used in speaking about the future: 'if I were given responsibility for this problem, I would resolve it quickly"' (pp. 118–21). The past/present/(future) distinction is malleable and subject to numerous forms of manipulation.

A particularly interesting example is the way time functions in narrative. Harald Weinrich has underscored the importance of the *foregrounding* of a given tense in narrative. Using a study by E. de Félice on medieval texts, he draws attention to the *attaco di raconto* (the narrative point of departure), distinguishing for example a narrative that begins in the preterit (*fuit*) from one that begins in the imperfect (*erat*). The past is not just the past; in its textual functioning it is, even before any exegesis, the bearer of religious, moral, and civic *values*. It can be the fabulous past of folk tales—"Once upon a time . . ." "In those days . . ."—or the sacralized past of the Gospels: "*In illo tempore . . .*"

André Miquel, using Weinrich's ideas to study a tale from the *Thousand and one Nights*, finds that it foregrounds an Arabic tense, the *mudi*, which expresses the past, the perfect or completed action, in relation to a subordinate tense, the *mudari*, which expresses concomitant or habitual action in the present (or imperfect). Since the past is authoritative, Miquel can show that this tale's goal or function is to recount for dispossessed Arabs a story about triumphant Arabs, to present them with a past conceived as a source, a foundation, or a guarantee of eternity.[4]

By charting changes in the way verb tenses and temporal expressions are used in language, historical grammar can also reveal the evolution of collective attitudes toward the past. For example, F. Brunot pointed out that in Old French (from the ninth to the thirteenth century) there was considerable confusion between tenses, a blurring of the past/present/(future), and that between the eleventh and the thirteenth centuries the use of the imperfect became increasingly important, while on the other hand in Middle French (fourteenth and fifteenth centuries) the use of each tense became more sharply delineated.[5] Paul Imbs has similarly maintained that language in the Middle Ages, at least in France, became clearer and clearer, more and more differentiated in order to express coincidence, simultaneity, posteriority, anteriority, etc. He also links different ways of conceiving and experiencing the relation between past and present with different social classes: the time of philosophers, theologians and poets oscillates between a fascination with the past and a drive toward future salvation; it is a time of both decadence and hope. The knight's time is characterized by speed, but it often turns in circles, confusing one point in time with another. The peasant's time is marked by regularity and patience; it is a past in which he seeks to maintain the present. The bourgeois's time, as we might expect, continually sharpens the distinction between past, present and future, and is characterized by the most insistent orientation toward the future.[6]

Finally, Emile Benveniste makes an important distinction between (1) physical time, which is continuous, uniform, infinite, linear, and can be segmented as one wishes, (2) chronological or "event" time, which is socialized as calendar time, and (3) linguistic time (tense), whose center is the present of the act of enunciation, the time of the speaker. "The only time inherent in language is the axial present of discourse, and this present is implicit. It determines two other temporal reference points; these are necessarily made explicit in a signifier, and in turn make the present appear as a line of demarcation between what is no longer present and what is going to become present. These two reference points do not relate to time, but to views of time, projected backward and forward from the present point" (1966:237–50).

Since historical time is usually expressed in the form of a *narrative*, both in the historian's work and in collective memory, it includes an insistent reference to the present, an implicit focus on the present. This is obviously especially true for traditional history, which has long been primarily a story-history, a narrative. Whence the ambiguity of even those historical discourses that seem to privilege the past, such as Michelet's program: history as the "integral resurrection of the past."

The distinction between past and present in primitive thought

The past/present distinction in "cold" societies, to borrow Claude Lévi-Strauss' terminology, is both weaker than that in "hot" societies and of a different order. It is *weaker* because in cold societies reference to the past is essentially to a mythical Creation or Golden Age (Le Goff 1986:227–61), and the time which is supposed to have to have elapsed between the Creation and the present is usually "flattened out." It is *different* because the "peculiarity of primitive thought is to be atemporal; it tries to grasp the world simultaneously as a synchronic and as a diachronic totality" (Lévi-Strauss 1962:348).

Through myths and rituals, primitive thought establishes a particular kind of relation between past and present: "mythical history is paradoxically both separated from the present and conjoined with it.... Through ritual, the mythical 'separate' past is connected on the one hand with biological and seasonal periodicity, and on the other with the 'conjoint' past which links, from one generation to another, the dead with the living" (Lévi-Strauss 1962:313).

In the case of Australian aborigines, for instance, one can distinguish between (1) *historical or commemorative rites* which "recreate the sacred and beneficent atmosphere of mythical times—a 'dream' age, the aborigines say—and mirror their protagonists and their high deeds," and which "transport the past into the present," and (2) *rites of mourning* which "correspond to an inverse procedure: instead of assigning to the living the task of playing the roles of distant ancestors, these rites guarantee that men who are no longer among the living will be converted into ancestors" and that they will bring "the present into the past" (Lévi-Strauss 1962:314).

Among the Samo tribes of the Upper Volta, rites whose purpose is to delay death through sacrifices reveal "a certain conception of an immanent time, which is not subject to the rules of chronological segmentation,"[7] or "relative temporalities."Among the Nuer, as among many "primitive" peoples, the past is measured according to different kinds of ages. One past concerns small groups, and quickly vanishes "in the mysterious distance of former times," while a second past constitutes "historical time, a sequence of remarkable and important events for the tribe" (floods, epidemics, famines, wars), which goes back much further than the historical time of small groups but is probably limited to about fifty years. Then comes a "level of traditions" at which time "is incorporated into a mythical complex." Beyond this extends the horizon of pure myth, where "the world, the peoples, the civilizations" which have "all existed simultaneously in the same immortal past" are conjoined. For the Nuer, "time does not extend very far: what one can take as history stops a century back, and tradition, carefully measured, carries us back only ten or twelve generations in the structure of descent. One can see how short Nuer time is by considering that the tree under which humanity came into being was still standing a few years ago in the western region of the Nuer country!" (Evans-Pritchard 1940:128–33).

But the sense of a historical past is hidden at the heart of primitive thought, which is nevertheless profoundly synchronic in nature. Lévi-Strauss thought he could glimpse it in the *charinga* of the central Australian Aranda. Charinga are "objects made of stone or wood, more or less oval in form, and with pointed or rounded extremities often incised with symbolic signs," in which he saw striking analogies with our own archival documents. "Charinga are tangible witnesses to the mythical period . . . , similarly, if we were to lose our archives, our past would not thereby be completely destroyed: it would be covered with what we might be tempted to call its diachronic savor. It would still exist as a past, but it would be preserved only in reproductions, books, institutions, even a situation, all of them contemporary or recent. Consequently, it would also be laid out synchronically" (1962:316–21). Among certain peoples of the Ivory Coast, the consciousness of a historical past has developed alongside a multiplicity of other times. Thus the Guéré seem to have five different kinds of temporal categories: (1) mythical time, which is the time of the mythical ancestor, after whom a past exists until the first actual forebear; (2) historical time, which is a sort of epic of the clan; (3) genealogical time, which can go back more than ten generations; (4) lived time, which is subdivided into ancient times (a very hard time, characterized by tribal wars, famines, dissatisfaction, a time of a colonization both liberating and enslaving), and the time of Independence, paradoxically viewed as a time of oppression because of the effects of a policy of modernization; (5) projected time, the time of an imagined future (A. Schwartz, in *Temps et développement*, pp. 60–61).

General reflections on the distinction between past and present in historical consciousness

Eric Hobsbawm has recently (1972) raised the problem of the "social function of the past," the past being defined as the period anterior to the events an individual remembers directly. Most societies consider the past as the model for the present. But there are interstices in this devotion to the past through which innovation and change slip in. What is the role of innovation in societies attached to the past? Only a few sects succeed in isolating themselves in order to completely resist change. The societies we call traditional, and particularly peasant societies, are not at all as static as they are thought to be. But if the attachment to the past can admit novelties and transformations, the direction of the evolution it perceives is usually that of a decadence or a decline. Thus innovation presents itself in a society in the form of a return to the past: that is the central idea of "renaissances."

Many revolutionary movements take a return to the past as their motto and ambition: for instance, Zapata's effort to restore peasant society in Morelos to the state in which it existed forty years earlier by erasing the intervening age of Porfirio Diaz. We have to take into account symbolic restorations such as the reconstruction of the old city of Warsaw as it existed before the destruction of the Second World War. A demand for a return to the past may conceal very new projects: the name "Ghana" transfers history from one part of Africa to another, geographically distant area that is also historically completely different. The Zionist movement resulted not in the restoration of the ancient Jewish Palestine, but in an entirely new state: Israel. Nationalist movements, including Nazism and fascism, which tend to inaugurate a completely new "order," present themselves as traditionalist, as returning to the past. The past is rejected only when innovation is judged to be both unavoidable and socially desirable. When and how did the words "new" and "revolutionary" become synonymous with "better" and "more desirable"?

Two special problems have to do with the past conceived as genealogy and as chronology. Individuals composing a society almost always feel the need to have ancestors, and one of the roles of great men is to fill that need. The customs and the artistic taste of the past are often aped and adopted by revolutionaries. As for chronology, it remains essential to a modern, historical sense of the past, for history is a directional change. Historical and nonhistorical chronologies coexist, and it must be recognized that the sense of the past persists in diverse forms. We swim in the past like fish in water, and we cannot escape from it (Hobsbawm).

Studying the birth of history in ancient Greece, François Châtelet tried first to define the characteristic features of "the historical Spirit." He began by presenting the past and the present as categories that are simultaneously identical and different.

> The historical Spirit believes in the *reality* of the past, and maintains that the past, in its mode of being and, to a certain extent, in its content, is not different in nature from the present. Recognizing what is no longer as *having been*, he acknowledges that what happened did formerly exist, in a specific time and place, just as what we now see exists. . . . That means, in particular, that it is not in any way acceptable to treat what has happened as fictive, as unreal, and that the nonpresence of the past (and of the future) cannot in any manner be identified with its nonreality. (p. 11)

But the past and the present are also differentiated and even opposed:

> If the past and the present belong to the sphere of the *same*, they are also in the sphere of *alterity*. If it is true that the past event is gone forever and that this dimension constitutes its essence, it is also true that its "pastness" differentiates it from any other event that might resemble it. The idea that there are repetitions in history . . . that there is "nothing new under the sun," and even that we can learn from the past, can be meaningful only for a mentality that is not historical. (1:12)

Finally, history, the science of the past, makes use of scientific methods for studying the past.

> It is indispensable that the past, which is held to be real and decisive, be studied rigorously insofar as past times are considered as having a claim on our attention, insofar as a structure is assigned to them, insofar as their traces are visible in the present. It is necessary that every discourse concerning the past be able to clearly show why—on the

> basis of which documents, and what evidence—it proposes a particular sequence of events, a particular version, rather than another. It is especially important that great care be taken in dating and locating the event, since the latter acquires historical status only to the extent that it is determined in this way. (1:21–22)

Châtelet maintains that "this concern with precision in the study of what formerly happened appears clearly only at the beginning of the last century," and that "the decisive impetus" was given by Leopold von Ranke (1795–1886), professor at the University of Berlin from 1825 to 1871 (1:22).

The evolution of the relation between past and present in European thought from ancient Greece to the nineteenth century[8]

Collective attitudes toward the past, the present, and the future can be schematically expressed as follows: in pagan antiquity, the valorization of the past predominated along with the idea of a decadent present; in the Middle Ages, the present is trapped between the weight of the past and the hope of an eschatological future; in the Renaissance, on the contrary, the primary stress is on the present, while from the seventeenth to the nineteenth centuries, the ideology of progress turns the valorization of time towards the future.

In Greek culture the sense of time is oriented toward either the myth of the Golden Age, or toward memories of the heroic era. Even Thucydides sees in the present no more than a sort of future anterior, and he brackets future entirely,[9] even when he knows how things will turn out, in order to absorb himself completely into the past moment.[10] Roman historiography is dominated by the idea of the morality of the ancients, and the Roman historian is always more or less a *laudator temporis acti*, a praiser of the past, as Horace puts it. Livy, for example, who is writing within the framework of Augustus' project of "restoration," exalts "the most distant past" and in his preface he indicates that the decline from past to present is his leading theme: "let us then follow in spirit, along with the gradual relaxation of discipline, first the appearance of cracks in morality, so to speak, and then its progressive destruction, and finally its rapid collapse, in order to arrive at our own time."

Studying the beginnings of history in the Bible, Pierre Gibert underlined one condition that must be met for the collective memory of the past to become history: the sense of continuity. He believes this can be seen in the institution of monarchy (Saul, David, Solomon): "It is to the institution of monarchy that we must attribute Israel's acquisition of a sense of continuity in the knowledge of its past, for even if it possessed a certain sense of this past through the corpus of its legends, even if had a certain concern for exactitude, it is only with the monarchy that the sense of a continuity without ruptures appears" (Gibert, p. 391). But in the Bible, Jewish history is on the one hand fascinated by its own origins (the creation and then the covenant between Yahweh and his people), and on the other drawn toward an equally sacred future: the advent of the Messiah and of the Heavenly Jerusalem which, in Isaiah, is opened to all nations.

Between our origins, darkened by original sin and the Fall, and the end of the world, the Parousia, the expectation of which should not disturb Christians, Christianity strives to focus attention on the present. From Saint Paul to Saint Augustine and the great theologians of the Middle Ages, the Christian Church attempts to concentrate Christians' minds on a present which, with the incarnation of Christ, the central point of history, is the beginning of the end of time. Mircea Eliade, referring to various Pauline texts (Thessalonians 1:4, 16–17; Romans 13, 11–12; Thessalonians 2:3, 8–10), shows the ambiguities involved in this attempt: "The consequences of this ambivalent valorization of the *present* (while waiting for the Parousia, history continues and must be respected) will soon make themselves felt. In spite of the countless solutions proposed from the end of the first century onward, the problem of the *historical present* continues to haunt contemporary Christian thought."[11]

In fact, medieval time confines the present between a retro-orientation toward the past and a futuro-tropism that is particularly strong among millenarians (Le Goff 1978 5:712–46). Just as the Church *restrained* or condemned millenarian movements, it privileged the past. This privilege was reinforced by the theory of the six ages of the world, according to which the world had entered its sixth and final stage, that of decrepitude and old age. In the twelfth century Guillaume de Conches declares: "We are only commentators on the ancients, we invent nothing new." The term "antiquity" (*antiquitas*) is synonymous with authority (*auctoritas*), value (*gravitas*), greatness and majesty (*majestas*).

S. Stelling-Michaud has maintained that the men of the Middle Ages, tossed back and forth between the past and the future, tried to live the present non-temporally, as an instant that was supposed to be a moment of eternity. This is what Saint Augustine urges Christians to do: "Who can arrest this thought (floating at the mercy of the waves of the past and the future), who can immobilize it and give it a little stability, in order to open it to the intuition of the splendor of eternity, which is always immobile?" (*Confessions*, XI, 13). Again: "Your years are like a single day . . . and this today does not give way to a tomorrow, any more than it follows a yesterday. Your today is Eternity" (*Confessions*, XI, 13). And in *The City of God*, he writes: "Compared with a moment of eternity, the longest time is nothing" (XII, 12). Dante expresses this magnificently in his image of the *point* as a lightning flash of eternity: "A single moment makes for me greater oblivion than five and twenty centuries have wrought upon the enterprise that made Neptune wonder at the shadow of the Argo" (*Paradiso*, XXXIII, 94–96).[12]

In the same way, medieval artists, caught between the attraction of the past, the mythical time of Paradise, and the search for the *prerogative* moment that is oriented toward the future, whether salvation or damnation, sought above all to express the atemporal. Motivated by a "desire for eternity," they frequently resorted to the symbol, which puts the past, the present and the future spheres in communication. Christianity is the religion of intercession (J. S. Morgan).

The present is further diminished by the tendency of medieval man to constantly actualize the past, especially the biblical past. The man of the Middle Ages lives in a constant anachronism, ignoring local color, and attributing to ancient people medieval costumes, feelings, and modes of behavior. The Crusaders believed that in Jerusalem they were punishing the true tormentors of Christ. But can one say: "the past is not studied as past, it is relived, brought into the present"? (Rousset, p. 631) Is it not rather that the present is eaten away by the past, for only the past gives the present its sense and its significance?

Nevertheless, at the end of the Middle Ages, the past is increasingly understood in relation to the time of the chronicles, to progress in dating, and to the measuring of time brought about by mechanical clocks. "Present and past are distinguished in the consciousness of the late Middle Ages not only in terms of their historical aspect, but also through a painful and tragic sensibility" (R. Glasser, p. 95). The French poet Villon was tragically aware of this flight of time, of the irremediable passing away of the past.

The Renaissance seems to be caught between two contradictory tendencies. On one hand, progress in measuring, dating, and chronology permit the past to be put in perspective (P. Burke). On the other, the tragic sense of life and death (A. Tenenti, 1957), can lead to epicureanism, to the enjoyment of the present, expressed by poets from Lorenzo the Magnificent to Ronsard:

> But gentle ladies, handsome youths,
> Who sing and play upon your lutes,
> Drink the joy of every day,
> For hour by hour it slips away.[13]

Scientific development, starting with Copernicus and especially Kepler, Galileo, and Descartes, gives rise to the Enlightenment optimism that leads to an affirmation of the superiority of the moderns over the ancients (see essay "Ancient/Modern"). Accordingly, the idea of *progress* becomes the leading theme of history, which turns toward the future.

The nineteenth century is divided between the economic optimism of the partisans of material progress and the disillusions of those disappointed by the aftermath of the French Revolution and the Napoleonic empire. Romanticism turns deliberately toward the past. The pre-Romanticism of the eighteenth century had already taken an interest in the ruins of Antiquity. The great master was Winckelmann (1717–1768), a German historian and archeologist who saw in Greco-Roman art the model of true perfection (*The History of Ancient Art*, 1764), and published a noted archeological study, *Ancient Monuments Explained and Illustrated*, in 1767. The first excavations at Herculaneum and Pompeii took place at this time. The French Revolution promoted this taste for Antiquity. Later, Chateaubriand's *Spirit of Christianity* (1802), Scott's historical novels (*Ivanhoe*, 1819; *Quentin Durward*, 1823), and Novalis' essay *Christianity or Europe* (1826) all helped focus the predilection for the past on the Middle Ages. The figure of the *troubadour* became fashionable in the theater, painting, watercolors, woodcuts, and lithographs.

In this period, art in France was a veritable "factory of the past" (F. Haskell). Three main stages can be distinguished. In 1792, in the former convent of the Grands-Augustins, the archeologist Alexandre Lenoir opened a museum that in 1796 became the Museum of French Monuments. Among the many contemporary visitors deeply impressed by this museum was Jules Michelet, who first discovered the French past there. Napoleon strongly favored the painting of scenes from French history. In the 1801 and 1802 exhibitions two paintings dealt with the history of

France; in 1814, eighty-six were devoted to this subject. Finally, Louis-Philippe decided in 1833 to restore Versailles and to make it a museum dedicated to "all the glories of France."

The Romantic taste for the past, which nourished European nationalist movements in the nineteenth century, and which was in turn developed by nationalism itself, extended to ancient law and philology and to popular culture. The best example of this latter tendency is doubtless the work of the brothers Jakob (1785–1863) and Wilhelm (1786–1859) Grimm, the authors of the famous collection of *Kinder- und Hausmärchen* (1812; known in English as *Grimm's Fairy Tales*), a *History of the German Language* (1848), and a *German Dictionary* (1852–1858).

The ghost of the past, the history of the present, and the fascination with the future in the twentieth century

Millenarianism is far from dead in nineteenth century Europe. It is hidden deep within Marxist thought, which claims to be scientific, as well as within positivist thought. When Auguste Comte sees, in his *Brief Overall Estimate of the Modern Past* (1820), the decline of a theological and military system at the dawn of the new scientific and industrial system, he is casting himself in the role of a modern Joachim of Floris. In the same way, the nineteenth century—which was *the* century of history—continued, beyond Romanticism, to bring the medieval past to life (F. Graus). But at the beginning of the twentieth century, a crisis concerning the idea of progress (Le Goff 1986:187–284) leads to new attitudes with respect to the past, the present, and the future. On the one hand, the attachment to the past at first takes exasperated, reactionary forms, and later, caught between the anguish of the atomic age and the euphoria of scientific and technological progress, it turns both toward the past with nostalgia and toward the future with fear or hope. However, after Marx, historians try to establish new relations between the present and the past. Marx had decried the paralyzing weight of the past, which had been reduced to the exaltation of "great memories." This weight was felt by nations, for example, by the French: "The drama of the French, as well as that of the workers, is great memories. These events must put an end once and for all to this reactionary cult of the past" (Letter to César de Paepe, September 14, 1870). At the end of the nineteenth and at the beginning of the twentieth century, this cult of the past was one of the essential elements of right-wing ideologies and a component of fascist and Nazi ideology. Even today, the cult of the past accompanies social conservatism, and Pierre Bourdieu locates it particularly in declining social categories: "A class or a fraction of a class is in decline, and therefore oriented toward the past, when it is no longer able to reproduce with all its properties of condition and position" (p. 530).

On the other hand, the acceleration of history has led the masses in industrial nations to cling nostalgically to their roots; whence the fashion of earlier clothing styles, the predilection for history and archeology, the interest in folklore, the vogue of ethnology, the fascination with photography that evokes memories and reminiscences, and the prestige of the idea of *patrimony*.

In other domains, the attention given to the past and to duration played a growing role in literature (Proust and Joyce), in philosophy (Bergson), and finally in a new science: psychoanalysis. In the latter, psychic life is in fact presented as dominated by unconscious memories, by the buried history of individuals, and notably by the most distant past, that of earliest infancy. However, the importance accorded to the past by psychoanalysis has been denied; for instance, by Marie Bonaparte citing Freud: "The processes of the unconscious system are atemporal, that is, they are not temporally organized, they are not modified by passing time; in short, they have no relation to time. The relation to time is linked to the workings of the conscious system"(p. 73).

Jean Piaget makes another criticism of Freudianism:the past which the psychoanalytic experience grasps is not a true past but a reconstructed past: "What this operation yields is the subject's current conception of his past, and not a direct knowledge of this past. . . . And as I believe Erikson (an unorthodox psychoanalyst, with whom I nevertheless entirely agree) has said, the past is reconstructed in relation to the present just as the present is explained by the past. There is interaction. For orthodox Freudians the past determines the adult's current behavior. But then how can this past be known? Through memories which are themselves reconstituted in a context, which is the context of the present and in relation to this present."[14]

In the final analysis, Freudian psychoanalysis is part of a vast antihistorical movement which tends to deny the importance of the past/present relation, and whose roots are, paradoxically, in positivism. Positivist history, which through increasingly scientific modes of dating and textual criticism seemed to make a solid study of the past possible, actually immobilized history in the event itself and thereby eliminated duration. In England, the study of history at Oxford led by different paths to the same result. Freeman's aphorism, "history is the politics of the past and politics is the history of the present" perverted the past/present relation. Gardiner (1829–1902), declaring that "he who studies the society of the past will do a great service to the society of the present insofar as he does not take the latter into account," tended in the same direction (Marwick, pp. 47–48). These remarks either seek merely to warn against anachronism and are thus thoroughly banal, or else they sever any rational link between present and past. Positivism also had another attitude which, notably in France, resulted in the negation of the past that was supposed to be venerated. This is the "desire for eternity" in a new secular guise. In the twelfth century Otton de Freising had thought that with the realization of a feudal system controlled by the Church, history had reached its goals and had come to an end. Positivist historians thought that with the French Revolution and then with the Republic, history, and first of all the history of France, had attained its final development. As Alphonse Dupront insightfully put it, after 1789 and 1870 there was nothing left except eternity, "because the republican form of government definitively established the revolutionary spirit of France." School texts suggest that history has reached its goal and arrived at stability forever: "Republic and France, these are, my children, the two words that should remain engraved in your deepest hearts. Let them be the object of your constant love, and of your eternal gratefulness as well." And Alphonse Dupront adds: "The mark of eternity is henceforth on France" (p. 1466).

In another way, new scientific developments—psychoanalysis, sociology, structuralism—stimulate the quest for the atemporal and seek to empty out the past. Philip Abrams has shown that even if sociologists (and anthropologists) based themselves on the past, their enterprise was in reality very ahistorical: "The essential point was not to know the past, but to establish an idea of the past that could be used as a term of comparison in order to understand the present."[15] Specialists in the human sciences have recently reacted against this elimination of the past. For example, the historian Jean Chesneaux has asked: Should we turn the past into a *tabula rasa*? That is the temptation felt by many young revolutionaries, or simply by young people concerned with freeing themselves from any constraints, including those of the past. Chesneaux is aware of the manipulation of the past by the dominant classes. Thus he thinks that peoples, and particularly those of the third world, should "liberate the past." But we must not reject it, we must make it serve social and national struggles: "If the past counts for the popular masses, it is on the other side of social life, when it takes part directly in their struggles" (J. Chesneaux, p. 32). But this recruitment of the past for revolutionary and political ends results in a confusion of the two attitudes a historian may take with respect to the past, and which he must not confuse: his professional attitude as a historian and his political engagement as a man and as a citizen.

The anthropologist Marc Augé also takes as his point of departure the recognition of the repressive aspect of memory, history, and the call to order based on the past or—for that matter—on the future: he calls it "the past as constraint." As for the future: "Messianic and prophetic movements also link constraint to the future anterior, deferring the appearance of the signs that will express, when the moment comes, a necessity anchored in the past" (Augé, p. 149). But "every current society demands that history have a meaning and a direction . . . in every case the demand for meaning is mediated by reflection on the past" (pp. 151–52). What is necessary, then, is a constant rereading of the past in relation to the present, which must constantly be questioned anew.

This questioning of the past from the point of view of the present is what Chesneaux calls "inverting the past/present relation," and he sees its origin in Marx. Henri Lefebvre also addresses this issue, citing Marx's statement in the *Grundrisse*: "Bourgeois society is the most highly developed and diversified historical organization of production. The categories that express the relations in this society and make it possible for us to understand its structure also allow us to grasp the structure and the relations of production in past societies." Lefebvre comments: "Marx has clearly indicated the way historical thought proceeds. The historian starts from the present . . . at first he moves backward, from the present to the past. Afterward he comes back toward the present, which is now analyzed and known, instead of offering a confused totality to analysis" (H. Lefebvre 1970).

Similarly, Marc Bloch has described a double movement in the historian's method: he must understand the past through the present: "Incomprehension of the present is the inevitable result of ignorance of the past. But it is perhaps just as fruitless to struggle to understand the past if one knows nothing about the present" (p. 47). Whence the importance of the movement from present to past in history: "It would indeed be a serious error to believe that the order adopted by historians in their investigations should necessarily be modeled on that of events. On the condition that they later restore history's true movement, historians have often profited from starting by reading it, as Maitland put it, "backwards." This conception of past/present relations, which played a major role in the journal *Annales* founded in 1929 by Lucien Febvre and Marc Bloch, has even inspired a British historical journal to take *Past and Present* as its name, and in its first issue to declare that "history cannot logically separate the study of the past from the present and the future."

The future, no less than the past, attracts people today who are searching for the roots of their identity (see F. Hincker and A. Casanova, eds.. *L'Historien entre l'ethnologue et le futurologue),* and fascinates them more than ever. But the old apocalypses, the old millenarianisms are reborn, and are nourished by a new form of popular writing, science fiction. *Futurology* is developing, but at the same time philosophers or biologists are making notable contributions to the insertion of history into the future. For example, the philosopher Gaston Berger has examined the idea of the future and the prospective attitude. Starting out from the observation that "men have only recently recognized the meaning of the future" (G. Berger, p. 227), and from Paul Valéry's remark that "we go into the future facing backward," he has recommended a conversion of the past toward the future and an attitude with regard to the past that does not turn away from the present or the future, but on the contrary, helps to predict and even to shape the future.

At the end of his book *From Biology to Culture* (1976), the biologist Jacques Ruffié also examines the prospective attitude and "the call of the future." For him, humanity is on the threshold of a "new evolutionary jump" (p. 569). Perhaps a profound transformation of the relations between past and present is on the horizon.

In any case, the acceleration of history has made the official definition of contemporary history untenable. A true contemporary history must be brought into being, a history of the present. It would presuppose that history is no longer concerned only with the past, that "a history" based on a sharp break between present and past is over, and that we reject the "abdication of our responsibility to know the present at the very moment when the present is changing in nature and incorporating the elements science exploits in order to know the past"(Nora 1978:468).

ANTIQUE (ANCIENT)/ MODERN

An ambiguous Western pairing

Although equivalents can be found in other civilizations and in other historiographies, the "antique/modern" pair is linked to the history of the West. During the preindustrial age, from the fifth to the nineteenth centuries, it organizes a cultural opposition that from the end of the Middle Ages to the Enlightenment forces its way onto the center of the intellectual stage. In the middle of the nineteenth century, it is transformed with the appearance of the concept of *modernity*, an ambiguous reaction of culture under attack by the industrial world. In the second half of the twentieth century, it is found throughout the Western world, whereas elsewhere, and especially in the third world, it is introduced with the help of the notion of *modernization*, which arises from contact with the West.

The *antique-modern* opposition developed in an equivocal and complex context. First of all, this was because each of the terms and concepts is not always opposed to the other: *antique* can be replaced by "ancient" or *traditional*, and *modern* by *recent* or *new*. The second complexity arose because each of the two terms has been accompanied by laudatory, pejorative, or neutral connotations. When *modern* appears in vulgar Latin it has only the meaning *recent*, which it keeps well into the Middle Ages; *antique* can mean "belonging to the past" and more precisely, to the historical period known in the West since the sixteenth century as *Antiquity*, that is, to the period before the triumph of Christianity in the Greco-Roman world and before the great demographic, economic, and cultural regression of the High Middle Ages, which is marked by the decline of slavery and an intense ruralization.

When, starting in the sixteenth century, the dominant Western historiography (developed first by independent scholars and later by university professors) divides history into three periods, *antique*, *medieval*, and *modern* (*neuere*, in German), each adjective often refers only to a chronological period, and *modern* is opposed to *medieval* rather than to *antique*. Moreover, this way of organizing the past does not always correspond to what the people of the past thought. Stefan Swiezawski, discussing the "*via antiqua—via moderna*" schema that since the nineteenth century has dominated historians' analyses of late medieval thought, suggests that this model "cannot be used by the doctrinal historiography of the period without numerous reservations and restrictions." Swiezawski adds: "This schema is not general in either time or space; the concept of progress and vitality then in force did not always coincide with what was considered new at the time, and the pair of concepts 'modern-ancient' thus had ambiguities that leave the historian perplexed."[1]

Finally, modernity can camouflage or express itself under the auspices of the past—of Antiquity, for example. That is the peculiarity of *renaissances* and particularly of the sixteenth- century European *Renaissance*. Today, taste for the fashions of earlier decades is one of the components of modernity.

In this pair the modern is the main problem

If antique complicates matters because alongside the meaning of "ancient" it has taken on a special meaning in reference to the period of Antiquity, it is *modern* that plays the major role in the couple. What is at stake in the antagonism between *antique* and *modern* is the attitude of individuals, societies, and periods with respect to the past, that is, to *their* past. In so-called traditional societies, antiquity is a firm value, and the Ancients, old people who are repositories of the collective memory and guarantors of authenticity and property, are dominant. These societies look for guidance to the Ancients, to Senates, to a gerontocracy tempered by its retirement from active life. Among the Alladjan of the Ivory Coast before colonization, the supreme chief of the phratry was the *nanan*, the oldest man of the oldest age group, and the *akoubeote* or village chiefs were probably automatically designated using the criterion of age. In the Middle Ages, in common law lands, the antiquity of a right attested by the oldest members of a community is a juridical argument of considerable weight. We should not however imagine that in antique or archaic societies, there is not also a negative side to age and antiquity. Alongside the respect for age, there is also scorn for decrepitude. The etymology that linked the Greek word *geron*, old man, with the term *geras*, honor, has been shown to be false. Emile Benveniste has reminded us that *geron* has to be seen in relation to the Sanskrit *jarati*, "to be decrepit," and he adds: "Certainly old age is surrounded with respect; old men make up the counsel of Ancients, the Senate; but royal honors are never given them, an old man never receives a royal privilege, a *geras* in the precise sense of the term."[2] In warrior societies, the adult is exalted by contrast with the child and to the old man. That is the case in ancient Greece, as it is depicted in Hesiod: the gold and silver ages are ages of vitality, ages in which youth and old age are unknown, whereas the age of iron is that of old men, and if it indulges in hubris, it will end with death striking down grey-haired men born old. Through the metaphor of the ages of life, the term *antique* thus participates in the ambiguity of a concept caught between wisdom and senility.

But it is *modern* that gives rise to the pair and to its dialectical operation. In fact, the consciousness of modernity arises from the feeling of having broken with the past. Is it legitimate for the historian to see modernity where the people of the past saw nothing of the sort? In reality, even if they did not perceive the extent of the mutations they underwent, historical societies had the feeling of modernity, and created a vocabulary for it at the turning points in their history. The word *modern* comes into being in the fifth century, with the collapse of the Roman empire; the periodization of history into ancient, medieval, and modern is established in the same sixteenth century whose "modernity" Henri Hauser has stressed; Théophile Gautier and Baudelaire launch the concept of modernity in Second Empire France at the time that the industrial revolution is taking hold; economists, sociologists, and political scientists spread and discuss the idea of modernization on the eve of the

Second World War, in the context of decolonization and of the emergence of the third world. The study of the pair *antique (ancient)/modern* must include the analysis of a historical moment that ushers in the idea of *modernity* and thereby simultaneously creates an *antiquity*—to denigrate it, exalt it, or simply to distinguish it and put it at a certain distance. For modernity can be located in order to praise it as well as to decry it.

The ambiguity of the antique (ancient): Greco-Roman antiquity and other antiquities

Even if the main developments take place on the modern side of the distinction, the historical content acquired through the term *antique* in Western culture has had great weight in the struggle of the term *modern* to emerge as designating a value.

To be sure, just as *modern* could have the neutral meaning of recent, *antique* could have the neutral sense of ancient, or refer to a period other than Greco-Roman antiquity, a period sometimes exalted, sometimes deprecated. Thus the Middle Ages and the Renaissance use the expression "antique serpent" (*antiquus serpens*) to refer to the Devil, and the expression "antique mother" (*antiqua mater*) to refer to the Earth, apparently in a neutral sense, alluding merely to the origins of humanity. But whereas the Devil's antiquity only reinforces his wickedness and his evil nature, that of the Earth confers on it the highest virtues.

For Christianity, the terms *Old Testament*, *Old Law* (where *old* [*ancien*] is opposed to *new*, not to *modern*) are explained by reference to the anteriority of the Old Testament with respect to the New Testament, but they still have an ambivalent value. At first sight, since the new Law replaced the old, and as charity (*caritas*, love) replaced justice, to which it is superior, the old Law is inferior to the new but nevertheless enjoys the prestige of the ancient, of origins. The giants of the Old Testament surpass the men of the New, even if the latter are not reduced to dwarfs, as they were in the twelfth century in a new *topos*, attributed by John of Salisbury to Bernard, the director of the cathedral school at Chartres. This topos is illustrated by a thirteenth-century stained glass window in the Cathedral that shows tiny evangelists perched on the shoulders of the great prophets.

At the very time when *antique* comes to denote Greco-Roman antiquity and takes on all the values that the Renaissance invested in it, the humanists call the script of the Carolingian age (tenth and eleventh centuries) *antique* writing. Salutati, for instance, tried to obtain Abelard's manuscripts "en antica." Thus in the sixteenth century, according to Robert Estienne, "*à l'antique*" is a pejorative expression in French, because it was associated with "uncultivated" antiquity—that is, with the *gothic* antiquity of the Middle Ages.

But in general, from the Renaissance onward, and especially in Italy, the term *antique* (*antico*) refers to an age that is distant, exemplary, and unfortunately gone forever. The *Grande Dizionario della Lingua Italiana* gives (under "antico") these significant quotations: "Virtù contra favore / prenderà l'arme, e fia 'l combatter certo, / ché l'*antiquo* valore / ne l'italici cor non è ancor morto" (Petrarch); "Oh gran bontà de cavallieri *antiqui*!" (Ariosto); "E di bellisima architettura in tutte le parti, per avere assai imitato *l'antico*" (Vasari); "Quella dignità che s'ammira in tutte quelle prose che sanno *d'antico*" (Leopardi).[3]

In most European languages, *antique* is distinguished from all the neighboring terms that can lend value to ancientness, and in particular from *old*, which tends to be pejorative. In his *Historical Dictionary of Old French*, La Curne de Saint-Palaye (d. 1781) put *antique*, *ancient*, and *old* in a curious hierarchical order: "Antique is above ancient, and ancient above old: to be antique, something must have existed more than a thousand years ago; to be ancient, more than two hundred years ago; to be old, more than a hundred years."

More precisely, the conceptual stake hidden within the antique/modern opposition was transformed in the Renaissance, when *antique* came to denote primarily Greco-Roman antiquity, which the humanists regarded as *the* model to be imitated. Petrarch already exclaims: "Is all of history anything but the praise of Rome?" ("Quid est enim aliud omnis historia quam Romana laus?").[4] What will henceforth give the *modern/antique* conflict an almost sacrilegious character is that *antique* designates a period and a civilization that have not only the prestige of the past, but also the halo of the Renaissance that idolized and served them. The combat between *antique* and *modern* becomes less a combat between past and present, between tradition and innovation, than between two forms of progress: on the one hand, a progress by recourse to origins and the Eternal Return, a circular progress that puts Antiquity at the apogee of the cycle, and on the other hand a linear progress that privileges everything that moves away from Antiquity. It is the *antique* on which the Renaissance and Humanism relied to create the "modernity" of the sixteenth century that will rise in opposition to the ambitions of the modern. The modern will be led to present itself as "antihumanist," given the virtual identification of humanism with love for the only valid Antiquity—that is, Greco-Roman antiquity. In the same way, the modern, in its struggle against the antique, comes to ally itself with different antiquities, precisely those that Greco-Roman antiquity replaced, destroyed, or condemned: primitive and barbarous antiquities. But while *antique* wins an early, easy victory over its neighbors in the semantic field of ancientness, *modern* remains for a long time at grips with its competitors: the new and progress.

The Modern and its competitors: Modern and New, Modern and Progress

If the term *modern* marks the recognition of a rupture with the past, it is not as loaded with meaning as its neighbors *new* and *progress*. *New* implies a birth, a beginning, which in Christianity takes on an almost sacred baptismal character. It is the *New* Testament or Dante's *Vita nuova* that are born with love. *New* signifies more than a break with the past, a forgetting, an erasure, or an absence of the past. To be sure, in ancient Rome the word can have an almost pejorative sense, for example in the expression *homines novi*, that is, men with without a past, born to parents who are outside the social hierarchy, commoners or parvenus. In certain expressions, Christian medieval Latin accentuates this sense of a sacrilegious novelty that is not connected with the primordial values of the origins. The "new apostles" (*novi apostoli*) that Abelard scornfully mentions in his twelfth century *Historia Calamitatum* are the hermits, itinerant preachers, canons, and reformers of monastic life who, in the intellectual Abelard's view are no more than crude, uncivilized caricatures of the true apostles—those of the past, of the true origins. Since Antiquity, the superlative of *novus*, *novissimus*, had taken on the meaning of *last*, *catastrophic*. Christianity pushes this superlative to the point of an apocalyptic paroxysm. In a thirteenth-century treatise on the perils and calamities of the last times (*De periculis novissimorum temporum*), the Parisian master Guillaume de Saint Amour plays on the double meaning of *novissimus*, which denotes both the most recent time and the end of the world. But *new* (*novus*) also has above all the prestige of the newly bloomed, the newborn, the pure.

Similarly, *modern* is contrasted with *progress*. Insofar as this term, which emerges from Latin into the Romance languages only in the sixteenth century, is used solely as a noun, to a large extent it carries *modern* along in its wake. The *recent*, as opposed to the past, thus takes its place in a positive evolutionary line. However, when in the nineteenth century the noun *progress* gives rise to verbal and adjectival forms—*to progress, progressive*—*modern* is left up in the air, outside the valorizing trajectory of the other terms.

Thus at the dawn of the Industrial Revolution, *modern* is caught between *new*, whose freshness and innocence it lacks, and *progressive*, whose dynamism it also lacks. It finds itself opposed to *antico*, but deprived of some of its advantages over the latter. Before examining *modern*'s forward movement toward *modernity*, however, we must first consider what history has made of the opposition *antique (ancient)/modern*, and analyze *modernism* before turning to *modernity*.

Antique (ancient)/modern and history: Quarrels between Ancients and Moderns in preindustrial Europe from the sixth to the eighteenth centuries

Generational conflicts opposing "Moderns" to "Ancients" already appeared in Antiquity. Horace (*Epistles*, II, 1, 76–89) and Ovid (*The Art of Love*, III, 121) complained about the prestige of ancient writers (*"antiqui"*), and rejoiced to live in their own time, but they did not have a word for "modern," since they did not contrast *novus* with *antiquus*. The neologism *modernus* first appears in the sixth century, derived from *modo* ("recently"), just as *hodiernus* ("of this day") was derived from *hodie* ("today"). Cassiodorus speaks of the "antiquorum diligentissimus imitator, *modernorum* nobilissimus institutor" (*Variae*, IV, 51). As E. R. Curtius has put it, *modernus* is "one of the last legacies of vulgar Latin."[5] One of the marks of the Carolingian Renaissance is the consciousness of "modernism" on the part of some of its representatives, such as Walahfrid Strabo, who calls the age of Charlemagne *"saeculum modernum"* ("the modern age"). For another author of the ninth century, the line of demarcation passes not between Antiquity and the Christian era, but between ancient authors (*"veteres"*, including both ancient pagans and early Christians, notably the Church Fathers) and the writers of his own time.

In the Middle Ages, from the twelfth to the fifteenth centuries, there are two waves of conflict between Ancients and Moderns. The first occurs in the twelfth century. As E. R. Curtius has noted, in the domain of

Latin poetry after 1170 there is a genuine quarrel between Ancients and Moderns. Recalling Bernard of Chartres' comment about dwarfs perched on the shoulders of giants, Alain de Lille condemns "modern crudeness" (*modernum ruditatem*).

Two notable authors of the second half of the twelfth century stressing the modernism of their time—one to deplore it, the other to praise it—show the bitterness of this first phase of the quarrel between Ancients and Moderns. John of Salisbury exclaims: "Everything was becoming new; by discarding the rules of the ancients, grammar was renewed, dialectic overthrown, rhetoric scorned, and new paths for the *quadrivium* were proposed." But the opposition is between *nova* ("novelties"—implicitly pernicious) and *priores* ("the earlier masters"). For his part, Gautier Map, in *De nugis curialem* (between 1180 and 1192), insists on a "modernity" that is the end result of a secular progress: "I call our age to this modernity, that is, to this period of one hundred years whose last part is still going on, whose recent and manifest memory gathers together everything that is remarkable. . . . The hundred years that have elapsed, that is our 'modernity.'" And there we find the term *modernitas*, which will not emerge in the vernacular until the nineteenth century.

The opposition, if not the conflict, persists in thirteenth- century scholasticism. Thomas Aquinas and Albert the Great considered antique the old masters who taught at the University of Paris two or three generations earlier, around 1220 to 1230, the date at which the intellectual revolution connected with Aristotelianism replaced them with the *moderni*, among whom Thomas and Albert counted themselves. But it is in the fourteenth and fifteenth centuries, in the same cultural climate if not in direct connection, that several movements arise, appealing openly to novelty or modernity and opposing it explicitly or implicitly to earlier, ancient ideas and practices.

These appear first of all in the domain of music, where the *ars nova* triumphs in the work of Guillaume de Machaut, Philippe de Vitry (the author of a treatise entitled *Ars Nova*), and Marchetto of Padua. Jacques Chailley says that this new art is "a conception of pure music, in which words were only a pretext."[6] Then a similar movement arises in theology and philosophy, where the *via moderna* is championed in opposition to the *via antiqua*. The modern path is followed by very different minds, but they all pursue the way opened up by Duns Scotus when he broke with Aristotelian scholasticism in the twelfth century, and they are all more or less *nominalists* or at least flirt with nominalism. The most famous and important of these "*logici moderni*" or "*theologi moderni*" or "*moderniores*" are Ockham, Buridan, Bradwardine, Gregory of Rimini, and Wycliff. A special place must be set aside for Marsilius of Padua, who has been seen as the precursor of modern political science, the first theoretician of the separation of Church and State, of secularization, and who, in the *Defensor Pacis* (1324), tends to give *modernus* the sense of *innovative*. This is also the period of Giotto, whom the sixteenth century considered the first "modern" artist. For Vasari, he is the one "who revived the modern and goodd art of painting"(che risuscito la moderna e buona arte della pittura). In his *Libro dell'arte*, Cennino Cennini credits Giotto with having "adapted to the modern," that is, with having abandoned convention for "nature," and with the invention of a new figurative language. Finally, in the fifteenth century, the *devotio moderna* establishes itself in the domain of religion, marking a break with scholasticism, and with the "superstitious" religion of the Middle Ages. It returns to the Fathers of the Church, to primitive monastic asceticism, purifies religious feeling and practice, and promotes an individual and mystical religion.

The Renaissance changes the course of this periodic emergence of the *modern* as opposed to the *antique* by establishing the meaning of *Antiquity* as denoting the pagan culture of ancient Greece and Rome and by giving it precedence over other cultures. The *modern* has a right to preference only insofar as it imitates the *ancient*. That is the meaning of the famous passage in Rabelais celebrating the renewal of classical studies: "Now all the disciplines have been revived." The modern is elevated through the ancient.

But the Renaissance makes an essential distinction between the antique period and the modern. As early as 1341, Petrarch distinguishes between *storia antica* and *storia nova* (*ancient* history and *new* history). Different languages will later sometimes choose *modern* (*storia moderna* in Italian), sometimes *new* (*neuere Geschichte* in German). In any case, the relationship between the antique and the modern is established at the expense of the Middle Ages. Between *storia antica* and *storia nova*, Petrarch places the dark ages (*tenebras*), which extend from the fall of the Roman empire to his own time. In the evolution of Western art, Vasari distinguishes a "*maniera antica*" from a "*maniera moderna*" (which begins with the *rinascita*, the "rebirth," in the middle of the thirteenth century and culminates in Giotto), separated by a "*maniera vecchia*" ("old manner") located between the two.

Nevertheless, protests against this superiority of the Ancients begin to be heard. There is a desire to use the image of "dwarves mounted on the shoulders of giants" to stress—as Bernard of Chartres did in the twelfth century—that the modern dwarves have at least the advantage of long experience over the antique giants. All the same, in the first half of the sixteenth century, the Spanish humanist Luis Vives protested that the men of his time were no more dwarfs than the men of antiquity were giants, and that at the very least, his contemporaries had, thanks to the ancients, risen higher than they had (*De causis corruptarum artium*, I, 5). A century later, Gassendi declares that nature was no less generous to the men of his time than to the men of antiquity, but that zeal and the spirit of competition must be instilled in them. And he takes up the idea that the moderns can rise higher than the antique giants (*Exercitationes paradoxicae adversus Aristotleos, lib.* I, *Exercitatio*, II, 13).

The second and most famous quarrel of the Ancients and the Moderns breaks out at the end of the seventeenth century and the beginning of the eighteenth. It lasts practically throughout the eighteenth century and ends in Romanticism. The triumph of the Moderns is signaled by Stendhal's *Racine and Shakespeare* and by Hugo's preface to *Cromwell* (1827), in which the opposition between romantic and classic is only the latest guise taken by the conflict between Moderns and Ancients; things are chronologically confused, since the hero of the Moderns, Shakespeare, is earlier than the classical models of the seventeenth century.

It is true that since the end of the sixteenth century, the superiority of the true ancients, the people of Antiquity, was occasionally challenged. For example, at the beginning of the seventeenth century, Secondo Lancelotti founded a sect in Italy, the *Hoggidi*, that praised the present, and in 1623 he published *L'Hoggidi overo gli ingegni moderni non inferiori ai passati* (Today's People or Modern Talents Not Inferior to Those of the Past). But at the end of the seventeenth century the quarrel heats up both in England and in France. Whereas Thomas Burnet and William Temple publish respectively a *Panegyric of Modern Learning in Comparison of the Ancient*, and *An Essay upon the Ancient and Modern Learning*, Bernard le Bovier de Fontenelle wrote his *Digression on the Ancients and the Moderns* (1687) and Charles Perrault, after having touched off an explosion by presenting *The Century of Louis the Great* (*Le siècle de Louis le grand*) to the French Academy in January 1687, committed a further offense by publishing *Parallels Between the Ancients and the Moderns* (*Parallèles des anciens et des modernes*, 1688).

Confronted by the partisans of the Ancients who could see nothing but decadence among the Moderns, the partisans of the latter proclaimed the equality of the two ages, crediting the Moderns with the advantage of having simply accumulated more knowledge and experience, or else they invoked the idea of a genuinely qualitative progress.

As an example of the first position, consider these lines from Perrault's *The Century of Louis the Great*:

> I always considered antiquity venerable,
> But I never thought it adorable.
> I contemplate the Ancients not on bended knee;
> True, they are great, but only men such as we,
> And we can compare without fear of injustice
> The age of Louis with that of Augustus.

As an example of the second position, consider what Malebranche wrote as early as 1674/1675 in *The Quest for Truth* (*La Recherche de la vérité*): "The world is older by two thousand years, and it has more experience than in the time of Aristotle and Plato." Or Terrasson's *Philosophy Made Applicable to all Objects of the Mind and Reason* (*La Philosophie applicable à tous les objets de l'esprit et de la raison*, Paris, 1754): "The moderns are in general superior to the ancients: that is a proposition bold in its utterance, and modest in its principle. It is bold, insofar as it attacks an old prejudice; it is modest, insofar as it makes us understand that we do not owe our superiority to the capacity of our own minds, but to the experience acquired through the examples and reflections of those who have preceded us."

Nevertheless, even among the partisans of the Moderns, the idea of old age and decadence remained the explanatory curve of history. Perrault wrote in the *Parallels*: "Is it not true that the development of the world is usually regarded as comparable to that of a man's life, that it has had its infancy, its youth, and its maturity, and is presently in its old age?"

Not until the eve of the French Revolution did the century of the Enlightenment adopt the idea of progress without restrictions. Tocqueville places the decisive turning point in 1780. However, in 1749 the young Turgot wrote his *Reflections on the History of the Progress of the Human Spirit* (*Réflexions sur les progrès de l'esprit humain*). In 1781 Servan published his *Discourse on the Progress of Human Knowledge* (*Discours sur le progrès des connaissances humaines*), and the masterpiece of belief in indefinite progress was written by Condorcet shortly before his death: *An Outline of the Progress of the Human Spirit* (*Esquisse d'un tableau des progrès de l'esprit humain*, 1794).

Antique (ancient)/modern and history: modernism, modernization, modernity in the nineteenth and twentieth centuries

Starting from the historical heritage of the Quarrel of the Ancients and the Moderns, the industrial revolution radically changes the conflict between *antique (ancient)* and *modern* in the second half of the nineteenth century and in the twentieth century. Three new poles of evolution and conflict appear at the turn of the twentieth century: literary, artistic and religious movements appeal to, or are accused of, *modernism*, a term which marks the hardening into doctrine of modern tendencies that had earlier been diffuse. The encounter between developed and underdeveloped countries outside Western Europe and the United States poses problems of *modernization* that are radicalized by decolonization after the Second World War. At the heart of the acceleration of history in Western culture, through both forward impetus and reaction, a new concept appears and expands in the area of esthetic creation, mentality, and manners: *modernity*.

Modernism

Around 1900, three very different movements are labeled "modernist"—one of them at its own request, the other two under protest: a limited literary movement in the area of Hispanic culture, a set of artistic tendencies whose principal denomination was *Modern Style*, and diverse kinds of dogmatic inquiry within Christianity and principally within Catholicism.

1. MODERNISMO

The term *modernismo* "indicates, since about 1890, a group of authors writing in Spanish who chose this name to show their common desire to renew themes and forms" (Berveiller 1971:138). It included especially poets, and it was particularly vital in Latin America. Its principal representative is the Nicaraguan writer Rubén Dario. The characteristics of his work that are of special interest for the general problem of the couple *antique (ancient)/modern* are the very different aspects of its reaction to historical evolution. On the one hand, there is a reaction to the rise of the power of money, of materialist ideals, and of the bourgeoisie (modernism is an "idealist" movement); on the other, there is a reaction to the irruption of the masses into history (modernism is an "aristocratic" movement of aesthetes: "I am not a poet for the masses," Dario says in the preface to *Cantos de vida y esperanza*). But in reaction against the culture of classical Antiquity, Dario chooses his models in the cosmopolitan literature of the nineteenth century, and especially the second half of the nineteenth century. Dario declares: "Verlaine means much more to me than Socrates." A reaction against the Spanish-American war of 1898 and against the bitterness that arose from the Spanish defeat, his work is also a reaction against the emergence of Yankee imperialism and shares the "reactionary" tendencies of the Spanish "Generation of '98" and of Latin Panamericanism.

2. MODERNISM

In the strict sense, modernism is a movement internal to the Catholic Church during the first years of the twentieth century. The term appears in Italy in 1904, and its use culminates in Pope Pius X's 1907 encyclical *Pascendi*, which condemns it. But it is situated within the long-standing tension that has agitated Christianity and particularly the Catholic Church from the French Revolution down to the present, the Second Vatican Council marking an important but not final stage in the development of this tension. The Catholic aspect of the conflict *antique (ancient)/modern* became a confrontation between the conservative Church and Western society of the industrial revolution. In the nineteenth century, the term *modern* becomes a pejorative term that the leaders of the Church and its traditionalist elements apply either to the ideology born of the French Revolution and progressive movements in nineteenth-century Europe (liberalism, and later socialism and naturalism), or—and in their eyes this is still graver—to Catholics seduced by these ideas or simply lukewarm in their opposition to them (for example, Lamennais). The official Catholic Church of the nineteenth century declares itself *antimodern*. Pius IX's *Syllabus* (1864) is representative of that attitude. The last "error" it condemns is the proposition: "The Roman Pontiff can and must reconcile himself to and come to terms with progress, with liberalism, and with modern civilization." To be sure, here *modern* still has the neutral sense of "recent," but it moves decisively in the direction of the pejorative. At the end of the nineteenth and at the beginning of the twentieth century, the conflict *antico/moderno* within Catholicism flares up again, and becomes more concentrated and venomous, in relation to two problems: (1) dogma, and especially Biblical exegesis; (2) social and political evolution.

More than the ambiguous social Catholicism, which in any case did not directly confront the official Church (provided since Leo XIII's 1891 encyclical *Rerum Novarum* with an equally ambiguous but open social doctrine), it was the theological and exegetical movement that was at the center of the crisis of *modernism*. The crisis came from "the lagging behind of ecclesiastical science, as they called it, with respect to lay culture and scientific discoveries . . . It was occasioned by the brutal encounter between traditional ecclesiastical teaching and the new religious sciences that were developed far away from the control of orthodoxies, and often in opposition to them, on the basis of a revolutionary principle: the application of positive methods to a domain and to texts that were heretofore considered beyond their grasp" (E. Poulat 1971:135–36). This modernism, which is linked with issues concerning the freedom of higher education (the law of 1875) and the creation of five Catholic institutes, caused a particularly grave crisis in France, notably in the case of Alfred Loisy, Monseigneur Louis Duchesne's pupil, who was ultimately excommunicated in 1902.

Three phenomena having to do with the development of the *antique (ancient)/modern* conflict should be noted in connection with this modernism. First, in Italy, the modernist movement results in mass, propagandistic action and ends up challenging the retrograde control of the Church over political, intellectual, and everyday life. Three priests illustrate the diverse tendencies of this movement at the beginning of the twentieth century: Father Giovanni Semeria (1867–1931), Romolo Murri (1870–1944), the founder of Christian Democracy, and the historian Ernesto Buonaiuti (1881–1946). Semeria was exiled, and Murri and Buonaiuti were excommunicated. In Italy, the modernist movement thus confronts the Catholic Church as the principal obstacle to the modernization of society.

Second, modernism broadens *modern*'s field of action by opposing it less to *ancient* than to *traditional*, and in a more precise religious sense, to *integrationist*. But this broadening is produced above all by the way it lends itself an array of combinations and nuances: for instance, it becomes possible to speak of ascetic modernism or military modernism, *semimodernism* or *modernizationism* (*modernisantisme*).

Third, Emile Poulat has well described the final scope of this modernism. Within Catholicism and beyond it, in all the Western milieux in which its influence makes itself felt in some degree, it limits the domain of the "believable" and expands that of the "knowable." *Modern* thus becomes the touchstone of a fundamental reorganization of the field of knowledge.

3. MODERN STYLE

One can—at the level of vocabulary, which is after all very important—contest the annexation by the *modern* of a whole constellation of esthetic movements that around 1900 took or were given various names in Europe and in the United States, and were called *Modern Style* only in France. But most of these names echo the modern through the intermediary of youth or novelty—*Jugendstil*, *arte joven*, *nieuwe Kunst*—or allude to the rupture that it implies—*Sezessionstil*, *style Liberty*. These movements indicate decisively the rejection of academic traditions, the farewell to antique (Greco-Roman) models in art. In a way, they put an end to the life-breath of the *antique/modern* opposition in art. What will henceforth be opposed to them will no longer be a return to the antique.

R. H. Guerrand has derived Modern Style and its cognates from a double trend visible in the second half of the nineteenth century: the struggle against academicism and the theme of art for everyone.[7] It is thus intimately bound up with three ideological aspects of the industrial revolution: liberalism, naturalism, and democracy.

In this essay, which concerns not art and its history, but rather the metamorphoses and meanings of the antithesis *antique (ancient)/modern*, we will focus only on a few significant episodes, figures, and principles. Since the enemy is the Antique, which has produced the artificial, the masterpiece, and is addressed to an elite, Modern Style will be naturalistic and take its inspiration from a nature in which sinuous lines predominate, to the detriment of straight or simple lines. It will have as its goal to produce objects, to invade everyday life, and thus to remove the barrier between high arts and minor arts. Finally, it will not be addressed to an elite, but to everyone, to the people; it will be social.

Modern Style is born in England with William Morris (1834–1896), a disciple of Ruskin who wanted to change the way *homes* looked. Morris launched the "decorative revolution," created in London the first shop selling decorative ensembles, and was the originator of *design*. In Belgium the movement is placed under the sign of the moderne with the foundation, in 1881, of the review *L'Art Moderne*. It is in Belgium, too, that the link between modern art and social policy is first asserted. One of the founders of an association called *La Libre Esthétique*, whose goal was to promote the new trends, was the editor of *Peuple*, the organ of the Belgian labor party. Victor Horta (1861–1947), an architect who exploited all the resources of steel and created buildings which he decorated and furnished, was one of the pioneers of social art and the builder of the Maison du Peuple in Brussels. And it was in Belgium that modern art found an architect and decorator, Henry Van de Velde (1863–1957), who, at the school that he directed at Weimar (where Gropius succeeded him), prepared the way for the great architectural art of the twentieth century, the Bauhaus. In the Netherlands, the *Nieuwe Kunst* used materials of all kinds: wood, porcelain, and silver, and made the new lines triumphant in the illustrated book, the calendar, and the poster.

In France, where Modern Style's first capital was in Nancy, with the Gallé glassworkers (1816–1904), the Dareux brothers, and the architect Victor Prouvé (1858–1943), who practiced all the arts, Modern Style descends into the street with Hector Guimard (1867–1942), the "Ravachol of architecture," who made of the Paris metro stations temples of modern art, and with the poster-artist Alphonse Mucha (1860–1939). The modern took over jewelry and goldsmithing with René Lalique (1860–1945) and opened shop with Samuel Bing (1838–1905), who made objects in the Modern Style fashionable.

In Germany, in Munich, modern art allied itself, under the sign of Youth (*Jugendstil*) with pacifism and anticlericalism. In Spain, or rather in Catalonia, modern art produced the genius of naturist architecture: Gaudi (1854–1920). In Italy, the *Liberty* style (taking its name from a British merchant who had founded a home furnishings shop in London in 1875) triumphed in the first International Exposition of modern decorative arts (Turin, 1902). In the United States, the exemplary figure is Tiffany (1848–1933), whose "art workshop" in New York excelled in all the so-called minor arts and promoted blown glass by making it the décor of the most familiar of modern inventions: electrical lighting.

Modern Style, an ephemeral phenomenon that lasted less than twenty years (from 1890 to 1910), was overshadowed by a movement that arose out of the rejection of decoration, curves, and flourishes, and that first appears in Darmstadt, Germany, and culminates in Austria with Adolph Loos (1870–1933). Amid the ruins of ornamentation, Loos made himself the prophet of a "new age" of "great walls, all white," the reign of concrete. Nevertheless, since 1970 Modern Style has emerged from a long purgatory to assert itself once again in the wake of *modernity*, thanks to characteristics that R. L. Delevoy has well analyzed: *Kitsch*, "the dimension of the gratuitous," a system of objects, structures of ambience, a language of ambiguity.

The essential point here is that the *antique* spirit was attached to heroes, to masterpieces, to exploits, while the *modern* spirit is henceforth nourished by the everyday, by the massive, by the diffuse.

Modernization

The first total confrontation between the antique and the modern was perhaps that between the Indians of the Americas and the Europeans. But the result was clear: the Indians were vanquished, conquered, reduced, or absorbed. The different forms of imperialism and colonialism in the nineteenth and early twentieth centuries rarely arrived at such radical outcomes. The nations touched by occidental imperialism, when they more or less succeeded in preserving their independence, were led to consider the problem of their backwardness in certain domains. Decolonization after World War II permitted the new nations to examine this problem in turn.

Nearly everywhere the nations that lagged behind found themselves facing the equation: modernization = westernization, and the problem of the modern was thus associated with that of national identity. Nearly everywhere too a distinction was drawn between social and cultural modernization and technological, economic, material modernization.

Here we can consider only a few examples intended to bring out the avatars of the couple *antique (ancient)/modern*. We will distinguish—while acknowledging the relatively arbitrary nature of this distinction—three types of modernization: (1) a balanced modernization in which the successful inroads of the *modern* have not destroyed the values of the *antique* (ancient); (2) a conflictual modernization in which the trend toward the *modern*, while affecting only part of the society, has created serious conflicts with ancient traditions; (3) a hesitant modernization which, taking various forms, seeks to reconcile *modern* and *antique (ancient)*, not through a new general equilibrium, but through partial choices.

The model of balanced modernization is Japan. Determined from the top of a hierarchical society, at a moment when the spread of the industrial revolution and the discoveries of the nineteenth century allowed

Japan to rapidly take its place among the leading modern nations, the modernization carried out by the Meiji (from 1867 onward) was characterized by the "reception of Western techniques and the conservation of indigenous values." But the autocratic-militarist regime that emerged from this process ended in 1945, a defeat that was, in some way, a major crisis in the modernization of Japan. In 1976, Japanese society, in spite of its progress toward democratic politics, is still experiencing the tensions inherent in an equilibrium between *antique (ancient)* and *modern.*

It may be that in another way, and on the basis of much more complex elements, Israel also represents a contemporary model of balanced modernization. But in this case the tensions are located within the geographical and cultural factors composing a new Israeli people, between these factors, and generally, between Jewish traditions (and their religious foundation) and the new State's need for a modernization which is one of the essential guarantees of its existence. For the same reasons concerning its survival, Israel must at all costs safeguard both its *antique (ancient)* and its *modern.*

The majority of Islamic countries can serve as examples of conflictual modernization. In these countries, modernization has usually come about not by choice but by invasion (military or other), and in any case through a shock administered from the outside. Almost everywhere in the Islamic world modernization has taken the form of Westernization, and this has reawakened or created a fundamental problem: West or East? Without entering into the details of this conflict, it can be said that historically, it appears in three forms: in the nineteenth century, as a reaction to European imperialism, whether colonialist or not; after World War II, in the framework of decolonization and the emergence of the third world; and in the 1970s with the boom in the oil market.

Although individual cases vary in many ways, on the whole, up to now, modernization has affected only a few sectors of the Islamic countries' economies and touched only the surface of their national life. It has been welcomed only by the governing elites and certain parts of the "bourgeoisie." It has exasperated nationalisms, deepened the gulfs between classes, and introduced a profound cultural malaise.

Jacques Berque and Gustav von Gruenebaum, among others, have analyzed this malaise.[8] For Gruenebaum, modernization raises for Islamic peoples and nations the essential problem of their identity. Jacques Berque has seen in "current Arab languages" the rupture that economists deplore in their own domain: "modern sector"/"traditional sector." Studying literary and artistic forms in the Arab world, which a hundred years ago "was ignorant of painting, sculpture, and even literature in the sense modern times have given to these words," he indicates the contradictions in the essay, the novel, music, theater, and paradoxically, even in film—an art without a past—which agitate and to a certain extent paralyze the culture. In this world where "the exception proceeds directly or indirectly from the foreign," modernity does not function as a creative process but as "acculturation, or a transaction between the archaic and the imported" (pp.292–93).

The black African countries can be considered a kind of laboratory of hesitant modernization. Whatever the variety of heritages and orientations, two basic givens dominate the *antique (ancient)/modern* problem in these countries. The first of these is the fact that their independence is of recent date, and the elements of modernization brought in by the colonizers are weak, fragmented, and poorly adapted to the real needs of the peoples and nations; in short, the *modern* is very young. The second is that the historical lag is great, and the *antique(ancient)* a very heavy burden.

As a result, through diverse and even opposed political and ideological formulas can be discerned two general desires: a) to find that which in the *modern* is suitable for Africa, to practice a selective, partial, loopholed, empirical, modernization; b) to seek a specifically African equilibrium between tradition and modernization.

Despite undeniable successes and considerable effort, it seems that modernization in black Africa often remains at the stage of moving incantations, and that Africa is not only groping its way but hesitating to face up to it except through a mixture of empiricism and rhetoric (although perhaps Africans are right to proceed in this way, and may be developing a specific, efficacious mode of modernization). For example, Amadou Hampaté Ba, then director of the Institute of Human Sciences in Mali, declared in 1965 that "To speak of 'tradition' is to speak of a heritage accumulated by a people over millions of years, and to speak of 'modernism' is to speak of a taste or even a mania for whatever is current. I do not think everything that is modern always represents an absolute progress with respect to the customs handed down to us from generation to generation. Modernism can represent moral, administrative, or technical progress on a particular point or a move backwards on this same point."[9] Moreover, he writes, "tradition is not opposed to progress; it seeks progress, it demands it, it demands it from God, and even from the Devil himself" (p. 45).

One case that may be aberrant with respect to the problem of modernization remains to be discussed. If Louis Dumont is right, the sense of time and history in India has so far remained untouched by the notion of progress. In India "people discussed the respective merits of the ancients and the moderns," but on a single level, so to speak, comparing them without any idea of progress (or regression). "History was only a repertory of high deeds and models of conduct, of examples" (1975:36), situated at a greater or a lesser distance, much as they might be located to the right or left, to the north or south, in a world that is not oriented by topological values.

Moreover, according to Dumont, the conditions of independence, far from simplifying the way the problem of modernization is raised, have made it more complicated:

> Adaptation to the modern world demands a major effort from Indians. Independence has created a misunderstanding, because having obtained it, Indians find themselves regarded as equals by other nations, and they have thus been able to imagine that the adaptation has essentially already been completed. Their success was established, and now they have only to make minor adjustments. The opposite was true. . . . For India has succeeded in ridding itself of foreign domination *while achieving a minimum of modernization.* This is doubtless a remarkable success, which is due in great part to the genius of Gandhi, whose policy can be summed up, I believe, by this very formula. (pp. 72–73)

If Dumont is correct, there would thus be an important segment of humanity that has up to now escaped the dynamic dialectic of the pair *antique (ancient)/modern.*

Modernity

The term *modernity* was coined by Baudelaire in his article "The Painter of Modern Life," which was written around 1860 and published in 1863. The term gained currency primarily in literary and artistic circles during the second half of the nineteenth century, and was later revived and much more widely used after World War II.

Baudelaire—and this is new—does not offer any reason for valuing the present, and thus the modern, other than that it is present. "The pleasure we derive from the representation of the present," he writes, "comes not only from the beauty it may have, but also from its essential quality of being present." The beautiful is partly eternal, but "academicians" (i.e., the partisans of the antique) do not see that it is necessarily also partly linked to "the times, to fashion, morality, passion." The beautiful must be at least partly modern. What is modernity? It is the "poetic in history," the "eternal" in the "transitory." Modernity derives from "mode." Thus in the examples he gives, Baudelaire speaks of feminine fashion, of the "study of the military man, the dandy, even animals, dogs or horses." He pushes the meaning of the word "modern" in the direction of behaviors, customs, settings. He claims that every period has "its bearing, its look, its gesture." What should interest us in the "antique" is only "the art itself, the logic, the general method." As for the rest, we have to retain "the memory of the present," and carefully study "everything that makes up the external life of a period."

Modernity is thus connected with fashion, with dandyism, with snobbery. Baudelaire stresses that "fashion should be considered a symptom of the taste for the ideal rising up in the human brain over everything crude, earthly, and revolting that natural life accumulates there . . ." We can understand the success enjoyed by the term among the cultural dandies, the Goncourt brothers, who wrote in their *Journal* (1889, p. 901): "Ultimately, the sculptor Rodin allows himself to be too much taken in by old-fashioned literature, and he lacks the natural taste for the modern that Carpeaux had."

In our own time Roland Barthes—one of the cantors of modernity who has also championed fashion—has written of Michelet: "He was perhaps the first author of modernity who could only sing what could not be spoken." Modernity here becomes an attack on limits, an adventure in marginality, as opposed to a conformity with the norm, a refuge in authority, a gathering in the center in the manner characteristic of the cult of the *antique*.

Modernity has found its theoretician in the philosopher Henri Lefebvre. In his *Introduction to Modernity*, Lefebvre distinguishes *modernity* from *modernism*: "Modernity differs from modernism in the way a concept that is being formulated in a society differs from social phenomena, as reflection differs from fact . . . The first tendency—certitude and arrogance—corresponds to Modernism; the second—a questioning and reflection that are already critical—corresponds to Modernity. These tendencies are inseparable, and both are aspects of the modern world" (p. 10).

Modernity, by turning toward what is unfinished, sketchy, ironic, thus tends to realize, in the second half of the twentieth century, and on the eve of postindustrial society, the program outlined by Romanticism. In this way, seen in a longer perspective, the conflict between *antique (ancient)* and *modern* persists, rearticulating the conjunctural opposition between classical and romantic in Western culture.

Modernity is the ideological outcome of modernism. But as an ideology of the unfinished, of doubt, and of criticism, modernity is also a drive toward *creation*—an explicit break with all ideologies and all theories of *imitation* founded on reference to the antique and tending toward academicism.

Going still further, Raymond Aron thinks that the ideal of modernity is "Promethean ambition," "the ambition to reclaim the old formula and become masters and possessors of nature through science and technology" (1969:287). But this stresses only the conquering side of modernity, and thus perhaps attributes to modernity what should be attributed only to modernism. In any case, it is a call to inquire, as we will do in conclusion, into the ambiguities of modernity.

Domains that reveal modernism

The oldest forms of the confrontation between *antique (ancient)* and *modern* were the quarrels of the Ancients and the Moderns; in other words, this confrontation took place primarily on a literary or, more generally, cultural terrain. Up until the recent battles concerning modernity (i.e., at the turn of the twentieth century), literature, philosophy, theology, art, and music have been particularly involved in these debates (in the realm of music, there is the *ars nova* dating from the fourteenth century, and then in the eighteenth century, Jean-Jacques Rousseau's "Treatise on Modern Music"). These realms of inquiry were even more beset by struggles over modernity in Antiquity, the Middle Ages and the Renaissance.

From the end of the Middle Ages a general vision—which was, however, limited to the clergy and the intellectuals—entered the field of battle. This was religion. Certainly, the *devotio moderna* did not attack the foundations of Christendom, the Reformation of the sixteenth century did not present itself as a "modern" movement (rather the reverse, with its references to the Old Testament, to the early Church, etc.), and even the "modernist" movement of the early twentieth century would have had a limited effect had the Church's highest authorities not lent it a significance that went far beyond its objectives. But the entry of religion into the *antique/modern* conflict marks a broadening of the debate.

It has not been sufficiently noticed that from the sixteenth to the eighteenth centuries, this debate, as it was experienced by contemporaries, was extended to two essentially new domains. The first of these is history. It is well known that the Renaissance created the concept of the Middle Ages, but only when it necessary as a bridge between two historical periods that were positive, full, significant: ancient history and modern history. The true innovation, from which everything else derived, was the idea of a "modern" history.

The second new domain was that of science. Here again the progress of "modern" science affects only the intellectual elite. It is true that the discoveries of the late eighteenth and nineteenth centuries were known and recognized by the masses. But Copernicus, Kepler, Galileo, Descartes, and later Newton, were able to convince part of the learned world that even if Homer, Plato, and Virgil remained unsurpassed, Archimedes and Ptolemy had been overthrown by modern scientists. The British were the first to notice this. Fontenelle, in the preface to his *History of the Academy of Sciences, 1666–1699*, ranked "the renewal of mathematics and physics" foremost among the advances made by the modern spirit of which he himself was one of the heralds. He goes on: "Descartes and other great men have labored with such success that this kind of literature has entirely changed its face." For Fontenelle, the chief point is that progress in these sciences has affected the human spirit as a whole: "Authority has ceased to have more weight than reason. . . . As these sciences have extended their scope their methods have become simpler and easier to use. In short, mathematics has not only recently yielded an enormous number of truths of its own kind, but also produced fairly generally an exactitude of thought that is perhaps more valuable than all these truths themselves."

The revolution in the area of the modern dates from the twentieth century. Modernity, considered up to that point primarily in relation to "superstructures," henceforth takes shape at all levels in the spheres that seem to twentieth-century men the most important: economics, politics, everyday life, mentalities.

As we have seen, it is with the intrusion of modernity into the third world that the economic criterion becomes primordial. Moreover, in the complex of modern economy, the touchstone of modernity is mechanization, and more precisely industrialization. But just as Fontenelle saw in the progress of certain sciences the progress of the human spirit, the economic criterion of modernity is perceived above all as a progress in mentality. Here again it is the *rationalization* of production that is the essential sign of modernity. The great minds of the nineteenth century had already recognized this, as Raymond Aron has noted: "Auguste Comte held the rational exploitation of natural resources to be the most important project of modern society, and Marx offered an interpretation of the permanent, constitutive dynamism of capitalist economy that still remains valid today" [*Les désillusions du progrès*, p. 299]. Gino Germani, returning to a text published in 1960 in Rio de Janeiro [*Resistencia a Mudança*], says much the same thing: "In *economics* the process of secularization means first of all the differentiation of *specific economic institutions* incorporating instrumental rationality as a fundamental principle of action and the institutionalization of change."[10]

This "intellectual" conception of economic modernity has led a group of social scientists to inquire into the problem of the relations between the Protestant ethic and economic development, thus extending to contemporary non-Western countries the theses that Max Weber and R. H. Tawney had defended concerning the sixteenth and seventeenth centuries in Europe (Eisenstadt 1968). These theses, which I believe to be false, have the merit of raising the problem of the relations between religion and modernity on a broader basis than that of quarrels between exegetes or theologians. In the same perspective, modernity can be examined—today—from the point of view of demography. First of all, the demography of the family: Gino Germani, for example, sees in the "secularization" of the family (divorce, birth control, etc.) an important aspect of the process of modernization and links the "modern" family to industrialization—a link demonstrated, he believes, by the case of Japan. Henri Lefebvre counts the appearance of "the modern woman" among the prominent traits of modernity.[11]

With this primacy of the economic and this definition of modernity by abstraction two new concepts come into play in the opposition between *antique(ancient)* and *modern* (ibid.). First, along with economics, the *modern* is associated not with *progress* in general, but with *development*, or in a more restricted sense, according to certain liberal economists, with *growth*. Second, *modern* is no longer opposed to *antique* but to *primitive*.

It is in the area of religion that G. Van Leeuw opposes a "primitive mentality" incapable of objectivizing to a "modern mentality" defined by the "faculty of abstraction".[12] But the twentieth century has also defined *modernity* by reference to certain political attitudes. Pierre Kende writes: "It is a commonplace to observe that the structures of modern life are the direct product of two series of revolutions: the one occurring in the sphere of *production* (the passage from artisanal to industrial modes of production), and the other in the *political* sphere (the replacement of monarchy with democracy)."[13] Kende adds: "Productive usage presupposes rational calculation, which is another aspect of lay and scientific thought." Marx, in his 1844 article "Zur Kritik der hegelschen Rechtsphilosophie" ("Critique of Hegel's Philosophy of Law"), wrote: "The abstraction of the State as such belongs only to modern times, and the abstraction of the political State is a modern product. The Middle Ages are characterized by real dualism, modern times by abstract dualism."

Raymond Aron, while essentially concerned with the problem of "the *social order* of *modernity*" (1969:298), starts out from *economic fact* and more precisely from the *productivity of labor*, and seems to arrive, as we have seen, at the idea of *Promethean ambition* founded on science and technology as "*the source of modernity*." He nevertheless defines "modern civilization" by three values whose political resonance is clear: "equality, personality, universality" (p. 287).

Studying "traditional political structures and modern political structures" in black Africa, Christian Vieyra observes that if most of the new African states have adopted political institutions of the Western type (universal and direct suffrage, separation of powers), the modernization of these states has not always succeeded in overcoming a "vicious circle": the transformation of these states into modern countries presupposes national unity, while the latter is based on structures (ethnic groups and leaders) tied to tradition and opposed to modernization.

Since Marx, the modern state is more or less defined by capitalism. Thus it is not surprising that for many people, and sometimes naively, the model of modernism, and particularly political modernism, is the United States. Kenneth S. Sherril has a offered a definition (based on research done in the United States) of the "politically modern man"; the chief interest of this definition is that it may influence (or reflect) the foreign policy of the United States. According to Sherril, the politically modern man (1) identifies with the national political community; (2) is able to distinguish between the personal and the political spheres; (3)

has a strong *ego*; (4) has firm opinions, (4a) is powerfully influenced by the mass media, and as a result, (4b) is well-informed; (5) is fundamentally optimistic, (6) needs to associate with others; (7) is inclined toward participation; (8) is concerned about political events without being either obsessed or upset by them, (8a) is partisan, but "openly partisan"; (9) has the feeling of having an influence on the decisions made by public authorities; and (10) is characterized by a general faith in government. More generally, the American is often presented as the prototype of the modern man, as a "new man."[14]

Finally, modernity has recently been defined by its massive character: it is a culture of everyday life and a mass culture. Baudelaire, in spite of his elitist definition of modernity, had from the beginning oriented it toward what Henri Lefebvre (himself a philosopher of modernity and of everyday life) has called "the flower of the everyday." The artistic movements known as "Art Nouveau" at the turn of the century also invested modernity in everyday objects as well as in artworks, and modernity thus leads to *design* and to gadgets. Pierre Kende sees one of the characteristics of modernity and one of the causes of its acceleration in the "massive diffusion of ideas," "mass communications." If McLuhan was wrong in predicting the disintegration of the Gutenberg galaxy, he correctly stressed the role of the audiovisual in modernity, as did Leo Bogart in *The Age of Television* (1968).

Edgar Morin has no doubt best described and explained modernity as "mass culture." He sees it as being born in the United States in the 1950s, and then spreading to other Western societies. He defines it this way:

> The popular masses in the cities and in part of the countryside accede to new standards of living; they enter progressively into the universe of well-being, leisure, consumption, which had previously been reserved for the middle classes. The quantitative transformation (increase in buying power, the substitution of machines for human labor, the augmentation of leisure time) bring about a slow qualitative metamorphosis: the problems of individual, private life, of the realization of a personal life thenceforth arise, insistently, no longer only at the level of the middle classes, but also at that of the developing salaried class. (1975:119–21)

Morin sees its chief novelty in the way mass culture subjects the relation between the *real* and the *imaginary* to an unprecedented transformation. This culture, which is "a great producer of myths" (happiness, well-being, leisure, etc.) functions not only from the real toward the imaginary but in the reverse direction as well. "It is not only an *evasion*, but at the same time and paradoxically an *integration*."

The twentieth century has in the past projected modernity into periods or societies that had no consciousness of modernity or had defined their modernity otherwise. Thus in 1930 an eminent French historian, Henri Hauser, saw in the sixteenth century (which had put the Ancients on a pedestal and saw itself as modern only in art, letters, and history and only in relation to the Middle Ages) five kinds of modernity: an "intellectual revolution," a "religious revolution," a "moral revolution," a "new politics," and a "new economy." And he concluded: "From any point of view, the sixteenth century thus appears to us as a prefiguration of our own time. In its conception of the world and of moral, individual, and social knowledge, in its feelings regarding the internal freedom of the soul, in its domestic and international politics, in the appearance of capitalism and the formation of a proletariat, and, we might add, in the birth of a national economy—in all these domains the Renaissance brought with it new elements that were singularly fertile even when they proved to be dangerous . . ." But can we speak of modernity in a case where the supposed moderns had no consciousness of being modern or at least did not mention it?

The historical conditions of the recognition of modernism

Our goal here is not to explain the causes of the accelerated transformation of societies in the course of history, or to explore the difficult history of changes in collective mentalities, but rather to shed light on the ways people come to recognize breaks with the past and on the collective will to assume these breaks that we call modernism or modernity. We will focus on four elements that frequently come into play separately or together in this process of recognition [*prise de conscience*]. The first of these is the perception of what has been commonly called in certain periods the "acceleration of history." But in order for there to be a conflict between Ancients and Moderns, this acceleration must allow a conflict between generations. For instance, the quarrel between the nominalists and the Aristotelians, the humanists and the Scholastics (let us recall here the cunning of history that makes the supporters of Antiquity the Moderns in this case), the Romantics and the Classicists, the partisans of modern art and the defenders of academicism, etc. The *antique (ancient)/modern* opposition, which is one of the conflicts through which societies experience their contradictory relations with their past, becomes acute when the Moderns have to struggle against a past present, a present that is experienced as a past, when the quarrel between Ancients and Moderns takes on the form of a settling of accounts between fathers and sons.

The second element is the pressure that material progress exercises on mentalities, contributing to their transformation. It is true that changes in mentality are seldom sudden, and that they take place primarily at the level of the mentalities themselves. What changes is the mental equipment. The recognition of modernity is expressed most often through an affirmation of reason—or rationality—against the authority of tradition, as in the case of the "modern" thinkers of the Middle Ages opposing the "authorities," Enlightenment writers from Fontenelle to Condorcet, or Catholic modernists who opposed traditionalists at the beginning of the twentieth century. But modernity can also—in the cases of Ruysbroeck, Gérard Groote, Baudelaire, or Roland Barthes—privilege the mystique of the contemplative over intellectuality, "the transitory, fugitive, and contingent" over the "eternal and immutable" (Baudelaire). Henri Lefebvre adds the "aleatory" as a characteristic of modern modernity. But the technological and economic "revolution" of the twelfth and thirteenth centuries, the science of the seventeenth century, the inventions and the industrial revolution of the nineteenth century, and the atomic revolution of the second half of the twentieth century are all factors stimulating the recognition of modernity whose action should be carefully studied.

In some cases an external shock facilitates the recognition. Greek philosophy and the works of the Arab thinkers, if they did not launch, certainly nourished the "modernist" consciousness of the medieval Scholastics; Western technology and thought created the conflict between Ancients and Moderns in non-European societies; and Japanese and African art played a role in the coming to consciousness of the new art of the West around 1900.

Finally, the affirmation of modernity, even if it goes beyond the borders of culture, is restricted to a limited group of intellectuals and technocrats. A phenomenon of the recognition of progress often contemporaneous with a democratization of social and political life, modernity remains, at least at the level of its development, limited to an "elite," to groups and coteries. Even when modernity has a tendency, as it does today, to incarnate itself in a mass culture, as Edgar Morin has suggested, those who develop that culture, through television, posters, design, comic strips, etc., belong to a restricted group of intellectuals. This is just one of modernity's ambiguities.

The ambiguity of the modern

We should note first that the modern has a tendency to *deny itself*, to *destroy itself*. From the Middle Ages onward one of the arguments of the Moderns has been that the Ancients were Moderns in their own time. Fontenelle, for example, reminded his readers that the Latins had been modern with respect to the Greeks. By defining the modern as the present one can make of it a *future* past. One thus privileges not a content but an ephemeral container. Baudelaire, pushing this meaning of the modern to the limit in his concept of modernity, and drawing on fashion in order to define it, dooms the modern to be perpetually on the way toward obsolescence. "The pleasure we derive from the representation of the present comes not only from the beauty it may possess, but also from its essential quality of being present."

Thus the modern is not only linked to fashion ("Fashion and the modern are both attached to time and to the moment, and mysteriously connected with the eternal, mobile images of an immobile eternity," says Henri Lefebvre, commenting on Baudelaire [1962:172]), it can scarcely escape snobbery. The modern tends to privilege the new for its own sake, to empty out the content of the work, of the object, of the idea. "Since the sole interest for modern art," writes H. Rosenberg, "lies in the novelty of a work, and since this novelty is not determined by analysis but by social and pedagogical power, avant-garde painting exercises its activity in a milieu totally indifferent to the content of its work" (1959:37).

Ultimately, modernity can designate anything at all, and notably the ancient. "Everyone knows," H. Rosenberg observes, "that the label *modern art* no longer has any relation to the words that compose it. In order to be modern art, a work does not need to be modern, nor art, nor even a work. A three-hundred-year-old mask from the South Pacific can be called modern and a piece of wood found on a beach becomes art" (p. 35). The modern is caught up in an unrestrained process of acceleration. It has always to be more modern, and it is whirled about in the vertiginous vortex of modernity.

Here is another paradox—or ambiguity: the "modern" at the edge of the abyss of the present turns back toward the past. If it attacks the ancient, it nevertheless tends to take refuge in history. Modernity and the taste for earlier styles go together. "This period, which calls itself and wants to be entirely new, allows itself to be obsessed by the past: memory, history." Thus Jeanne Favret has shown by studying the local politics of rural Algeria how one can fall into "traditionalism through an excess of modernity." Among the inhabitants of Kabylia in particular, the penetration of the Industrial Revolution destroyed the traditional structures, but a hundred years later, traditionalism reappears, not to fulfill the old functions, which no longer exist, but a new function of calling for modernization.

The ambiguities of modernity are especially relevant to revolution. As Henri Lefebvre has shown, modernity is "the shadow of the revolution, its dispersion and sometimes its caricature." But paradoxically, this break that individuals and societies make with their past, or the modernist reading of history that is not so much revolutionary as disrespectful, can become, through what Edgar Morin has called "the impregnation of cultural and daily life," an instrument that makes its users more adaptable to change and better able to integrate themselves into their surroundings.

MEMORY

The idea of memory is an intersection. Although the present essay is devoted exclusively to memory as it appears in the human sciences—primarily in history and anthropology—and is therefore chiefly concerned with collective rather than individual memories, it is important to sketch out briefly the contours of the amorphous phenomenon we call memory as it appears generally within the field of knowledge.

Memory, the capacity for conserving certain information, refers first of all to a group of psychic functions that allow us to actualize past impressions or information that we represent to ourselves as past. From this point of view the study of memory is related to psychology, psychophysiology, neurophysiology, biology, and where disturbances of memory—the principal one being amnesia—are concerned, to psychiatry.[1] Certain aspects of the study of memory in one or the other of these sciences may allude, either metaphorically or concretely, to traits or problems of historical and social memories (Morin and Piatelli-Palmarini 1974).

The notion of apprenticeship, which is important in the phase of memory acquisition, leads us to pay attention to the different systems of training memory that have existed in various societies and in various periods: mnemotechnologies. All the theories leading in some measure to the idea of a more or less mechanical actualization of memory *traces* have been abandoned in favor of more complex concepts of the mnemonic activity of the nervous system: "the process of memory in human beings involves not only the establishment of traces, but the rereading of these traces," and "the processes of rereading can involve very complex nerve centers and a large part of the cortex," even if there are "some cerebral centers that specialize in the fixing of memory traces" (Changeux 1974:356).

In particular, the study of childhood memory acquisition has allowed us to observe the major role played by intelligence (Piaget and Inhelder 1968). In line with that thesis, Scandia de Schonen declares that "The characteristic of perceptual-cognitive behavior patterns that seems to us most fundamental is their active, constructive aspect" (1974:294), and she adds: "Therefore one can conclude by hoping that further research will investigate the problem of mnesic activities by resituating them in the ensemble of perceptual-cognitive activities, in the ensemble of those activities that aim either at organizing themselves in a different way in the same situation, or at adapting to new situations. Only in this way will we someday be able to understand the nature of human memory, which causes us so much trouble in our fields" (p. 302). Whence the various recent conceptions of memory that emphasize aspects of structuration and self-organizing activities. The phenomena of memory, in their biological as well as their psychological aspects, are only the result of dynamic systems of organization and exist only "insofar as the organization maintains or reconstitutes them."[2]

Researchers have thus been led to relate memory to phenomena having to do directly with the human and social sciences. For example, Pierre Janet in his book *L'évolution de la mémoire et la notion du temps* (1922) regards the fundamental mnemonic act to be the "conduct of the story," which he defines as *social function* because it is the communication of information from one person to another in the absence of the actual event or object concerned; here we encounter "language as a product of society." Similarly, Henri Atlan, studying self-organizing systems, relates "languages and memories": "The utilization of a spoken and then a written language is a powerful extension of the storage capacity of our memory, which can thereby move beyond the limits of our bodies and locate itself either in others or in libraries. That means that before being spoken or written, a certain language exists in our memory as a form of information storage" (Morin and Piatelli-Palmarini, p. 461).

It is even more evident that the memory disturbances which, alongside amnesia,[3] can also appear at the level of language in aphasia, must also be explained in many cases by reference to the social sciences. Moreover, at a metaphorical but important level, in the same way that amnesia is not merely a local disturbance of the individual's memory but causes more or less serious perturbations in his personality, the absence, or voluntary or involuntary loss, of collective memory among peoples and nations can cause serious problems of collective identity. The connections between different forms of memory may also be not metaphorical but real in character. Jack Goody has observed, for example, that "in all societies individuals hold a large quantity of information in their genetic heritage, in their long-term memory, and temporarily, in their active memory" (1977a:3–5).

André Leroi-Gourhan, in *La mémoire et les rythmes*, the second part of *Le Geste et la parole*, takes memory in a very broad sense, but also distinguishes three types of memory: *specific* memory, *ethnic* memory, and *artificial* memory.

> Memory is understood in this work in a very extended sense. It is not only a property of intelligence but, whatever it may be, the support on which sequences of acts are inscribed. In this way one can speak of a "specific memory" to define the fixation of the behavior in animal species, of an "ethnic" memory which ensures the reproduction of behaviors in human societies, and, by the same token, of an "artificial" memory, which is electronic in its most recent form, and which ensures, without recourse to instinct or reflection, the reproduction of linked mechanical acts. (p. 269)

Recent developments in cybernetics and biology have considerably enriched the notion of memory, especially metaphorically, in relation to human conscious memory. People now speak of the memory of computers, and the genetic code is presented as a memory for heredity.[4] But paradoxically, this extension of memory to machines and to life has at the same time directly affected psychological research on memory, passing from a primarily empirical stage to a theoretical stage: "From 1950 on, interests shifted radically, partly under the influence of new sciences such as cybernetics and linguistics, and took a clearly more theoretical turn."[5]

Psychologists and psychoanalysts have insisted, in the case of memory as well as in that of forgetting (notably following Ebbinghaus), on the conscious or unconscious manipulations that interest, affectivity, desire, inhibition, and censorship exercise on individual memory. Similarly, collective memory has been an important issue in the struggle for power among social forces. To make themselves the master of memory and forgetfulness is one of the great preoccupations of the classes, groups, and individuals who have dominated and continue to dominate historical societies. The things forgotten or not mentioned by history reveal these mechanisms for the manipulation of collective memory.

The study of social memory is one of the fundamental approaches to the problems of time and history, in relation to which memory is sometimes retreating, sometimes overflowing. In the historical study of historical memory, we must accord a special importance to the differences between societies whose memory is essentially oral and those whose memory is essentially written, and to the phases of the passage from orality to writing—what Jack Goody calls "the domestication of primitive thought." We will therefore take up in succession: (1) ethnic memory, in societies without writing, called "primitive"; (2) the rise of memory, from orality to writing, from prehistory to Antiquity; (3) medieval memory, in equilibrium between the oral and the written; (4) the progress of written memory, from the sixteenth century to the present; (5) the current overflowing of memory. This procedure is inspired by that of André Leroi-Gourhan: "The history of collective memory can be divided into five periods: oral transmission, written transmission with tables or indices, simple file cards, mechanical writing, and electronic sequencing" (1964/65:65).

In order to bring out more clearly the relations between memory and history that constitute the principal horizon of this essay, it has seemed to me preferable to discuss separately memory in societies without writing, whether ancient or modern, and to distinguish the following phases in the history of memory in societies that have both oral and written memories: (1) the antique phase in which oral memory predominates alongside the particular functions of written or figured memory; (2) the medieval phase of equilibrium between the two memories along with the important transformations in the functions of each of them; (3) the modern phase characterized by decisive advances in written memory connected with printing and literacy, and finally; (4) the phase corresponding to the revolutionary changes of the past century that Leroi-Gourhan calls "memory in expansion."

Ethnic Memory

Contrary to Leroi-Gourhan, who uses the term "ethnic memory" for all human societies, I will use it only to refer to the collective memory of people without writing. Let us note, without paying it undue attention, but without forgetting its importance, that outside of writing mnesic activity is constant not only in societies without writing, but also in those that have it. Jack Goody has recently pertinently reminded us that "In most cultures without writing, and in many sectors of our own culture, the accumulation of elements within memory is part of everyday life" (1977a:35).

This distinction between oral and written cultures by reference to the tasks assigned to memory seems to me, as to Goody, to be based on the fact that relations among these cultures are situated at the midpoint between two currents of thought that are equally wrong in their radicalism—"one affirming that all men have the same possibilities, the other drawing, explicitly or implicitly, a distinction between 'them' and 'us' " (p. 45). The truth is that the culture of people without writing is different, but it is not other.

The principal domain in which the collective memory of peoples without writing crystallizes is that which provides an apparently historical foundation for the existence of ethnic groups or families, that is, myths of origin. Georges Balandier, discussing historical memory among the inhabitants of the Congo, notes that "The beginnings seem all the more impressive because they have survived in memory with less precision. The Congo has never been so vast as it was in the time of its obscure history."[6] "Ritual . . . accentuates certain aspects of power. It evokes its beginnings, its roots in a history that has become mythic, and it makes this history sacred."

Apropos of the Nupe of Nigeria, Nadel distinguishes two types of history: on the one hand, the history he calls "objective," which is "the series of facts that we, as researchers, describe and establish in accord with certain criteria that are 'objective, universal, and concern their relations and succession," ' and on the other the history he calls "ideological," which "describes and organizes these facts in accord with certain established traditions" (1976:127). This second kind of history is the collective memory that tends to confuse history with myth. And this "ideological history" turns its attention more readily toward "the earliest beginnings of the kingdom," toward "the figure of Tsoede or Edegi, the cultural hero and mythical founder of the Nupe kingdom." The history of beginnings thus becomes, to adopt Malinowski's expression, a "mythical charter" of the tradition.

This collective memory of so-called "primitive" societies is also particularly interested in practical, technical, and professional knowledge. As Leroi-Gourhan has pointed out, in acquiring this "technical memory" through apprenticeship "the social structure of trades plays an important role, whether we are concerned with blacksmiths in Africa or Asia, or with trade associations in the West up to the seventeenth century. Apprenticeship and the conservation of trade secrets is at stake in each of the social sciences of the ethnic groups" (1964/65:66). Georges Condominas has found among the Moïs of central Vietnam the same orientation of collective memory toward the time of origins and mythical heroes (1965:). This attraction of the ancestral past for "primitive memory" can also be verified in the case of proper names. In the Congo, Balandier notes, after the clan has given the newborn child a first name known as a "birthname," he is given a second, more official name, which displaces the first. This second name "perpetuates the memory of an ancestor, who is chosen because of the veneration in which he is held."[7]

In these societies without writing, there are memory specialists, memory-men—"Genealogists, guardians of the royal lawbooks, historians of the court, traditionists"—of whom Balandier says that they are "the memory of the society" and that they are at once the conservators of "objective" history and of "ideological history," to use Nadel's terms (19 :207). But they are also "aged heads of families, bards, priests," according to Leroi-Gourhan, who attributes to these figures "in traditional humanity, the very important role of maintaining the cohesion of the group" (1964/65;660).

But it must be emphasized that contrary to what is generally thought, the memory transmitted through apprenticeship in societies without writing is not a "word-for-word" memory. Goody has proven this by studying the myth of the Bagre among the Lo Dagaa in northern Ghana.

He has pointed out the numerous variants in the different versions of the myth, even in the most stereotypical fragments. The memory-men, in this case storytellers, do not play the same role as schoolmasters (the school appears only with writing). A mechanical, automatic apprenticeship does not develop around them. But according to Goody, in dealing with societies that lack writing, we have to consider not only the objective difficulty involved in word-for-word, total memorization, but also the fact that "this kind of activity is rarely felt to be necessary"; "the product of an exact act of memory" seems to these societies as "less important, less useful, less valuable than the fruit of an inexact evocation" (1977a:38). Thus one seldom finds mnemotechnical procedures in these societies (one of the rare exceptions is the case of the Peruvian Quipu, a classic of ethnographic literature). Collective memory seems to function in these societies in accordance with a "generative reconstruction" rather than with a mechanical memorization. In this way, Goody says, "the support of rememoration is not situated on the superficial level on which memory operates word-for-word, nor on the level of "deep" structures that many mythologists discern . . . on the contrary, it seems that the important role is played by the narrative dimension and by other structures at the level of particular events" (p. 34). On this view, while mnemonic reproduction word-for-word would be linked to writing, societies without writing (though they may have certain practices of memorization *ne varietur*, the principal one being song) grant memory more freedom and creative possibilities.

Perhaps this hypothesis would explain an astonishing comment in Caesar's *Gallic Wars* (VI, 14). Concerning the Druids who lived amongst the Gauls, around whom many young people gathered to learn from them, Caesar writes:

> There, they learn by heart, people say, a large number of verses, and some of them spend twenty years studying with the Druids. They believe that religion forbids these courses to be written down, whereas for almost everything else, both public and private accounts, they use the Greek alphabet. They seem to me to have established this custom for two reasons: because they do not wish to divulge their doctrine, or to see their pupils neglect their memory by relying on writing, for it almost always happens that making use of texts has as its result decreased zeal for learning by heart and a diminution of memory.

The transmission of knowledge considered to be secret, the will to safeguard in proper form a more creative than repetitive memory—are these not two of the principal reasons for the vitality of collective memory in societies without writing?

The Rise of Memory: From Orality to Writing, from Prehistory to Antiquity

In societies without writing, collective memory seems to organize itself around three major interests: the collective identity based on myths, and more particularly on myths of origin, the prestige of the leading families that is expressed by genealogies, and the technical knowledge that is transmitted by practical formulas that are deeply imbued with religious magic.

The appearance of writing is linked to a profound transformation in collective memory. As early as the "middle paleolithic age," figures appear which have been seen as "mythograms" paralleling the "mythology" that develops in the verbal order. Writing permits collective memory to make a double advance with the rise of two forms of memory. The first is the commemoration or celebration of a memorable event by a commemorative monument. In this case memory takes the form of an inscription and leads in modern times to the development of a science auxiliary to history, epigraphy. To be sure, the world of inscriptions is very diverse. Louis Robert has stressed its heterogeneity: "Runes, the Turkish epigraphy of Orkhon, Phoenician, Neopunic, Hebraic, Sabean, Iranian, and Arabic epigraphies, the Khmer inscriptions—these are all very different things" (Samaran 1961:453). In the ancient Middle East, for example, commemorative inscriptions were the occasion for multiplying monuments such as steles and obelisks. Mesopotamia was the domain of steles, where as early as the third millennium B.C. kings tried to immortalize their exploits by means of figured representations accompanied by an inscription. A notable case is the Vulture Stele now in the Louvre, on which the king Eannatoum of Lagash, around 2470 B.C., had the memory of a victory preserved in images and inscriptions. The Akkadian kings made particularly frequent use of this form of commemoration, and the most famous of their steles is the one of Naram-Sim, in Susa, on which the king wished to perpetuate the image of a victory won over the people of Zagros (also in the Louvre). In the Assyrian period, the stele took the form of the obelisk, such as that of Assourbelkala (end of the second millennium B.C.) at Nineveh (in the British Museum) and the black obelisk of Salmanasar III, which comes from Nimrud, immortalizing the king's victory over the country of Mousri (853; in the British Museum). Sometimes, the commemorative monument lacks inscriptions and its meaning remains obscure, as in the case of the obelisks of the Obelisk Temple in Byblos (beginning of the second millennium B.C.).[8] In ancient Egypt steles fulfilled multiple functions in perpetuating a memory: funerary steles commemorating, as at Abydos, a pilgrimage to a familial tomb, or recounting the life of the deceased, like that of Amenenemphet under Thoutmosis III; royal steles commemorating victories such as that called "the Victory of Israel" under Minephtah (c. 1230 B.C.), the only Egyptian document mentioning Israel, probably from the period of the Exodus; juridical steles, like that at Karnak (let us recall that the most famous of these juridical steles of antiquity is the one on which Hammurabi, a king of the first Babylonian dynasty, c. 1792–1750 B.C., had his Code engraved, and which is preserved in the Louvre); sacerdotal steles on which priests had their privileges engraved.[9] But the great period of inscriptions was that of ancient Greece and Rome, about which Louis Robert has said, "one could call the Greek and Roman countries a civilization of epigraphy" (1961:454). In temples, cemeteries, public squares and avenues, along roads and even "deep in the mountains, in the greatest solitude," inscriptions accumulated and encumbered the Greco-Roman world with an extraordinary effort of commemoration and perpetuation of memory. Stone, usually marble, served as a support for an overload of memory. These "stone archives" added to the function of archives proper the character of an insistent publicity, wagering on the ostentation and durability of this lapidary and marmoreal memory.

The other form of memory connected with writing is the document written on a support specially designed for writing (after experiments with bone, cloth, skin, cinders and letters of clay or wax in Mesopotamia, birchbark in ancient Russia, palm leaves as in India, or tortoise shells as in China, and finally with papyrus, parchment, and paper). But it is important to note that, as I have tried to show (Le Goff 1978 5:38–48), every document has in itself the character of a monument and that there is no unmediated, raw collective memory.

In this type of document, writing has two principal functions: "the first is information storage, which allows communication across time and space and provides men with a means of marking, memorizing, and registering"; the other, "while ensuring the passage from the auditory to the visual domain," allows us "to examine in a different way, to rearrange, to rectify phrases and even isolated words" (1977b:145).

For Leroi-Gourhan, the evolution of memory, which is linked to the appearance and diffusion of writing, depends essentially on social evolution and particularly on urban development:

> Collective memory, when writing begins, does not have to interrupt its traditional movement, except when there is something a nascent social system has a special interest in preserving. It is therefore not a coincidence that writing notes what is normally neither made nor seen, but constitutes the framework of urban society, for which the heart of the vegetative system lies in an economy of circulation among producers, whether celestial or human, and rulers. The innovation affects the top of the system, and selectively includes financial and religious documents, dedications, genealogies, the calendar—everything that in the new city structures cannot be completely fixed in memory either by sequences of gestures or by products. (1964/65: 67–68)

Great civilizations, in Mesopotamia, Egypt, China, or pre-Columbian America, have at first tried to use written memory for the calendar and for distances. "The sum of the facts that must be passed on through successive generations" is limited to religion, history, and geography. "The threefold problem of time, space, and man constitutes what is memorable" (p. 68).

This is a specifically urban memory, and a royal one too. Not only does "the capital city become the pivot of the celestial world and of humanized space"—and, let us add, the center of a politics of memory—but the king himself deploys, on the whole terrain over which he holds sway, a program of remembering of which he is the center.

Kings constitute memory-institutions: archives, libraries, museums. Zimri-Lum (c. 1782/1789 B.C.) made of his palace in Mari, where numerous tablets have been found, an archival center. In Ras-Shamra, in Syria, the excavation of the building of the royal archives of Ougarit has made it possible to locate the archival depots in the palace: diplomatic, financial, and administrative archives. In this same palace, there was a library in the second millennium B.C., and in the seventh century B.C., the library of Ashurbanipal in Nineveh was famous. In the Hellenistic period the great library of Pergamum was founded by Attalus, and the celebrated library at Alexandria was combined with the famous Museum created by the Ptolemys. It is a royal memory, insofar as kings have *Annals* composed, and sometimes engraved on stone (at least in extracts), in which their exploits are especially recounted, and which bring us to the frontier where memory becomes "history" (see the final essay, "History").

In the ancient Orient before the middle of the second millennium B.C. there are only dynastic lists and legendary accounts of royal heroes like Sargon or Naram-Sim. Then sovereigns begin to have their scribes write more detailed accounts of their reigns, in which military victories, the bounty of their justice, and the progress of the laws emerge, three domains worthy of providing memorable examples for men to come. In Egypt, it seems that from the invention of writing, shortly before the beginning of the third millennium, up to the fall of the indigenous royalty in the Roman period, the royal *Annals* were continuously maintained. But the one and no doubt only copy preserved on papyrus has disappeared. There remain no more than a few extracts engraved on stone.[10] In China, the ancient royal annals on bamboo probably date from the eleventh century B.C., and they include mainly questions and the responses of oracles which form "a vast repertory of governmental formulas" and "the function of archivist gradually devolved on the diviners: they were the guardians of the memorable events proper to each reign."[11] Finally, there is also a funerary memory, as is shown, for instance, by the Greek steles and Roman sarcophagi—a memory that has played a capital role in the development of the portrait.

With the passage from oral to written transmission, collective memory, and especially "artificial memory," undergoes a profound transformation. Goody thinks that the appearance of mnemotechnical procedures allowing "word for word" memorization is linked to writing. But in his opinion the existence of writing "also implies internal modifications in psychic life," and "it is not a matter of simply a new technical capability, of something comparable, for example, to a mnemotechnical procedure, but of a new intellectual *aptitude*" (1977b:192–93). At the heart of this new mental activity, Goody places the *list*, the series of words, concepts, gestures, operations that are to be carried out in a certain *order*, and that allow a verbal given to be "decontextualized" and "recontextualized" in the manner of a "linguistic recoding." In support of this thesis, he points to the importance in antique civilizations of lexical lists, glossaries, and treatises on onomastics that are based on the idea that to name is to know. He underlines the significance of the Sumerian lists known as "Proto-Izi" and sees in them one of the instruments of Mesopotamian expansion: "This kind of educative method based on the memorization of lexical lists had extended over an area far exceeding Mesopotamia and played an important role in the diffusion of Mesopotamian culture and the influence it exercised on neighboring zones: Iran, Armenia, Asia Minor, Syria, Palestine, and even Egypt in the period of the New Empire" (p. 178).

We should add that this model must be refined according to the kind of society and the historical moment in which the passage from one kind of memory to the other takes place. It cannot be applied without qualification to the passage from oral to written in antique societies, in modern or contemporary "primitive" societies, in European societies of the Middle Ages, or in Islamic societies. Dale F. Eickelman has shown that in the Islamic world a type of memory based on the memorization of a culture at once oral and written lasts until around 1930, then changes and recalls the fundamental links between school and memory in all societies.

The oldest Egyptian treatises on onomastics, which were perhaps inspired by Sumerian models, date only from about 1100 B.C. The treatise by Amenope was published by Maspéro under the significant title "Un manuel de hiérarchie égyptienne."[12]

We should, in fact, ask ourselves what this transformation of intellectual activity revealed by written "artificial memory" is connected with in its turn. Writers have noted the need to memorize numerical values (regular notches, knotted cords, etc.) and proposed a link with the development of commerce. We must go further and resituate this expansion of *lists* within the establishment of monarchical power. Memorization by inventory, the hierarchized list, is not only an activity of organizing knowledge in a new way, but also an aspect of the organization of a new power.

It is thus that we must trace back to the royal period of ancient Greece the lists whose echo is found in the Homeric epics. In the second book of the *Iliad*, we find in succession the catalogue of ships, then the catalogue of the greatest warriors and the best Achaian horses, and immediately afterward the catalogue of the Trojan army. "The whole forms about half of the second Book, amounting to almost 400 lines, composed almost exclusively of a series of proper names, which presupposes a veritable training of the memory" (Vernant 1965:55–56). With the Greeks, we see in striking fashion the evolution of collective memory into history. Transposing a study by Ignace Meyerson (1956) from individual memory to collective memory as it appears in ancient Greece, Vernant emphasizes: "Memory, insofar as it is distinguished from habit, represents a difficult invention, the progressive conquest by man of his individual past, as history constitutes for the social group the conquest of its collective past" (p. 51). But among the ancient Greeks, in the same way that written memory added itself to, and transformed, oral memory, history takes over collective memory, modifying but not destroying it. This makes it all the more profitable to study the functions and evolution of collective memory. The divinization, and later the secularization of memory, the birth of mnemotechnology: that is the rich tableau offered by Greek collective memory between Hesiod and Aristotle, between the eighth and the fourth centuries B.C.

To be sure, the passage from oral memory to written memory is difficult to pinpoint. But one institution and one text may perhaps be able to help us reconstruct what might have happened in archaic Greece. The institution is that of the *mnemon*, which "allows us to observe the advent in the law of a social function of memory" (Gernet 1947:285). The mnemon is a person who maintains the memory of the past for the purpose of making juridical decisions. This can be a person whose role as "memory" is exercised only occasionally. For instance Theophrastus mentions that in the law of the Thurium the three neighbors closest to the property to be sold received a coin "for the purpose of *remembrance* and *testimony*." But the mnemon can also be a more durable function. The appearance of these memory officials recalls the phenomena we have already mentioned: the links with myth and with urbanization. In mythology and legend, the *mnemon* is the servant of a hero whom he constantly accompanies in order to remind him of the divine mission that will cause his death if he forgets it. The *mnemons* are used by cities as magistrates charged with keeping in their memories what is useful in religious matters (concerning the calendar in particular) and in jurisprudence. With the development of writing, these "living memories" are transformed into archivists.

On the other hand, in the *Phaedrus* (274C—275B), Plato places in the mouth of Socrates the legend of the invention by the Egyptian god Thot, the patron of scribes and literate officials, of numbers, calculation, geometry and astronomy, table games and dice, and the alphabet. And he stresses that in doing this, the god transformed memory but no doubt also contributed to weakening it more than to developing it: the alphabet, "by relieving men of the need to exercise their memories, will produce forgetfulness in the souls of those who learn it, so much so that trusting to writing, they will seek outside themselves, and on their own, the means of remembering; as a result, you have found a remedy, not for memory, but rather for the process of remembering." It has been suggested that this passage alludes to a survival of the traditions of oral memory (Notopoulos 1938:476).

The most remarkable thing is no doubt the "divinization of memory and the elaboration of a vast mythology of reminiscence in archaic Greece," as Vernant has well put it. Vernant generalizes his observation: "In different periods and cultures, there is a connection between the techniques of remembering that are practiced, the internal organization of that function, its place in the system of the self, and the image that people have of memory" (1965:51).

The Greeks of the archaic age made Memory a goddess—Mnemosyne. She is the mother of the nine muses, whom she has conceived in the course of nine nights spent with Zeus. She reminds men of the memory of heroes and their high deeds, and she presides over lyric poetry.[13] The poet is thus possessed by memory, the *aede* is a diviner of the past, as the seer divines the future. He is the inspired witness of the "ancient times," of the heroic age, and beyond that, of the age of origins.

When poetry is identified with memory, this makes the latter a kind of knowledge and even of wisdom, of *sophia*. The poet takes his place among the "masters of truth"[14] and at the origins of Greek poetics the poetic word is a living inscription inscribed on memory as it is on marble (J. Svenbro). It has been said that for Homer, "to versify was to remember." By revealing the secrets of the past to the poet, Mnemosyne introduces him to the mysteries of the beyond. Memory then appears as a gift reserved for initiates, and *amamnesis* or reminiscence as an ascetic and mystical technique. Thus Memory plays a prominent role in Orphic and Pythagorean doctrines. It is the antidote for Oblivion. In the Orphic underworld the dead must avoid the springs of oblivion; they must not drink the waters of the Lethe, but on the contrary drink from the fountain of Memory, which is a source of immortality.

Among the Pythagorean philosophers, these beliefs are combined with a doctrine of the reincarnation of souls, and the path to perfection is the one that leads to the remembrance of all previous lives. The adherents of these sects regarded Pythagoras as an intermediary between man and God because he had retained the memory of his successive reincarnations, and notably his existence, during the Trojan war, in the form of Euphorbus, whom Menelaus killed. Empedocles also remembered himself: "A wanderer exiled from the seat of the gods. . . . I have already been a boy and a girl, a bush and a bird, a silent fish in the sea." Thus in the Pythagorean apprenticeship "exercises in memory" played an important part. According to Aristotle (*Rhetoric*, III, 17, 10), Epimenides entered in this way into a state of ecstatic remembrance.

But as Vernant has profoundly remarked, "the transposition of Mnemosyne from the cosmological to the eschatological level changes everything in the equilibrium of myths about memory" (1965:61). This removal of Memory from the temporal realm radically separates memory from history. The mystical divinization of memory obstructs every "effort to explore the past" and "the construction of an architecture of time" (pp. 73–74). Thus, depending on its orientation, memory can lead toward history or away from it. When it is put in the service of eschatology it also nourishes itself on a veritable hatred for history (Le Goff 1978 5:712–46).

Even the greatest Greek philosophers never fully succeeded in reconciling memory and history. If memory in Plato and Aristotle is a function of the soul, it does not manifest itself at its intellectual level but only at its sensuous level. In a famous passage in Plato's *Theatetus* (191 C-D), Socrates speaks of the wax tablet that exists in our souls, which is "the gift of memory, the mother of the Muses," and which permits us to receive impressions in the way a signet ring imprints sealing wax. Platonic memory has lost its mythical aspect, but it does not try to make the past a source of knowledge; rather, it wants to escape from temporal experience.

Aristotle distinguishes between memory proper, *mneme*, the simple power of preserving the past, and reminiscence, *amamnesis*, the voluntary recall of the past. For Aristotle, memory, desacralized and secularized, is "now included in time, but in a time which for Aristotle continues to resist understanding" (Vernant 1965:78). But his treatise translated into Latin as *De memoria et reminiscentia* seemed to the great Scholastic philosophers of the Middle Ages, Albert the Great and Thomas Aquinas, to be an Art of Memory comparable to the *Rhetorica ad Herennium* attributed to Cicero.

However, this secularization of memory combined with the invention of writing allowed the Greeks to create new techniques of memory, a *mnemotechnology*. This invention has been attributed to the poet Simonides of Ceos (c. 556–468). The *Chronicle of Paros* engraved on a marble slab around 264 B.C. even mentions that in 477 "Simonides of Ceos, the son of Leoprepe, the inventor of the system of mnemonic aids, won the choral singing prize at Athens." Simonides was still close to mythical and poetic memory, and he composed songs in praise of victorious heroes and funeral songs; for example, in praise of the memory of the soldiers who fell at Thermopylae. In *De Oratore* (II, lxxxvi), Cicero told in the form of a religious legend the story of Simonides' invention of mnemotechnology. During a banquet given by Scopa, a Thessalian aristocrat, Simonides sang a poem in honor of Castor and Pollux. Scopa told the poet that he would pay him only half the price they had agreed on, and that he could ask the Dioscuri themselves for the other half. Shortly afterward, someone came to tell Simonides that two young men were looking for him. He went out, and saw no one. But while he was outside, the roof of the house collapsed on Scopa and his guests, whose bodies were so crushed as to be unrecognizable. Simonides, remembering the order in which they had been seated, was able to identify their bodies and return them to their families (Yates 1966:1–2, 27–29).

Thus Simonides established two principles of artificial memory as understood by the Ancients: the remembrance of *images*, which are necessary for memory, and the reliance on an *organization*, an *order*, which essential to a good memory. But Simonides had accelerated the secularization of memory and accentuated its technical and professional character by perfecting the alphabet and being the first to demand payment for his poems (Vernant 1965:78, n.98).

Simonides is also supposed to be responsible for an important distinction in mnemotechnology between the *places of memory* in which one can locate the objects of memory by association (the zodiac was soon to provide such a framework for memory, while artificial memory was constituted as an edifice divided into "rooms of memory"), and the *images*, forms, characteristic traits, and symbols that facilitate mnemonic recall. Another major distinction in traditional mnemonic technique is supposed to have appeared after Simonides: the one between "the memory by means of things" and "memory by means of words" that is found, for example, in a text dating from around 400 B.C., the *Dialexeis* (Yates 1966:41).

Curiously, none of the ancient Greek treatises on mnemotechnology has come down to us, neither that of the sophist Hippias, who, Plato says (*Hippias minor*, 368 B, f.), inculcated his pupils with an encyclopedic knowledge through the use of techniques of remembering that had a purely positive character, nor that of Metrodorus of Skeptis [?], who lived in the first century B.C. at the court of the King of Pontus, Mithridates, who was himself endowed with a famous memory and developed an artificial memory based on the zodiac.

Our knowledge of Greek mnemotechnology is based primarily on the three Latin texts, which were for centuries the definitive statement of the classical theory of artificial memory (an expression which they coined: *memoria artificiosa*): the *Rhetorica Ad Herennium* compiled by an anonymous teacher in Rome between 86 and 82 B.C., and which the Middle Ages attributed to Cicero, Cicero's own *De Oratore* (55 B.C.), and Quintilian's *Institutio oratoria* (end of the first century A.D.). These three texts refine Greek mnemotechnology, establishing the distinction between *places* and *images* (*loci* and *imagines*), clarifying the active character of these images in the process of remembering (*active images*, *imagines agentes*), and formalizing the division between memory of things (*memoria rerum*) and memory of words (*memoria verborum*).

Above all, these texts situated memory in the great system of *rhetoric* that was to dominate antique culture, be reborn in the Middle Ages (twelfth to thirteenth centuries), and be revived in our time in the work of semioticians and other new rhetoricians.[15] Memory is the fifth part of rhetoric: after *inventio* (the discovery of something to say), *dispositio* (the organization of what has been found), *elocutio* (ornamentation through words and figures), *actio* (the performance of the discourse in the manner of an actor, through gestures and diction), and *memoria* (*memoriae mandare*, to consign to memory). Roland Barthes observes that "The first three operations are the most important . . . the last two (*actio* and *memoria*) were soon abandoned, as soon as rhetoric no longer dealt only with the spoken (declaimed) discourses of lawyers or politicians or 'speakers' (in the epidictic genre), but also, and finally almost exclusively, with written works. However, there is no doubt that these two parts offer great interest . . . the second because it postulates a level of stereotypes, an inter-textuality that is stable and mechanically transmitted" (1964/65:197).

Finally, we must not forget that alongside the spectacular emergence of memory at the heart of rhetoric, that is, at the heart of an art of discourse that is linked to writing, the collective memory continues to develop through the social and political evolution of the ancient world. Paul Veyne has emphasized the confiscation of collective memory by the

Roman emperors, particularly by means of the public monument and by the inscription, in a sort of delirium of the epigraphical memory. But the Roman Senate, constantly vexed and sometimes decimated by the emperors, found a weapon against imperial tyranny. This weapon was the *damnatio memoriae*, which removes the name of a defiant emperor from archival documents and from monumental inscriptions. The power to destroy memory is a counterweight to power achieved through the production of memory.

Memory in the Middle Ages—Western Europe

Whereas the "popular" or rather "folklore" social memory remains almost completely beyond our grasp, the collective memory formed by the leading classes of society undergoes profound transformations in the Middle Ages. The essential change derives from the spread of Christianity as a religion and as a dominant ideology and from the quasi-monopoly the Church acquires in the intellectual domain.

The Christianization of memory and of mnemotechnology, the division of collective memory between a circular liturgical memory and a lay memory little influenced by chronology, the development of the memory of the dead and especially of dead saints, the importance of memory in an educational system depending on both the oral and the written, and finally the appearance of treatises on memory (*artes memoriae*)—these are the most characteristic traits of memory in the Middle Ages.

If ancient memory was strongly influenced by religion, Judeo-Christianity contributed something additional and different to the relation between memory and religion, between man and God.[16] Judaism and Christianity, both firmly anchored historically and theologically in history, have been described as "religions of remembrance" (Oexle 1976:80). And this is true in several respects, because "divine acts of salvation situated in the past form the content of faith and the object of rites," but also because the Holy Book on one hand, and the historical tradition on the other, insist, essentially, on the necessity of remembrance as a fundamental religious activity.

In the Old Testament, it is especially Deuteronomy that calls the faithful to the duty of remembrance and of the memory that constitutes it: a memory that is first of all a recognition of Yahweh, the memory that founds Jewish identity: "Take heed lest you forget the Lord your God, by not keeping his commandments and his ordinances and his statutes" (8:11); "Do not forget the Lord your God, who brought you out of the land of Egypt, out of the house of bondage' (8:14); "You shall remember the Lord your God, for it is he who gives you power to get wealth; that he may confirm his covenant which he swore to your fathers, as at this day. And if you forget the Lord your God and go after other gods and serve them and worship them, I solemnly warn you this day that you shall surely perish" (8:18 –19). A memory of Yahweh's anger: "Remember, and do not forget how you provoked the Lord your God to wrath in the wilderness" (9:7); "Remember what the Lord your God did to Miriam,[17] when you were on your way out of Egypt" (24:9). A memory of the offenses of enemies: "Remember what Amalek did to you as you came out of Egypt, how he attacked you on the way, when you were faint and weary, and cut off at your rear all who lagged behind you; and he did not fear God. Therefore when the Lord your God has given you rest from all your enemies round about, in the land which the Lord your God gives you for an inheritance to possess, you shall blot out the remembrance of Amalek from under heaven; you shall not forget" (25:17–19).

And in Isaiah (44:21), an appeal to remembrance and the promise of memory between Yahweh and Israel:

> Remember these things, O Jacob,
> and Israel, for you are my servant;
> I formed you, you are my servant;
> O Israel, you will not be forgotten by me.

A whole family of words derived from the root *Zâkar* (Zachariah, from Zkar-yû, "Yahweh remembers") makes the Jew a man of tradition whom memory and mutual promise link to his God (Childs). The Jewish people are the people of memory par excellence.

In the New Testament, the Last Supper founds redemption on the remembrance of Jesus: "And he took bread, and when he had given thanks he broke it and gave it to them, saying, 'This is my body, which is given for you. Do this in remembrance of me' " (Luke 22:19). John puts the remembrance of Jesus in an eschatological perspective: "But the Counselor, the Holy Spirit, whom the Father will send in my name, he will teach you all things, and bring to your remembrance all that I have said to you" (John 14:26). And Paul extends this eschatological perspective: "For as often as you eat this bread and drink the cup, you proclaim the Lord's death until he comes" (1 Corinthians 11:26). Thus, as among the Greeks—and Paul is in fact thoroughly imbued with Hellenism—memory can eventuate in eschatology, denying temporal existence and history. This will be one of the paths taken by Christian memory.

But more commonly, the Christian is called to live in the memory of Jesus' words: "one must help the weak, remembering the words of the Lord Jesus" (Acts 20:35); "Remember Jesus Christ, risen from the dead" (2 Timothy 2:8), a memory that will not be lost in a future life, in the beyond, according to Luke (16:25), who makes Abraham say to the evil rich man in Hell: "Son, remember that you in your lifetime received your good things."

More historically Christian teaching presents itself as the memory of Jesus transmitted by the series of Apostles and their successors. Thus Paul writes to Timothy: "what you have heard from me before many witnesses entrust to faithful men who will be able to teach others also" (2 Timothy 2:2). Christian teaching is memory (cf. Nils Dahl); Christian ritual is commemoration.

St. Augustine bequeaths to medieval Christianity a deepening and a Christian adaptation of the ancient rhetorical theory of memory. In his *Confessions*, he starts out from the ancient conception of *places* and *memory images*, but he gives them an extraordinary psychological depth and fluidity, speaking of the "immense hall of memory":

> I come to the fields and spacious palaces of memory, where are the treasures of innumerable images, brought into it from things of all sorts perceived by the senses. There is stored up whatever besides we think, either by enlarging or diminishing, or any other way of varying those things which the sense hath come to; and whatever else hath been committed and laid up, which forgetfulness hath not yet swallowed up and buried. When I enter there, I require instantly what I will to be brought forth, and something instantly comes; others must be longer sought after, which are fetched, as it were out of some inner receptacle; others rush out in troops, and while one thing is desired and required, they start forth, as who should say, 'Is it perchance I?' These I drive away with the hand of my heart from the face of my remembrance; until what I wish for be unveiled, and appear in sight, out of its secret place. Other things come up readily, in unbroken order, as they are called for; those in front making way for the follow-

ing; and as they make way, they are hidden from sight, ready to come when I will. All which takes place when I recite a thing by heart.[18]

Frances Yates has written that these Christian images of memory harmonized with the great Gothic churches, in which we should perhaps see a symbolic memory-place. Where Panofsky sees a relation between the Gothic and Scholasticism, we should perhaps also see a relation between architecture and memory.

But Augustine, moving forward "into the fields and caverns, into the incalculable caverns of my memory" (*Confessions*, X, 17), seeks God in the depths of memory but does not find him in any image or in any place (*Confessions*, X, 25–26). With Augustine, memory sinks into the *interior man*, into the heart of that Christian dialectic between the inside and the outside from which will come the examination of conscience, introspection, and even perhaps psychoanalysis.[19]

However, Augustine also bequeaths to medieval Christianity a Christian version of the ancient trilogy of the three powers of the soul: *memoria*, *intelligentia*, *providentia* (Cicero, *De inventione*, II, liii, 160). In his treatise *De Trinitate* the triad becomes *memoria*, *intellectus*, *voluntas*, and these are, in man, images of the Trinity.

If Christian memory manifests itself chiefly in the commemoration of Jesus—annually in the commemorative liturgy from Advent to Pentecost, by way of the essential stages of Christmas, Lent, and the Ascension, and daily in the celebration of the Eucharist—at a more popular level it focuses particularly on the saints and on the dead.

The martyrs were witnesses. After their death, they crystallized Christian memory around their remembrance. They appear in the *Libri Memoriales* in which churches registered those whose memory they preserved, and to whom they prayed. Thus it is, for example, in the eighth-century *Liber Memorialis* of Salzburg, or in the eleventh-century one from Newminster (Oexle 1976:82). The tomb of a martyr was the center of a church, and was known not only as a *confessio* or *martyrium*, but also, significantly, as a *memoria*.[20] Augustine contrasts in a striking way the tomb of the apostle Peter with the pagan temple of Romulus, the glory of the *memoria Petri* with the abandonment of the *templum Romuli* (*Enar. in Ps.*, 44, 23). Deriving from the ancient cult of the dead and from the Judaic tradition of the tombs of the Patriarchs, this practice was particularly favored in Africa, where the word "*memoria*" became synonymous with "relic." Occasionally, the *memoria* involved neither a tomb nor relics, as in the Church of the Holy Apostles in Constantinople.

Elsewhere, a saint was commemorated on a liturgical feast day (and the most important might have several feast days, as did Saint Peter: in *The Golden Legend*, Joachim de Voragine explains three such commemorations associated with Peter's *pulpit*, his *captivity*, and his *martyrdom*; these recall his elevation as Pontiff of Antioch, his imprisonment, and his death), and ordinary Christians got into the habit of celebrating, along with their birthday, a custom inherited from antiquity, the day of the patron saint as well.[21]

The commemoration of the saints generally took place on the day known or supposed to be that of their martyrdom or death. The association between death and memory spread rapidly throughout Christianity, which developed it on the basis of the pagan cult of ancestors and the dead.

The custom of saying prayers for the dead became widespread early in the history of the Church. Very early, too, as in Jewish communities, the churches and Christian communities kept *Libri memoriales*, called only from the seventeenth century onward *necrologies* or obituaries (cf. Huyghebaert), in which were registered the living and especially the dead persons who had been the most frequent benefactors of their communities, whose memory the community wanted to preserve, and for whom it committed itself to pray. In the same way the ivory *diptychs*, which toward the end of the Roman empire, the consuls were in the habit of giving the emperor when they took office, were Christianized and henceforth served to commemorate the dead. The formulas invoking the memory of those whose names were inscribed on the diptychs or in the *Libri Memoriales* said much the same thing: "quorum quarumque recolimus *memoriam*" ("the men and women whom we recall to memory"), "qui in libello memorali . . . *scripti memoratur*" ("those who are inscribed in the book of memory in order that they be remembered"), "quorum nomina *ad memorandum* conscripsimus" ("those whose names we have inscribed in order to remember them").

At the end of the eleventh century, the introduction to the *Liber Vitae* of the monastery of Saint Benedetto di Polirone declares, for example: "The abbot has caused this book to be made, which will remain on the altar so that all the names of our brothers which are written in it may be always present to the eyes of God and so that the memory of all may be preserved by everyone throughout the monastery, during the celebration of the Mass as well as in all the other good works" (Oexle 1976:77).

Sometimes, the *Libri memoriales* betray the failures of those who are entrusted with memory. A prayer in the *Liber Memorialis* of Reichenau says: "The names that I have been given to inscribe in this book, but which I have through my negligence forgotten, I recommend to you, Christ, and to your mother, and to all the celestial power, in order that their memory be celebrated here below and in the beatitude of eternal life" (Oexle, p. 85).

In addition to forgetfulness, there was also the possibility that the names of the unworthy might be struck from the memory-books. Excommunication in particular entailed that kind of Christian "damnatio memoriae." Concerning an excommunicated person, the synod of Reisbach declared in 798 that "after his death let nothing be written in his memory," and the second synod of Elna in 1027 issued an edict concerning other condemned people: "and let their names not be read at the sacred altar along with those of the faithful dead."

Very early on, the names of the memorable dead had been introduced into the *Memento* of the Canon of the Mass. In the eleventh century, under pressure from Cluny, an annual celebration was established in memory of all the faithful dead, a *commemoration of the dead*, on the second day of November. The birth in the twelfth century of Purgatory, third place in the beyond located between Heaven and Hell, from which the living could help the souls of those in whom they had an interest to escape more or less rapidly through masses, prayers, or giving alms, intensified the efforts of the living on behalf of the memory of the dead. In any case, in the common language of the stereotyped formulas, memory enters into the definition of the mourned dead, they are "of good" or of "splendid memory" (*bonae, egregiae memoriae*).

With the saint, devotion crystallized around the miracle. Unknown in antiquity, ex-votos promising or dispensing recognition in the hope of a miracle or after its occurence enjoyed an immense popularity in the Middle Ages and maintained the memory of miracles.[22] On the other hand, between the fourth and the eleventh centuries, there is a diminution in the number of funerary inscriptions (Aries 1977:201 seq.).

Memory nevertheless played an important role in the social, cultural, and scholastic worlds and, of course, in the elementary forms of historiography.

The Middle Ages venerated old men above all because they were regarded as memory-men, prestigious and useful. One document among others, published by Marc Bloch, recounts that "toward 1250, when Saint Louis was on a Crusade, the canons of Notre-Dame de Paris tried to levy a tax on their serfs at Orly. The serfs refused to pay, and the regent Blanche of Castille was chosen as arbiter. The two parties produced as witnesses elderly men claiming that so long as anyone could remember the serfs of Orly had been—or had not been (depending on which side they were on)—subject to taxes: "ita usitatum est a tempore a quo non exstat memoria" ("that is what has been done since time immemorial—time out of memory").[23]

Bernard Guenée, trying to clarify the meaning of the medieval expression "modern times" (*tempora moderna*) after having carefully studied the "memory" of the Count of Anjou, Foulque IV le Rechin, who wrote a history of his house in 1096, of the Canon of Cambrai, Lambert de Wattrelos, who wrote a chronicle around 1152, and of the Dominican Etienne de Bourbon, the author of a collection of *exempla* compiled between 1250 and 1260, arrives at the following conclusions: "In the Middle Ages, some historians define modern times as the time of memory, many of them know that a reliable memory can cover about a hundred years, and modernity, modern times, is therefore for each of them the century in which they are living, or have just lived through the last years" (Guenée 1976/77:35). Moreover, an Englishman, Gautier Map, wrote at the end of the twelfth century:

> This began in our era. I mean by 'our era,' the period which is modern for us, that is, the extent of these hundred years whose end we now see and whose notable events are all sufficiently fresh and present in our memories, first because a few very old men are still alive and also because many sons have heard from their fathers and grandfathers very reliable stories about things they [the sons] have not seen. (quoted in Guenée, p. 35)

All the same, in this period when the written is developing alongside the oral and when there is, at least among clerks or *literati*, an equilibrium between oral memory and written memory, recourse to writing as a support for memory intensifies. Lords bring together in charter-books the documents they need to produce to defend their rights. Concerning the land, these charter-books constitute the *feudal memory*, whose other half, concerning men, is constituted by *genealogies*. The introduction to the charter granted in 1174 by Guy, Count of Nevers, to the inhabitants of Tonnerre, declares that "The use of letters was discovered and invented for the preservation of the memory of things. What we wish to retain and learn by heart, we cause to be written down, so that what we cannot keep perpetually in our weak and fragile memories may be preserved in writing and by means of letters that last forever."

For a long time, kings had only small and mobile archives. Philip Augustus left his behind in 1194 at Fréteval, where he was defeated by Richard the Lion-Hearted. The archives of the royal chancelleries began to take form around 1200. In the thirteenth century there were established in France, for example, the archives of the Chambre des Comptes (the royal acts of financial interest are collected in registers bearing the significant name of *memorials*) and of the Parlement. In the twelfth century, in Italy, and from the thirteenth and especially the fourteenth centuries elsewhere, *notarial archives* become increasingly common (Favier 1958:13–18). With the rise of cities urban archives are constituted, and jealously guarded by municipal bodies. Urban memory for these nascent and still threatened institutions is here clearly collective or communitarian. In this respect Genoa is a pioneer; it begins its archives as early as 1127 and still preserves today notarial registers from the middle of the eleventh century. The fourteenth century witnesses the first archival inventories (ordered by Charles V in France, by Pope Urban V for the pontifical archives in 1366, by the English monarchy in 1381). In 1356, for the first time, an international treaty (the Peace of Paris concluded between the dauphin and Savoy) contains an article concerning the fate of the archives of the countries involved.[24]

In the literary domain, orality continues for a long time alongside writing, and memory is one of the constitutive elements of medieval literature. This is particularly true for the eleventh and twelfth centuries and for the *chanson de geste* or epic song, which not only requires methods of memorization for the troubador or *jongleur* and for the audience, but integrates itself into the collective memory, as Paul Zumthor as shown in discussing the epic "hero": "The 'hero' exists only in the song, but he nevertheless also exists in the collective memory in which the men, both the poet and the audience, participate."[25] Memory plays the same role in schools. Concerning the High Middle Ages, Pierre Riché asserts:

> The pupil is supposed to register everything in his memory. One cannot overemphasize the importance of this intellectual aptitude, which characterizes and will continue for a long time to characterize not only the Western world but the Orient as well. Just like the young Muslim or the young Jew, the Christian schoolboy has to know the sacred texts

> by heart. First the psalter, which he learns more or less quickly (some take several years); then, if he is a monk, the Rule of St. Benedict (*Coutumes de Murbach*, III, 80).[26]

In this period, to know by heart is to know. The schoolmasters, following the advice of Quintilian (*Inst. Orat.* XI, 2) and Martianus Capella (*De Nuptiis*, ch. V), want their pupils to try to retain everything they read.[27] They think up different mnemotechnical methods, compose alphabetical poems (*versus memoriales*) that help the student remember grammar, computation, and history more easily" (p. 218). In this world which is passing from orality to writing, glossaries, lexicons, lists of cities, mountains, rivers, oceans proliferate (in conformity with Jack Goody's theory); and all these must be learned by heart, as Rhabanus Maurus indicated in the ninth century.[28]

In the Scholastic system of the universities, from the end of the twelfth century on, reliance on memory remains great, and it is founded even more on orality than on writing. In spite of the increase in the number of school manuscripts, the memorization of professorial lectures and oral exercises (*disputes*, *quodlibets*, etc.), remains central to the student's work.

At the same time, theories of memory develop in rhetoric and theology. In the fifth-century "Wedding of Philology and Mercury" (*De nuptiis Philologiae et Mercurii*), the pagan rhetorician Martianus Capella repeats, in inflated terms, the classical distinction between the *places* and the *images* of "memory by things" and a "memory by words." In Alcuin's treatise on *The Rhetoric of the Virtues*, we see Charlemagne inquiring into the five parts of rhetoric and arriving at memory:

> CHARLEMAGNE: And now what will you say about memory, which I consider the most noble part of rhetoric?
>
> ALCUIN: What can I do except repeat the words of Marcus Tullius (Cicero)? Memory is the storehouse of all things, and if it has not made itself the guardian of what one has thought, the other gifts of the orator, no matter how excellent they may be, will come to naught.
>
> CHARLEMAGNE: Are there no rules which teach us how one can acquire memory and increase it?
>
> ALCUIN: We have no rules about memory other than to learn by heart.

Alcuin obviously does not know the *Rhetorica ad Herrenium* which becomes, from the twelfth century onward, the great classic of the genre.

At that time it circulated widely in manuscript, and was attributed to Cicero (whose *De Oratore* and Quintilian's *Institutio oratoria* were then both practically unknown)

Starting at the end of the twelfth century, classical rhetoric takes the form of the *ars dictaminis*, a technique of epistolary art for administrative use of which Bologna becomes the major center. It is there that Boncompagno da Signa wrote in 1235 the second of the works in this genre that he composed, the *Rhetorica novissima*, in which memory in general is defined in these terms: "What is memory? Memory is a glorious and admirable gift of nature, by means of which we recall past things, embrace present things, and contemplate future things, thanks to their resemblance with past things."[29] Boncompagno goes on to recall the fundamental distinction between *natural memory* and *artificial memory*. Concerning the latter, he gives a long list of the "signs of memory" drawn from the Bible (p. 277); for example, the cock's crow that is for St. Pierre a "mnemonic sign." Boncompagno integrates into the science of memory the essential systems of the Christian morality of the Middle Ages, the virtues and vices which he makes into *signacula*, "memorial notes" (Yates 1966:59), and perhaps especially, beyond artificial memory, but as "a fundamental memory exercise," the remembrance of Heaven and Hell, or rather the "memory of Paradise" and the "memory of the infernal regions," at a moment when the distinction between Purgatory and Hell has not yet been entirely established. This is an important innovation which, after the *Divine Comedy*, will inspire countless representations of Hell, Purgatory, and Paradise, which should usually be regarded as "memory places" whose various levels or chambers recall the virtues and vices. We should look with "the eyes of memory" (Yates, p. 92) at Giotto's frescoes in the Scrovegni chapel in Padua and Ambrogio Lorenzetti's frescoes of Good Government and Bad Government in the Palace of the city of Siena. The remembrance of Paradise, Purgatory, and Hell finds its supreme expression in the *Congestorium artificiosae memoriae* by the German Dominican Johannes Romberch (first published in 1520; the most important edition, which includes illustrations of Romberch's figures, appeared in Venice in 1533), who knew all the ancient sources of the art of memory and relied especially on Aquinas. After bringing the system of *places* and *images* to a culmination, Romberch outlines a system of encyclopedic memory in which the medieval patrimony flourishes with the spirit of the Renaissance. But in the meantime, theology had transformed the ancient tradition of memory included in rhetoric. Following St. Augustine's lead, St. Anselm (d. 1109) and the Cistercian Ailred of Rievaux (d. 1167) revive the triad composed by *intellectus*, *voluntas*, and *memoria*. Anselm makes of these three elements the three "dignities" (*dignitates*) of the soul, but in the *Monologion*, the triad becomes *memoria*, *intelligentia*, and *amor*. There can be memory and intelligence without love, but there can be no love without memory and intelligence. Similarly, in his *De Anima*, Ailred de Rievaux is especially preoccupied with situating memory among the faculties of the soul.

In the thirteenth century two towering Dominicans, Albert the Great and Thomas Aquinas, accord memory an important role. To ancient rhetoric and to Augustine, they add above all Aristotle and Avicenna. Albert deals with memory in *De Bono*, *De Anima*, and in his commentary of Aristotle's *De memoria et remniscentia*. He starts out from the Aristotelian distinction between memory and reminiscence. By including *intention* (*intentio*) in the image of memory, he is in line with the Christianity of "the interior man." He anticipates the role of memory in the *imaginary* by conceding that *fable*, the marvelous, and the *emotions* that lead to *metaphor* (*metaphorica*) are an aid to memory, but just as memory is an indispensable auxiliary of prudence—that is, of wisdom (imagined as a woman with three eyes who can see past, present, and future things), Albert insists on the importance of training memory, on mnemonic techniques. Like a good "naturalist," Albert ultimately relates memory to temperaments. For him, the temperament most favorable to acquiring a good memory is "dry-hot melancholy, the intellectual, the inspired melancholy" (Yates, p. 69). Is Albert the Great thus a precursor of Renaissance "melancholy," in whom we should recognize a way of thinking and feeling based on remembrance?

Apart from any other aptitude, Thomas Aquinas was particularly qualified to deal with memory: he seems to have had a phenomenal natural memory, and his artificial memory had been exercised by Albert the Great's teaching at Cologne. Like Albert the Great, Thomas Aquinas deals in the *Summa Theologiae* with artificial memory under the rubric of prudence,[30] and again like Albert, he wrote a commentary on the *De memoria et reminiscentia*. On the basis of the classical doctrine of *places* and *images*, he formulates four mnemonic rules:

1. "Convenient similitudes of the things that one wants to remember" must be found; Frances Yates comments, "the images of

the artificial memory have turned into 'corporeal similitudes' through which 'simple and spiritual intentions' are to be prevented from slipping from the soul. And he gives again here the reason for using 'corporeal similitudes' which he gives in the Aristotle commentary, because human cognition is stronger in regard to the sensibilia, and therefore 'subtle and spiritual things' are better remembered in the soul in corporeal forms" (p. 75). Memory is linked to the body.

2. Next we must have "in considered determinate order the things that we want to remember so that, from one remembered point progress can easily be made to the next." Memory is reason.

3. We must "dwell with solicitude on, and cleave with affection to, the things we want to remember." Memory is connected with attention and intention.

4. We must "meditate frequently on what we want to remember." That is why Aristotle says that "meditation preserves memory," for "habit is like nature."

The importance of these rules comes from influence they have exerted, particularly from the fourteenth to the seventeenth centuries, on the theoreticians of memory, on theologians, teachers, and artists. Frances Yates thinks the fourteenth-century frescoes of the Capellone degli Spagnoli in the Dominican convent of Santa Maria Novella in Florence are an illustration of Thomist theories of memory, using "corporeal similitudes" to designate the liberal arts and the theologico-philosophical disciplines.

At the beginning of the fourteenth century, the Dominican Giovanni da San Gimignano, in his *Summa de exemplis ac similitudinibus rerum*, put the Thomist rules into brief formulas:

"There are four things that help a man have a good memory.

The first is to arrange the things to be remembered in a specific order.

The second is to pay careful attention to them.

The third is to relate them to unusual symbols.

The fourth is frequently to repeat them while thinking about them" (Book VI, ch. xiii).

Not long afterward another Dominican from the convent of Pisa, Bartolomeo da San Concordio (1262–1347), took up the Thomist rules of memory in his *Ammae stramenti degli antichi*, the first work to deal with the art of memory in the vernacular, in Italian, because it was addressed to lay people.

Among the many *Artes Memoriae* of the later Middle Ages—the period in which they flourished—we may mention the *Phoenix sive artificiosa memoria* by Pietro da Ravenna, of which the first edition appeared in Venice in 1491, and was followed by a second edition in Bologna in 1492. This was, it seems, the most widely read of these treatises. It went through several editions in the sixteenth century and was translated into various languages, for example by Robert Copland in London, about 1548, under the title *The Art of Memory That Is Otherwise Called the Phoenix*.

In his *De ratione studii* (1512), Erasmus is not enthusiastic about the art of memory: "Although I do not deny that places and images can aid the memory, the best memory remains that which is founded on three very important things: study, order, and application."[31] Fundamentally, Erasmus considers the art of memory as an example of medieval and Scholastic intellectual barbarism, and he warns particularly against magical practices of memory.

In his *Rhetorica elementa* (Venice, 1534), Melanchthon forbids students the use of mnemonic techniques or "tricks." For him, memory is integral to normal training in knowledge.

We cannot leave the Middle Ages without mentioning one theoretician who is also very original in the domain of memory, Ramón Lull. After having discussed memory in various works, Lull finally composed in 1316 three treatises on memory, *De Memoria*, *De intellectu*, and *De voluntate* (which are thus based on the Augustinian trinity), not to mention a *Liber ad memoriam confirmandam*. Very different from the Dominican *Artes Memoriae*, Lull's *Ars memorativa* is "a method of investigation, and a method of logical investigation" (Yates, p. 185), which is illuminated by Lull's *Liber septem planetarum*. The secrets of the *ars memorandi* are hidden in the seven planets. The Neoplatonic interpretation of Lullism in fifteenth-century Florence (Pico della Mirandola) led readers to see a cabalistic, astrological, and magical doctrine in Lull's *Ars memorativa*. He was thus to have a strong influence in the Renaissance.

The Progress of Written and Figured Memory from the Renaissance to the Present

Printing revolutionized Western memory, but slowly. It revolutionized memory even more slowly in China, where, even though printing had been invented in the ninth century A.D., printers did not discover movable type (typography), and thus remained content with xylography (printing by means of plates engraved in relief), up until the nineteenth century, when Western mechanical techniques were introduced. Printing did not therefore have a massive impact on China, but its effects on memories, at least in the cultivated strata of society, was significant, for it was primarily scientific and technical works that were printed, and these accelerated and extended the memorization of knowledge.

Things happened differently in the West. Leroi-Gourhan has described the revolution in memory brought about by printing:

> Up until the appearance of printing . . . it was difficult to separate oral from written transmission. Most of the known was buried in oral practices and techniques; the peak of the known, whose framework remained unchanged since Antiquity, was given fixed form in the manuscript in order to be learned by heart. . . . With the advent of printing . . . not only was the reader faced with an enormous collective memory whose subject matter he could no longer assimilate *in toto*, but he was frequently put in a position to exploit new works. We then witness a progressive exteriorization of individual memory; the work of orientation in a written text is accomplished from the outside. (1964/65:69–70)

Nevertheless, the effects of printing make themselves fully felt only in the eighteenth century, when the progress of science and philosophy has transformed the content and the mechanisms of collective memory:

> The eighteenth century in Europe marks the end of the ancient world in printing as in other techniques. . . . In the course of a few decades, social memory embodies in books all of Antiquity, the history of great peoples, the geography and ethnography of a world that has become definitively round, philosophy, law, the sciences, the arts, technology and a literature translated into twenty different languages. The flood-tide goes on swelling up to our own day, but without losing a sense of proportion one can say that no period in history has known a such a rapid expansion of the collective memory. Thus we already find in the

> eighteenth century all the formulas that can be used to bring a preconstituted memory to the reader. (Leroi-Gourhan 1964/65:70)

It is during this period from the end of the Middle Ages and the beginning of printing to the turn of the eighteenth century that Frances Yates has located the long death agony of the art of memory. In the sixteenth century, "the art of memory may be moving out of the great nerve centres of the European tradition and becoming marginal" (Yates, p. 127). Opuscules such as *Come migliorare la tua memoria* ("How to Improve your Memory") never stopped being printed (and are still printed today). But the classical theory of memory shaped in Greco-Roman antiquity and modified by Scholasticism, which was central to scholarly life, literature (cf. the *Divine Comedy*), and the arts in the Middle Ages, disappeared almost completely in the humanist movement.

However, the hermetic tradition, of which Lull had been one of the founders and which Ficino and Pico della Mirandola definitively established, continued to develop up until the beginning of the seventeenth century. It first inspired a curious figure, Giulio Camillo Delminio, "the divine Camillo" (Yates, p. 159). This Venetian was born about 1480, died in Milan about 1544. He built in Venice and then in Paris theaters made of wood of which we have no description but which one can imagine must have resembled the ideal theater that he describes in his *L'Idea del Teatro*, published posthumously in Venice and Florence in 1550. Constructed in accordance with the principles of classical mnemonic science, this theater is in fact a representation of the universe that develops from first causes through all the stages of creation. The foundations of this theater are the planets, the signs of the zodiac, and the books attributed to Hermes Trismegistus: the *Asclepius* in the Latin translation known in the Middle Ages and the *Corpus hermeticam* in Ficino's Latin translation. Camillo's *teatro* should be understood in the context of the Venetian Renaissance and in this case the "art of memory" reflects the context of this same Renaissance and particularly of its architecture. If Palladio, influenced by Vitruvius (notably in the Olympic Theater in Vicenza) and probably also by Camillo, did not fully realize a theatrical architecture founded on a hermetic theory of memory, perhaps it was in England that these theories were most fully developed. From 1617 to 1619, in Oppenheim (Germany) the two volumes (vol. 1: The Macrocosm; vol. 2: The Microcosm) of Robert Flood's *Utriusque Cosmia, maioris scilicet et minoris, metaphysica, physica atque technica Historia*, in which we find the hermetic theory of the theater of memory transformed from rectangular to round (*ars rotunda* instead of *ars quadrata*). Frances Yates thinks this was probably the model for the famous Globe Theater in London, Shakespeare's theater (pp. 342–67).

Meanwhile, occultist theories of memory had found their greatest theoretician in Giordano Bruno (1548–1600). These theories played a decisive role in the persecution, Church condemnation, and execution of this famous Dominican. For the details of these theories the fine book by Frances Yates may be consulted; they are expressed notably in Bruno's *De umbris idearum* (Paris, 1582), *Cantus Ciraeus* (1582), *Ars reminiscendi, explicatio triginta sigillorum ad omnium scientiarum et artium inventionem, dispositionem et memoriam* (published in England in 1583), *Lampas tringinta statuarum* (written in Wittenberg in 1587, first published in 1891), and *De imaginum, signorum et idearum compositione* (Frankfurt, 1591). Let us only say that for Bruno the wheels of memory turn by magic and that "Such a memory would be the memory of a divine man, of a Magus with divine powers through his imagination harnessed to the workings of the cosmic powers. And such an attempt would rest on the Hermetic assumption that man's *mens* is divine, related in its origin to the star-governors of the world, able both to reflect and to control the universe" (Yates, p. 224).

In Lyons, in 1617, a certain Johannes Paepp revealed, in his *Shenkelius detectus, seu memoria artificialis hactenus occultata*, that his master Lambert Shenkel (1547–c.1603), who had published two books on memory *De Memoria*, Douai, 1593, and *Gazophylacium*, Strasbourg, 1610) that are apparently faithful to ancient and Scholastic theories of memory, was in reality a secret adept of hermeticism. This was the swansong of mnemonic hermeticism. The scientific method elaborated in the seventeenth century was to destroy this second branch of the medieval *Ars Memoriae*.

The Protestant Pierre de la Ramée (known as Ramus), born in 1515 and a victim of the St.-Bartholomew's Day massacre in 1572, had already demanded in his *Scholae in liberales artes* (1569) that the ancient techniques of memorization be replaced with new ones founded on the "dialectical order," on a "method." This was an assertion of the claims of intelligence over those of memory which has continued up to our own time to inspire an "anti-memory" current of thought. For example, it demands the elimination or reduction in school curricula of the role played by "rote memory," whereas child psychologists such as Jean Piaget have shown, as we have seen, that memory and intelligence, far from being in conflict, mutually reinforce each other.

In any case, Francis Bacon said as early as 1620, in his *Novum Organum*: " There hath been also labored and put into practice a method, which is not a lawful method, but a method of imposture; which is, to deliver knowledges in such a manner, as men may speedily come to make a show of learning who have it not. Such was the travail of Raymundus Lullus in making that art which bears his name" (quoted in Yates, p. 374).

At the same period, in his *Cogitationes privatae* (1614–1621), Descartes attacked "Schenkel's ineptitudes" and proposed several logical "methods" for mastering the imagination: for instance, "through the reduction of things to their causes. Since all can be reduced to one, it is obviously not necessary to remember all the sciences" (Yates, p. 373).

Perhaps only Leibnitz tried, in the still-unpublished manuscripts preserved in Hanover, to reconcile Lull's *art of memory*, which Leibnitz described as a "*combinatoria*," with modern science (Yates, p. 382). Lull's wheels of memory, which were taken up again by Bruno, are moved by *signs, notations, characters, and seals*. It suffices, Leibnitz seems to think, to make out of the *notations* a universal mathematical language. His mathematization of memory, standing between the medieval Lullian system and modern cybernetics, is still impressive today.

Let us consider the evidence offered by vocabulary concerning this period of "memory in expansion" (Leroi-Gourhan). We will examine the two semantic fields in the French language that derive from *mneme* and *memoria*.

The Middle Ages contributed the central word *mémoire*, which appeared in French in the first monuments of the language in the eleventh century. In the thirteenth century the word *mémorial* (which has to do, as we have seen, with financial accounts) was added, and in 1320, *mémoire* in the masculine appears, designating an administrative dossier. *Mémoire* becomes bureaucratic, in the service of the monarchical centralism then establishing itself. The fifteenth century sees the appearance of *mémorable* at the period of the apogee of the *Artes Memoriae* and of the renewal of ancient literature: a traditionalist *mémoire*. In the sixteenth century, in 1552, personal *mémoires* usually written by an aristocrat, begin to appear. The eighteenth century contributes the word *mémorialiste* in 1726, and in 1777, the word *memorandum*, borrowed from the Latin via English. A journalistic and diplomatic *mémoire*: this marks the entry of public, national, and international opinion, which also makes its own *mémoire*. The first half of the nineteenth century witnesses a massive body of verbal creations: *amnésie* contributed in 1803 by medical science, *mnémonique* (1800), *mnémotechnie* (1823), *mnémotechnique* (1836), and *mémorisation* was created in 1847 by Swiss educators, a group that shows the progress of teaching and pedagogy, *aide-mémoire*, which in 1853 shows that everyday life is imbued with the need for memory. Finally, in 1907, the pedantic *mémoriser* seems to sum up the acquisitions of memory in expansion.

However, as Leroi-Gourhan has pointed out, the eighteenth century plays a decisive role in this broadening of collective memory:

> Dictionaries reach their limits in the encyclopedias of all kinds that are published for the use of manufacturers or tinkerers as much as for pure scholars. The first true boom of technical literature occurs in the second half of the eighteenth century. The dictionary constitutes a very evolved form of external memory, but one in which thought is infinitely moralized; the Great Encyclopedia of 1751 is a series of little manuals bound up in a dictionary . . . the encyclopedia is a dispersed, alphabetical memory in which each isolated cog contains an animate part of the total memory. The relation between Vaucanson's automaton and the Encyclopedia contemporary with it is the same as that between electronic machines and calculators with memory today. (Leroi-Gourhan 1964/65:70–71)

The memory that has accumulated will explode in the French Revolution of 1789. Was it not the great detonator?

While the living have at their disposal an increasingly rich technical, scientific, and intellectual memory, memory seems to turn away from the dead. From the end of the seventeenth to the end of the eighteenth centuries, at least in the France described by Philippe Ariès and Michel Vovelle, the commemoration of the dead grows steadily weaker. Tombs, including those of the kings, become very simple. Sepulchers are left to nature, and cemeteries are deserted and poorly kept up. The Frenchman Pierre Muret, in his *Cérémonies funèbres de toutes les nations*, finds the forgetting of the dead particularly shocking in England, and attributes it to Protestantism: "Formerly, people remembered the deceased every year. Today, people no longer talk about them, for that would smell too much of Papistry." Michel Vovelle believes that in the age of the Enlightenment, people want to "eliminate death."

On the eve of the French Revolution, a return of the memory of the dead asserts itself in France as it does elsewhere in Europe. The great period of cemeteries begins, with new kinds of monuments, funeral inscriptions, and the rite of the visit to the cemetery. The tomb outside the Church has become once again the center of remembrance. Romanticism accentuates the attraction of the cemetery linked to memory. The nineteenth century sees, not so much in the order of knowledge, as in the eighteenth century, but rather in the order of feelings and also, it is true, in education, a development of the commemorative spirit.

Did the French Revolution set the example? Mona Ozouf has described this use of the revolutionary celebration in the service of memory. "Commemorating" is part of the revolutionary program: "All the calendar-makers and celebration-makers agree on the necessity of using the festival to maintain the memory of the Revolution" (Ozouf, p. 199). Title I of the Constitution of 1791 declares: "National celebrations will be established to preserve the memory of the French Revolution."

But soon thereafter, the manipulation of memory appears. After 9 Thermidor, people have become sensitive to the massacres and executions of the Terror, and it is therefore decided to delete from the collective memory "the multiplicity of victims," and "in the commemorative celebrations, censorship will henceforth oppose memory" (Ozouf, p. 202). In other cases a choice must be made. Only three revolutionary days seem to the Thermidorians worthy of being commemorated: July 14, the first of Vendémiaire, a revolutionary day unstained by blood, and with more hesitations, August 10, the date of the fall of the monarchy. On the other hand, the commemoration of January 21, the day of Louis XVI's execution, will not succeed in being commemorated; it is the "impossible commemoration."

Romanticism rediscovers, more in a literary than in a dogmatic way, the attraction of memory. In his translation of Vico's *On the Ancient Wisdom of Italy* (1835), Michelet could read this epigraph: "Memoria et phantasia." Vico wrote: "The Latins call memory *memoria* when it retains sense perceptions, and *reminiscentia* when it gives them back to us. But they designated in the same way the faculty by which we form images, which the Greeks called *phantasia*, and which we call *imaginativa*; for where we vulgarly say *imaginare*, the Latins said *memorare*. . . . Thus the Greeks say in their mythology that the Muses, the powers of imagination, are the daughters of Memory."[32] Here the link between memory and imagination, between memory and poetry is rediscovered.

However, the secularization of festivals and of the calendar in many countries facilitates a multiplication of commemorations. In France, the remembrance of the Revolution allows itself to be absorbed into the celebration of July 14, whose avatars Rosemonde Sanson has described. Suppressed by Napoleon, the festival is reestablished, at Raymond Raspail's suggestion, on July 6, 1880. The reporter of the bill in the legislature had declared: "The organization of a series of national celebrations reminding the people of the memories that are linked to the existing political institution is a necessity that all governments have recognized and put into practice." Gambetta had already written in "La République française" (July 15, 1872): "A free nation needs national celebrations."

In the United States, shortly after the end of the Civil War, the Northern states decided to establish a day of commemoration; this was first celebrated on May 30, 1868. In 1882 this day was given the name of "Memorial Day."

The French revolutionaries wanted celebrations commemorating the Revolution, but the commemoration mania was even more intense among conservatives, and particularly among nationalists, for whom memory was both a goal and an important instrument of government. In 1881, Paul Déroulède, the founder of the "Ligue des Patriotes," exclaimed:

> I know people who think hatred fades—
> But it does not! We shall never forget;
> Too much French soil has been stolen from us;
> The conquerors have conquered too much.

French Catholics and nationalists had the celebration of Joan of Arc added to the Republican July 14. The commemoration of the past reaches its culmination in Nazi Germany and Fascist Italy.

Commemoration finds new means: coins, medals, postage stamps multiply. From about the middle of the nineteenth century, a new wave of statuary, a new civilization of inscriptions (monuments, street signs, commemorative plaques on the houses of famous people) floods Europe. This is a major area, in which politics, sensibilities, and folklore mingle, and which awaits its historians. For nineteenth-century France, Maurice Agulhon, in his studies on the mania for statues and Republican imagery and symbolism, has shown the way. The rise of tourism leads to an unheard-of development in the sale of "souvenirs."

At the same time, the scientific movement that will supply the national collective memories with monuments of remembrance accelerates. In the eighteenth century, centralized archival depositories were created (by the House of Savoy in Turin in the early eighteenth century, by Peter the Great in 1720, at St. Petersburg, by Maria-Theresa at Vienna in 1749; at Warsaw, in 1765, at Venice in 1770, at Florence in 1778, etc.). In France, the Revolution created the National Archives (decree of September 7, 1790). The decree of July 25, 1794, opening the archives to the public begins a new phase in which documents containing the national memory will be accessible to the public. Following France, England established a Public Record Office in London in 1838. In 1881, the Pope Leo XIII opened to the public the *Archivo segreto vaticano*, which had been established in 1611.

Specialized institutions were created to train specialists in the study of these materials: L'Ecole des Chartes in Paris, in 1821 (reorganized in 1829); the Institut für Osterreichische Geschichtsforschung was begun by Theodor von Sickel in Vienna in 1854; the Scuola di Paleografia was begun in Florence by Bonaini in 1857.

Much the same can be said about museums. After timid eighteenth-century efforts at opening them to the public (the Louvre between 1750 and 1774, the public Museum in Cassel established in 1779 by the Landgrave of Hesse), and the housing of great collections in special buildings (the Hermitage in St. Petersburg under Catherine II, in 1764, the Museo Clementino in the Vatican in 1773, the Prado in Madrid in 1785), we finally arrive at the period of public and national museums. The *Grande Galerie* in the Louvre was opened on August 10, 1793; the Convention established a technical museum with the revealing name of "The Conservatory of Arts and Crafts"; in 1833, Louis-Philippe founded the Museum of Versailles, which was devoted to all the glories of France. The French national memory was extended in the direction of the Middle Ages by the housing of the Du Sommerard collection in the Musée de Cluny, and in the direction of prehistory by the Musée de Saint-Germain, established by Napoleon III in 1862.

The Germans created the Berlin Museum of National Antiquities in 1830, and the Germanic Museum of Nuremberg in 1852. In Italy, the House of Savoy, which was in the process of bringing about Italian national unity, created the Bargello national museum in Florence in 1859. The collective memory in Scandanavian countries was more open to "popular" memory; museums of folklore opened in Denmark (1807), in Bergen, Norway (1828), in Helsingfors, Finland (1849), before the creation of the first open-air museum (skansen) in Stockholm in 1891. The attention to technical memory, which D'Alembert had called for in the *Encyclopedia*, was realized in the creation in 1852 of a museum of manufacturing at Marlborough House in London.

Libraries underwent a parallel process of development and opening to the public. In the United States, Benjamin Franklin opened a lending library in Philadelphia in 1731.

In addition to these important or significant manifestations of the collective memory, the appearance of two phenomena in the nineteenth century and at the beginning of the twentieth century also merit attention.

The first is the erection of monuments to the dead after the First World War, through which funerary commemoration reached new heights. In a number of countries a "Tomb of the Unknown Soldier" was built, seeking to push back the boundaries associated with anonymity, and proclaiming, over a nameless body, the cohesiveness of a nation united in a common memory.

The second phenomenon is that of photography, which revolutionizes memory: it multiplies and democratizes it, gives it a precision and a truth never before attained in visual memory, and makes it possible to preserve the memory of time and of chronological evolution.

Pierre Bourdieu and his group have demonstrated the significance of the "family album":

> The portrait gallery has become democratic, and each family has in the person of its head, its official portrait-maker. To photograph one's children is to make oneself the historiographer of their childhood, and to create for them, as a sort of inheritance, the image of what they have been. . . . The family album expresses the truth of social remembrance. Nothing is less like the artistic search for lost time than the showing of these family pictures, accompanied by commentaries—an initiation rite families impose on all their new members. The images of the past arranged in chronological order,"the natural order" of social memory, arouse and transmit the remembrance of events worthy of preservation because the group sees a unifying factor in the monuments of its past unity, or what amounts to the same thing, because it derives from its past the confirmation of its present unity. That is why there is nothing more decent, more reassuring, or more edifying than a family album: all the particular adventures that enclose individual remembrance in the particularity of a secret are excluded from it, and the common past, or if one prefers, the lowest common denominator of the past, has the almost coquettish neatness of a frequently visited funeral monument.[33]

Let us add to these penetrating lines just one correction and one addition. The father is not always the official family portrait-maker. The mother often fills this role. Should we see in this a relic of the feminine function of the conservation of remembrance or, on the contrary, a conquest of the group memory by feminism?

In addition to the photos people take, we should also consider postcards they buy. Both make up the new familial archives, the "iconothèque" of family memory.

Contemporary Revolutions in Memory

As we have already seen, André Leroi-Gourhan, focusing on the processes by which collective memory is constituted, has divided its history into five periods: "oral transmission, written transmission with tables of contents or indices, simple file cards, mechanical writing, and electronic sequencing" (1964/65:65).

We have just discussed the advance made by collective memory in the nineteenth century, of which file-card memory is only an extension, just as printing was ultimately the conclusion of the accumulation of memory since Antiquity. Leroi-Gourhan has defined the progress of file-card memory and its limits:

> Collective memory acquired in the nineteenth century such a volume that it became impossible to expect the individual memory to contain the contents of libraries. . . . The eighteenth century and a significant part of the nineteenth still lived on notebooks and catalogs of works; next came documentation on file cards, which is not really organized until the beginning of the twentieth century. In its most rudimentary form, it already corresponded to the constitution of a veritable exteriorized cerebral cortex, since a simple bibliographical file-collection permits, in the hands of a user, various kinds of organization. . . . The image of the cortex is to some extent misleading, however, for if a file-collection is a memory in the strict sense, it is a memory that lacks its own means of remembrance and to become active it must be introduced into the visual and manual operational field of the researcher. (pp. 72–73)

But the radical changes in memory in the twentieth century, and especially after 1950, constitute a genuine revolution in memory, of which electronic memory is only one element, though no doubt the most spectacular one.

The appearance in the course of the Second World War of large calculating machines (which is linked to the enormous acceleration of history, and particularly of technical and scientific history, since 1960) can be seen as part of a long history of automatic memory. The arithmetical machine invented by Pascal in the seventeenth century, which marked a significant advance over the abacus and has been seen as a precursor of modern computers, added to the *faculty of memory* a *calculative faculty*.

The function of memory is situated in the following fashion in a computer, which includes:

a) means of entering data and the program;
b) elements endowed with *memory*, constituted by magnetic devices, which preserve the information introduced into the machine and the partial results obtained in the course of its operation;
c) very rapid means of calculation;
d) means of verification;
e) means of extracting the results.[34]

We distinguish between memories that register the data to be dealt with and memories that temporarily preserve the intermediate results and certain constants (p. 12). In a way, we rediscover in the computer the distinction psychologists make between short-term and long-term memory.

In summary, memory is one of the three fundamental operations of a computer operation that can be analyzed into "writing," "memory," and "reading" (p. 28, fig. 10). This memory may be "unlimited" in some cases.

To this first distinction between human memory and electronic memory with regard to duration, we must add that "human memory is particularly unstable and malleable (a criticism that has become traditional in modern psychology, with reference to judicial testimony, for instance), whereas the memory of machines is respected for its great stability, which is comparable to the memory represented by books, but combined with a previously unheard-of ease of recall" (p. 83).

It is clear that the construction of artificial brains, which is still in its beginnings, is leading to the existence of "machines that will surpass the human brain in operations having to do with memory and rational judgment," and to the recognition that "the cerebral cortex, as admirable as it is, is insufficient, just like the hand or the eye" (Leroi-Gourhan 1964/

65:75). But we must note that electronic memory operates only on human command and in accord with human programming, that human memory preserves a large sector that cannot be reduced to "information," and that, like all the forms of automatic memory that have appeared in the course of history, electronic memory is only an aid, a servant of memory and of the human mind.

Beyond the services rendered in different technical and administrative domains in which information theory finds its first and most important information, we should note two consequences of the appearance of electronic memory that are relevant to our subject.

The first is the use of computers in the area of social sciences and in particular in the area in which memory is both the material and the object: history. History has undergone a genuine documentary revolution, in which the computer is moreover only one element, and archival memory has been radically changed by the advent of a new kind of memory: the *data bank* (Le Goff 1978 5:38–48). Basic works on the use of electronic memory are multiplying. Let us cite the works of Father Busa on Thomas Aquinas, the study by David Herlihy and Christiane Klapisch-Zuber, *Les Toscans et leurs familles.*

The second consequence is the "metaphorical" effect of the extension of the concept of *memory* and the importance of the influence *by analogy* of electronic memory on other kinds of memory. The most striking example is that of biology. Our guide here will be the Nobel Prize-winner François Jacob, in his book *La logique du vivant.* The computer was among the points of departure for the discovery of biological memory, of the *memory of heredity*: "With the development of electronics and the advent of cybernetics, organization itself became the object of study for physics and technology" (p. 267). Organization soon became important for molecular biology, which discovered that "heredity functions like the memory of a calculating machine" (p. 274).

Research on biological memory goes back to at least the eighteenth century. Maupertuis and Buffon glimpsed the problem: "The reproduction of an organization constituted by the assemblage of elementary units requires the transmission of a 'memory' from one generation to another" (p. 142). For the Leibnitzian Maupertuis, "the memory that directs the living particles to form the embryo is no different from the psychic memory" (p. 92). For the materialist Bouffon, "the interior model represents a hidden structure, a 'memory' that organizes matter in such a way as to produce a child in the image of its parents" (p. 94).

The nineteenth century discovers that "whatever the name and the nature of the forces through which the organization of the parents is reproduced in the child, they must henceforth be located in the cell" (p. 142). But for the first half of the nineteenth century "there is only the 'vital movement' to play the role of memory and to ensure the fidelity of reproduction" (p. 142). Like Buffon, Claude Bernard still "locates memory, not in the particles constituting the organism, but in a particular system that guides the multiplication of cells, their differentiation, the progressive formation of the organism," while Darwin and Haeckel "make memory a property" of the particles constituting the organism. In 1865, Mendel discovered the great law of heredity. In order to explain it, "it is necessary to call on a structure of a higher order, still more hidden, even more deeply buried in the body; it is in a third-order structure that the memory of heredity is located" (p. 226). But Mendel's discovery remained unknown for a long time. Not until the twentieth century and the development of genetics was it discovered that this organizing structure is buried in the nucleus of the cell and that "it is in it that the 'memory' of heredity is located" (p. 198).

Molecular biology finally finds the solution. "It is the organization of a macro-molecule, the 'message' constituted by the arrangement of chemical relays along a polymer, that holds the memory of heredity. It becomes the fourth-order structure by means of which the form of a living being, its properties and functioning, are determined" (p. 269).

Curiously, biological memory resembles electronic memory more than it does the nervous, cerebral memory. On one hand, it is also defined by a program in which two notions, "memory and the project" (p. 10) are fused. On the other hand, it is rigid: "In the suppleness of its mechanisms, nervous memory is particularly apt for the transmission of acquired characteristics. In its rigidity, heredity resists it" (p. 11). And unlike computers, "the message of heredity does not permit the slightest concerted intervention from the outside. There can be no change in the program through the action of men or of the environment" (p. 11).

To come back to social memory, the radical changes it has undergone in the second half of the twentieth century were prepared, it seems, by the expansion of memory in the area of philosophy and literature. As early as 1896, Bergson published *Matière et mémoire*. He rediscovers the central notion of the *image* at the intersection of memory and perception. At the end of a long analysis of deficiencies in memory (linguistic amnesia or *aphasia*), he discovers, beneath a superficial, anonymous memory that can be assimilated to habit, a deep, personal, "pure" memory that cannot be analyzed in terms of "things" but only of "progress."

This theory, which rediscovered the links between memory and the mind, and perhaps even the soul, had a great influence on literature. It left its mark on Marcel Proust's great novelistic project, *A la recherche du temps perdu* (1913–1927). A new novelistic memory is born, which should be situated in the sequence "myth, history, novel."

Surrealism, shaped by dreams, is led to reflect on memory. In 1922, André Breton had noted in his notebooks: "And what if memory were only a product of the imagination?" To learn more about dreams, men had to trust more in memory, which is normally so fragile and so deceptive. Whence, in the *Manifeste du surréalisme* (1924), the importance of the theory of *educable memory*—a new avatar of the *Artes Memoriae*.

We must mention here, of course, the inspiration of Freud, and especially the Freud of the *Interpretation of Dreams* (1st ed. 1899–1900; 8th ed. 1929), in which we read that "the behavior of memory during dreams is no doubt of enormous importance for any theory of memory." In chapter 2, Freud discusses "memory in dreams," where, commenting on a remark by Scholz, he thinks he sees that "nothing of what we have possessed intellectually can every be entirely lost." But he criticizes "the idea of reducing the phenomenon of dreaming to remembering," for the dream makes a specific choice in memory, a specific memory of dreams. This memory, in this case as well, is a *choice*. But isn't Freud tempted to treat memory as a thing, a vast reservoir? But by tying dreams to the *latent memory* and to the *unconscious memory*, and by insisting on the importance of childhood in the constitution of that memory, he contributes, at the same time as Bergson, to deepening the domain of memory, and to illuminating, at least at the level of the individual memory, the very important notion of the *censorship of memory*.

Collective memory has undergone enormous transformations with the constitution of the social sciences, and it plays an important role in the interdisciplinary relationships being established among them.

Sociology has stimulated the exploration of collective memory as it did the concept of time (see the section on *History* below). In 1950, Maurice Halbwachs published his book on *Les mémoires collectives*. Social psychology, insofar as this memory is associated with behavior, with *mentalities*, a new object of the new history, collaborates in this effort. Anthropology, to the extent that the term "memory" offers it a concept better adapted to the realities of "primitive" societies than the term "history," has welcomed the notion, and explored it along with history, particularly in the *ethnohistory* or *historical anthropology* that is among the most interesting recent developments in historical knowledge.

This pursuit, rescue, and celebration of collective memory, no longer in single events but over a long period, this quest for collective memory less in texts that in the spoken word, images, gestures, rituals and festivals, constitutes a major change in historical vision. It amounts to a conversion that is shared by the public at large, which is obsessed by the fear of losing its memory in a kind of collective amnesia—a fear that is awkwardly expressed in the taste for the fashions of earlier times, and shamelessly exploited by nostalgia-merchants; memory has thus become a best-seller in a consumer society.

Pierre Nora (1978) observes that *collective memory*, defined as "what remains of the past in the lived reality of groups, or what these groups make of the past," can at first sight seem to be almost completely opposed to *historical memory*, just as *affective memory* used to be opposed to *intellectual memory*. Up until our own time, "history and memory" had practically fused, and history seems to have developed "on the model of remembering, of amamnesis and of memorization." Historians proposed the expression "great collective mythologies," "we were passing from history to collective memory." But the whole evolution of the contemporary world, under the impact of an *immediate history* for the most part fabricated on the spot by the media, is headed toward the production of an increased number of collective memories, and history is written, much more than in earlier days, under the influence of these collective memories.

The so-called "new" history which seeks to create a scientific history on the basis of collective memory can only be interpreted as "a revolution in memory," that causes memory to "pivot" on a few fundamental axes: "an openly contemporary problematics . . . and a resolutely retrospective procedure," "the renunciation of linear temporality" in favor of multiple kinds of time as experienced "at the levels where the individual takes root in the social and the collective" (linguistics, demography, economics, biology, culture).

This is a history that would be based on the study of "places" in the collective memory: "topographical places, such as archives, libraries, and museums; monumental places, such as cemeteries or architectural edifices; symbolic places, such as commemorative ceremonies, pilgrimages, anniversaries or emblems; functional places, such as manuals, autobiographies, or associations: these memorials have their history." But we must not forget the true places of history, those in which not the elaboration or construction, but the creators and dominators of collective memory are to be sought: "States, social and political milieux, communities of historical experiences or of generations led to constitute their archives in relation to the different uses that they make of memory."[35] To be sure, this new collective memory constitutes its knowledge in the traditional vehicles, but it conceives them differently. Compare, for example, the *Enciclopedia Einaudi* or the *Encyclopaedia Universalis* with the venerable *Encyclopaedia Britannica*![36] Perhaps ultimately we would arrive at something more like the spirit of d'Alembert's and Diderot's great *Encyclopédie*, which was also the offspring of a period of active engagement and transformation of the collective memory.

The new collective memory manifests itself especially in the constitution of radically new kinds of archives, of which the most characteristic are oral archives. In the dictionary of the *Nouvelle Histoire* (Le Goff, ed.), Joseph Goy has defined and situated *oral history*, which no doubt originated in the United States, where, from 1952 to 1959, great departments of "oral history" were created at Columbia, Berkeley, and UCLA, and later developed in Quebec, England, and France. The case of Great Britain is exemplary. The University of Essex established a collection of "life histories," founded "The Oral History Society," and created numerous bulletins and journals such as *History Workshops*, one of whose main results was a brilliant rebirth of social history and above all labor history through attention to the industrial, urban, and working past of the largest segment of the population. Historians and sociologists played a particularly important role in this inquiry into the collective memory of workers. But historians and anthropologists also came together in other areas of collective memory, both in Africa and in Europe, where new methods of remembering such as "life histories" began to bear fruit. A new colloquium that met in Bologna under the title *Convegno Internazionale di Antropologia e storia: Fonti Orali*, whose proceedings were published in 1977 in a special issue of *Quaderni storici* ("Oral History: fra antropologia e storia"), demonstrated that the fertility of this research extended beyond African, French, English ("oral history and the history of the working class") and Italian ("oral history in a working quarter of Turin, oral sources and peasant labor apropos of a museum") examples.

In the area of history, under the influence of new conceptions of historical time, a new form of historiography is developing: "the history of history," which, in fact, is usually the study of the manipulation by collective memory of a historical phenomenon which up to this point only traditional history has studied.

In recent French historiography we find four remarkable examples of this. In two cases, the historical phenomenon through which collective memory has been manifested is a great individual; in a pioneering work, Robert Folz studied *Le souvenir et la légende de Charlemagne* (1950), and Jean Tulard analyzed *Le mythe de Napoléon* (1971). Closer to the tendencies of the new history, Georges Duby, in *Le dimanche de Bouvines* (1973), has renewed the history of a battle, first because he sees the event as the tip of an iceberg, and second because he considers, "in an anthropological perspective, both this battle and the memory it has left behind," and because he follows "through a whole series of commemorations, the destiny of a memory in the context of a moving ensemble of mental representations." Finally, through written documents of the past, and through oral testimony from the present, Philippe Joutard (1977) has discovered how a historical community established its collective memory and how this memory allowed the community to maintain itself in the face of events very different from those that established its memory on a single line, and even today enables the community to find its identity in this memory. After the ordeals of the religious wars in the sixteenth and seventeenth centuries, the Protestants of the Cévennes, reacted to the Revolution of 1789, the Dreyfus affair, and present-day ideological options by referring to their memory (faithful and mobile like any memory) of the local "Camisards" who opposed Louis XIV and his revocation of the Edict of Nantes in 1685.

Conclusion: The Stake of Memory

The evolution of societies in the second half of the twentieth century demonstrates the importance of the stake represented by collective memory. Overflowing history as both a form of knowledge and a public rite, flowing uphill as the moving reservoir of history, full of archives and documents/monuments, and downhill as the sonorous (and living) echo of historical work, collective memory is one of the great stakes of developed and developing societies, of dominated and dominating classes, all of them struggling for power or for life, for survival and for advancement.

The words of André Leroi-Gourhan are truer than ever: "Starting from *homo sapiens*, the constitution of the apparatus of social memory dominates all problems of human evolution," and further, "Tradition is biologically just as indispensable for the human species as genetic conditioning is to insect societies: ethnic survival depends on routine, and the dialogue that is established brings about the equilibrium between routine and progress, routine symbolizing capital necessary to the group's survival, and progress the intervention of individual innovation that produces a better survival." Memory is an essential element of what will henceforth be called individual or collective *identity*, the feverish and anxious quest for which is today one of the fundamental activities of individuals and societies. But collective memory is not only a conquest, it is also an instrument and an objective of power. It is societies whose social memory is primarily oral or which are in the process of establishing a written collective memory that offer us the best chance of understanding this struggle for domination over remembrance and tradition, this manipulation of memory.

The case of Etruscan historiography perhaps illustrates a collective memory so tightly bound to a dominant social class that the identification of that class with the nation brought about the absence of memory when the nation disappeared:

> We know the Etruscans, on the literary level, only through the intermediary of the Greeks and Romans: no historical account, even if we admit that such an account existed, has come down to us. Perhaps their national historical or parahistorical traditions disappeared along with the aristocracy that seems to have been the repository of the moral, juridical, and religious patrimony of their nation. When the nation ceased to exist as an autonomous nation, the Etruscans seem to have lost the consciousness of their past, that is to say, of themselves.[37]

Studying Greek and Roman philanthropy, Paul Veyne has shown admirably how the rich "sacrificed part of their wealth to ensure the memory of their role" (1973, p. 272), and how under the Roman empire the emperor monopolized philanthropy, and thereby the collective memory as well: "He alone caused all the public edifices to be built (with the exception of the monuments that the Senate and the Roman people erected in his honor)" (p. 688). And the Senate occasionally avenged itself by destroying this imperial memory.

Georges Balandier gives the example of the Beti of the Cameroon to illustrate the manipulation of the "genealogies" whose role in the collective memory of peoples without writing is well-known: "In an unpublished study on the Beti of southern Cameroon, the writer Mongo Beti reports and illustrates the strategy that permits ambitious and enterprising individuals to 'adapt' the genealogies in order to legalize a contestable preeminence."[38]

In developed societies, the new oral and audio-visual archives have not escaped the attention of governments, even if they cannot monitor or control this kind of memory as closely as they can the new tools for producing it—notably radio and television.

It is incumbent upon professional specialists in memory—anthropologists, historians, journalists, sociologists—to make of the struggle for the democratization of social memory one of the primary imperatives of their scientific objectivity. Taking his inspiration from Terence O. Ranger (1977), who criticized the subordination of traditional African anthropology to "elitist" sources and especially "genealogies" manipulated by the dominant clans, Alessandro Triulzi (1977) has called for an investigation of the memory of the African "common man." He recommends the study, in Africa as in Europe, "of family memories, local histories, histories of clans, families, villages, personal memories, and all the vast complex of unofficial, non-institutionalized knowledge which has not yet crystallized into formal traditions and which represents, so to speak, the collective consciousness of whole groups (families, villages) or individuals (memories and personal experiences) that form a counterweight to the knowledge which is privatized and monopolized by certain groups for the defense of established interests."

Memory, on which history draws and which it nourishes in return, seeks to save the past in order to serve the present and the future. Let us act in such a way that collective memory may serve the liberation and not the enslavement of human beings.

HISTORY

Almost everyone is convinced that history is not a science like other sciences, and some people even believe that it is not a science at all. It is not easy to talk about history, but examining the linguistic difficulties involved in doing so can lead us to the very center of history's ambiguities.

In this essay I shall try both to resituate reflection on history in its duration and to situate historical science itself in the periodizations of history, without reducing history to the European, Western vision, even if the latter leads me (because of the things I do not know and because of the—significant—state of the relevant documentation) to speak primarily of European and Western historical science.

The word "history" (in all the Romance languages and in English) comes from the ancient Greek word *historie*, in the Ionian dialect. This form derives from the Indo-European root *wid—weid*, "see." Whence the Sanskrit *vettas*, witness, and the Greek *istor*, a witness in the sense of "one who sees." This conception of vision as the essential source of knowledge leads to the idea that *istor*, the one who sees, is also the one who *knows*; *istorein*, in ancient Greek, means "to seek to know," "to in-form oneself." *Istorie* is thus inquiry. That is the sense of the word at the beginning of Herodotus' "Histories," which are investigations, inquiries.[1] The connection between *voir* and *savoir*, between seeing and knowing, is thus a first problem. But in Romance languages (as well as in others), *histoire*, *historia*, *storia*, etc. express two if not three different concepts. These are first, the inquiry into "the acts accomplished by men" (Herodotus) that has sought to establish itself as a science, the science of history; second, the object of that inquiry, what men have accomplished. As Paul Veyne puts it, "history is either a series of events, or the narrative of that series of events" (1968:423). But history can also have a third meaning, which is precisely that of *narrative*. A history is a narrative, which can be true or false, based on "historical reality" or on pure imagination; it can be a "historical" narrative or a fable. English avoids this last confusion by distinguishing between *history* and *story*. Other European languages seek more or less to avoid these ambiguities. Italian tends to distinguish, if not historical science, at least the productions of that science, by the word *storiografia*; German tries to distinguish between the "scientific" activity of *Geschichtschreibung* and historical science properly so called, *Geschichtswissenschaft*. This play of mirrors and ambiguities has continued throughout the ages. The nineteenth century, the century of history, invented doctrines that simultaneously accord history both a privileged place in knowledge, speaking, as we shall see, of either *historism* or *historicism*, and a function—I should rather say, a category of the real. This function or category is *historicity* (the word first appears in French in 1872, in English in 1880). Charles Morazé defines *historicity* in this way: "We must look beyond geopolitics, commerce, the arts, and even science to find the justification for people's obscure certainty that they are part of a unity, amputated as they are in the enormous flux of progress which defines them by opposing them. We have a strong feeling that this solidarity is linked to the implicit existence, which each person senses within himself, of a certain function" (p. 59). This concept of *historicity* has detached itself from its "historical" origins in the historicism of the nineteenth century in order to play a major role in the second half of the twentieth century. *Historicity* permits us, for example, to reject on the theoretical level the notion of a "society without history," which is, moreover, refuted by the empirical examination of the societies studied by ethnology (see Lefort 1952:30 ff). It obliges us to insert history itself into a historical perspective: "there is a historicity of history. It implies the movement that links an interpretive practice to a social praxis" (de Certeau 1970:484). A philosopher like Paul Ricoeur sees in the suppression of historicity by the history of philosophy the paradox of the epistemological foundation of history. In fact, according to Ricoeur, philosophical discourse splits history into two models of history, an event-model and a structural model, and this makes history disappear: "The system puts an end to history, because history is annulled in Logic; singularity also puts an end to history, because it denies all history. We arrive at the entirely paradoxical result that it is always at the frontier of history, of the end of history, that we are able to understand the general characteristics of historicity" (1961:224–25). Finally, Paul Veyne draws a double moral from the functioning of the concept of historicity. It permits the inclusion of new objects of history within the field of historical science: "That which does not have the character of an event, the '*non-événementiel*,' is an event that is not yet recognized as such: the history of regions, of mentalities, of madness or of the search for security through the ages. We will therefore call '*non-événementiel*' the historicity which we do not yet recognize as such" (1971:31). On the other hand, historicity excludes the idealization of history, the existence of History with a capital "H": "Everything is history, thus History does not exist."

But we have to live and think with this double or triple meaning of "history." We must struggle against the excessively crude and mystifying confusions of one sense with the others, and we must not confuse historical science with the philosophy of history. This latter confusion, which is "tenacious and insidious" (Lefebvre 1945/46:16), tends, in its various forms, to reduce historical explanation to the discovery or application of a single, first cause; for the scientific study of the evolution of societies, it tends to substitute that evolution itself, conceived in abstractions founded on a priori assumptions or on a very summary knowledge of scientific investigations. I find astounding the impact made, largely on nonhistorians, it is true, by Karl Popper's pamphlet, *The Poverty of Historicism*. He does not cite a single professional historian. We should not, however, make of this mistrust with respect to the philosophy of history a justification for rejecting this kind of reflection. The ambiguity of the vocabulary itself reveals that the frontier separating the two disciplines, the two orientations of research, is not—hypothetically—strictly drawn, or even drawable. The historian must not conclude that he should therefore turn away from a kind of *theoretical* reflection that is necessary for historical research. It is clear that the historians who are the most inclined to rely solely on facts are not only unaware that a historical fact results from a process of montage and that establishing it requires both technical and theoretical work, but also blinded by an unconscious philosophy of history that is often slender and incoherent. Certainly, I repeat, the ignorance of historical research among most philosophers of history—the corollary of historians' scorn for philosophy—has not facilitated dialogue. But for example, the existence of a high-quality journal such as *History and Theory: Studies in the Philosophy of History*, published since 1960 by Wesleyan University, proves the possibility and the value of common reflection on the part of philosophers and historians as well as the development of informed specialists in the field of theoretical reflection on history.

I think, therefore, that Paul Veyne's brilliant argument against philosophy of history goes slightly beyond the reality of the situation. He believes that philosophy of history is no longer anything but a dead genre, or one "that survives only among the epigones of a more or less popular knowledge," and that "it was a false genre." In fact, "unless it is a revealed philosophy, a philosophy of history will merely repeat the concrete explanation of facts and refer to the mechanisms and laws that explain these facts. Only the extremes are viable: either the Providentialism of the *City of God*, or historical epistemology; everything else is illegitimate" (Veyne 1961:40). Without going so far as to agree with Raymond Aron, who claims that "The absence and the need for a philosophy of history are thus equally characteristic of our time" (1961:38), I would say that on the margins of historical science a philosophy of history can legitimately develop like other branches of knowledge. We may hope that it will not be ignorant of the history of historians, but historians should admit that it can have cognitive relationships with the object of history that differ from theirs.

It is the duality of history as history-reality and as history-study of that reality which often explains, it seems to me, the ambiguities of certain statements concerning history made by Claude Lévi-Strauss. Thus, in a discussion with Maurice Godelier, Godelier having pointed out that the praise given, in *Du Miel aux cendres*, to history as irreducible contingency turns back against history, and that it "puts the science of history in an impossible position, reducing it to an impasse," Lévi-Strauss replies: "I do not know what you are calling a science of history. I would be satisfied to say simply *history*, and simple history is something we cannot do without, precisely because it constantly confronts us with irreducible phenomena" (1975:182–83). The whole ambiguity of the word "history" is in that statement.

I shall therefore approach history by borrowing my basic idea from a philosopher:

> History is history only insofar as it has not attained either absolute discourse or absolute singularity, insofar as its meaning remains confused, mixed. . . . History is essentially equivocal, in the sense that it is virtually *événementielle*, concerned with events, and virtually structural. History is truly the realm of the inexact. This is not an empty discovery; it justifies the historian. It justifies him in relation to the difficulties that confront him. The historical method can only be an inexact method. . . . History wants to be objective, and it cannot be. It wants to resuscitate and it can only reconstruct. It wants to make things contemporary, but at the same time, it has to restore the distance and the depth of historical time that separates it from its object. Finally, this reflection tends to justify all the aporias of the historian's craft, those that Marc Bloch pointed out in his defense of history and of the historian's craft. These difficulties do not arise from defects of method, they are well-founded ambiguities. (Ricoeur 1961:226)

This is a view that is a little too pessimistic on certain points, but which seems to me true. I shall therefore first present the paradoxes and ambiguities of history, but only the better to define it as a science—an unusual, but fundamental science.

I shall then deal with three essential aspects of history that are often mixed together, but which I believe should be distinguished: historical culture, the philosophy of history, and the historian's craft. I shall do so in a historical perspective, in the chronological sense. My criticism of a linear and teleological conception of history in the first part should ward off the suspicion that I identify chronology with qualitative progress, even if I stress the cumulative effects of knowledge, and what Ignace Meyerson has called "the rise of historical consciousness" (1956:354).

I shall not try to be exhaustive. (The bibliography, which could be enormous, is not exhaustive either. But it includes, in order to permit the reader to go further, and sometimes in another direction, works that are not cited in the text.) What interests me is to show, from the first point of view, through a few examples, the kind of relations that historical societies have entertained with their past, and the place of history in their present. In the perspective of the philosophy of history, I should like to show, through the cases of certain great minds and certain important currents of thought, how, beyond or outside of the disciplinary practice of history, people have, in certain milieux and in certain periods, conceptualized, and given ideological cohesion, to their history. The professional horizon of history will paradoxically give more attention to the notion of evolution and improvement. That is because by placing itself in the perspective of technology and science, it will inevitably encounter the idea of technical progress.

A final section devoted to the current situation of history will return to some of the fundamental themes of this essay and discuss certain new aspects.

Historical science has experienced a prodigious growth during the past half-century: the renewal and enrichment of its techniques and methods, of its horizons and domains. But maintaining with global societies relations that are more intense than ever, professional, scientific history is in a profound crisis. The knowledge of history is all the more troubled because its power is greater.

Paradoxes and Ambiguities of History

Is history a science of the past, or is it true that "there is only contemporary history"?

Marc Bloch did not like to define history as "the science of the past," and thought that "the very idea that the past as such could be the object of a science is absurd" (1941/42:32–33). He proposed to define history as "the science of men in time." He wanted thereby to stress three characteristics of history. The first of these is its human character. Although today historical research sometimes reaches into certain domains of natural history,[2] it is generally admitted that history is human history, and Paul Veyne has emphasized "the enormous difference" separating human history from natural history: "Man deliberates, nature does not; human history would become nonsensical if we were to ignore the fact that men have goals, ends, intentions" (1968:424). This conception of human history has, moreover, inspired in many historians the idea that the central, essential part of history is social history. Charles-Edmond Perrin has written about Marc Bloch: "He assigns to history as its object the study of man insofar as man is part of a social group," and Lucien Febvre goes even further: "Not man, I repeat, not man, never man. Human societies, organized groups."[3] Bloch thought next about the relations between past and present within history. In his opinion history must not only make it possible for us to "understand the present by means of the past"—a traditional attitude—but also to "understand the past by means of the present" (pp. 44–50). Firmly asserting the scientific, abstract character of the historian's work, he denied that this work was inseparable from chronology: "It would in fact be a serious error to believe that the order adopted by historians in their investigations has necessarily to model itself on that of events. On the condition that they afterward restore to history its true movement, historians may often profit by reading it, as Maitland put it, "backwards" (pp. 48–49). Whence the interest of "a prudently regressive method." "Prudent" in the sense that it does not naively bring the present into the past or follow in reverse a linear trajectory that would be just as illusory in the opposite direction. There are ruptures and discontinuities that cannot be leapt over in either direction.

The idea that history is dominated by the present rests largely on a famous phrase of Benedetto Croce's: "all history is contemporary history." Croce means thereby that "no matter how distant in time the events that history recounts may seem to be, in reality history is related to present needs and to the situations in which these events find their echoes." In fact, Croce thinks that the moment that historical events can be constantly rethought, they are no longer "in time," history is the "knowledge of the eternal present" (P. Gardiner). Thus this extreme form of idealism amounts to the negation of history. As E. H. Carr has observed, Croce inspired Colligwood's thesis in *The Idea of History*, a posthumous collection of articles published between 1932 and 1946 in which the British historian asserts—combining the two senses of history, the historian's investigation and the series of past events through which he carries out his investigation—that history is concerned with neither the past in itself nor with what the historian thinks about it, but rather with the relation between the two (Carr, pp. 15–16).

This conception is both fertile and dangerous. Fertile because it is true that the historian starts out from his own present in order to ask questions of the past. Dangerous because, if in spite of everything the past exists outside the present, it is vain to believe in a past independent of the one constituted by the historian.[4] This consideration dooms all conceptions of an "ontological" past—such as Emile Callot's definition of history: "an intelligible narration of a past that is definitively over."[5]

The past is constantly being constructed and reinterpreted, and it has a future that is an integral and significant part of history. This is true in two senses. First because the progress in methods and techniques allows us to think that an important portion of the documents of the past remains to be discovered. A material portion: archeology is always discovering buried monuments of the past, archives of the past never cease growing. But there are also new readings of documents, the results of a present to be born in the future, that will ensure the survival—or rather, the life—of a past which is not definitively over.

To the essential relation between past and present, we must therefore add the horizon of the future. Here again there are multiple meanings. The theologies of history have subordinated it to a goal defined as its end, its culmination and its revelation. This is true of Christian history, in the grip of eschatology, and it is also true of historical materialism (in its ideological version), which grafts onto a science of the past a desire for the future that does not depend solely on the fusion of a scientific analysis of past history and a revolutionary praxis enlightened by that analysis. One of the tasks of historical science is to find a way—other than ideology, and one that respects the unforeseeable nature of the future—to introduce the horizon of the future into its reflections (Erdmann, Schulin). Consider this observation, banal but full of consequences: historians who deal with ancient periods know what happened *afterward*; historians of present times do not. Contemporary history strictly speaking thus differs (and there are also other reasons for this difference) from the history of earlier periods.

This dependence of the history of the past on the historian's present should lead us to take certain precautions. It is inevitable and legitimate, insofar as the past does not cease to live and to make itself present. But this long duration of the past must not prevent the historian from establishing a certain distance with regard to the past, a reverential distance that is necessary if we are to respect it and avoid anachronism. In sum, I think history is indeed the science of the past, if it is acknowledged that this past becomes an object of history through a reconstitution that is constantly questioned. One cannot, for example, talk about the Crusades the way people would have before nineteenth-century colonization, but we have to ask if, and from what points of view, the term "colonialism" can be applied to the medieval Crusaders' occupation of Palestine.[6]

This interaction of past and present is what has been called the social function of the past or of history. Thus Lucien Febvre: "It is in relation to its present needs that history systematically harvests, and then classes and groups, past facts. It is in relation to life that it questions death. To organize the past in relation to the present: that is what one could call the social function of history" (p. 438). And Eric Hobsbawm has reflected on "the social function of the past" (1972). (See the opening essay, "Past and Present.")

Let us consider a few examples of the process by which "each period mentally fabricates its representation of the historical past."

Georges Duby has resuscitated or recreated the battle of Bouvines (July 27, 1214), a decisive victory of the French King Philip Augustus over the Emperor Otto IV and his allies. This battle, orchestrated and made legendary by French historians, fell into oblivion after the thirteenth century, then enjoyed a resurgence in the seventeenth century when memories of the French monarchy were lauded, and again under the July Monarchy because liberal and bourgeois historians (Guizot, Augustin Thierry) saw in it the beneficent alliance of the monarchy with the people, and again between 1871 and 1914 because it was seen as "the first great victory of the French over the Germans." After 1945, Bouvines sank into obscurity as a result of the general scorn for "battle-history" (Duby 1973).

Nicole Loraux and Pierre Vidal-Nacquet have shown how in France, from 1750 to 1850, from Montesquieu to Victor Duruy, a "bourgeois" image of ancient Athens was elaborated, whose principal characteristics were supposed to have been "respect for property, respect for private life, the flourishing of commerce, labor, and industry," and in which one even finds the hesitations of the nineteenth-century bourgeoisie: "Republic or empire? An authoritarian empire? A liberal empire? Athens takes on all these guises simultaneously" (Loraux and Vidal-Nacquet 1979:207–222). Zvi Yavetz, asking himself why Rome had been the historical model for Germany at the beginning of the nineteenth century, replied: "because the conflict between Prussian lords and peasants arbitrated after Jena (1806) through the reformist intervention of the State, without the counsel of Prussian statesmen, provided a model that was thought to be found in the history of ancient Rome: B. G. Niebuhr, the author of the *Römanische Geschichte* that appeared in 1811–12, was a close collaborator of the Prussian minister Stein" (Yavetz).

Philippe Joutard has traced the memory of the popular uprising of the Huguenot Camisards in the Cévennes at the beginning of the eighteenth century. In the written historiography a turning point appears around 1840. Up to that point, both Catholic and Protestant historians had nothing but scorn for this peasant revolt. But with the publication of *Histoire des Pasteurs du Désert* by Napoléon Peyrat (1842), *Les prophètes protestants* by Ami Bost (1842), and Michelet's *Histoire de France* (1862), a golden legend of the Camisards developed, which was countered by a dark Catholic legend. This opposition explicitly drew nourishment from the political passions of the second half of the nineteenth century that put in conflict the partisans of the movement and the partisans of order; the latter considered the Camisards the ancestors of all the rebels of the nineteenth century, the advance scouts of "the eternal army of disorder," "the first precursors of those who demolished the Bastille," the precursors of the Communards and of contemporary socialists, their "direct descendents," along with whom they were "supposed to have demanded the right to commit pillage, murder, and arson in the name of the freedom to strike." However, in another kind of memory which secretes "a different history," Joutard has found a positive, living legend about the Camisards, but one which also functions in relation to the present and makes the rebels of 1702 "the secular and republican" people of the end of Louis XIV's reign. Later, the regionalist revival transformed them into Occitan rebels, and during the Second World War, the French Resistance turned them into *maquisards.*

It is also in relation to contemporary positions and ideas that a polemic concerning the Middle Ages broke out in Italy after the First World War.[7] Still more recently, the medievalist Ovidio Capitani has discussed the distance and the proximity of the Middle Ages in a collection of essays significantly titled *Medioevo passato prossimo* (The Past, the Recent Middle Ages). He writes:

> The currentness of the Middle Ages consists in this: knowing one cannot act without seeking God where he is not. . . . The Middle Ages is 'current' precisely because it is past, but past as an element definitively attached forever to *our history*, and which obliges us to take it into account, because it includes a powerful body of answers that men have given, and cannot forget, even if they have proven their inadequacy. The only way to [forget them] would be to abolish history. (1979:276)

Thus, historiography appears as a series of new readings of the past, full of losses and resurgences, of memory gaps and revisions. These "aggiornamenti" [updatings] can also affect the historian's vocabulary and, through the anachronism of concepts and words, they can seriously flaw the quality of his work. Thus it is that relying on examples drawn from English and European history between 1450 and 1650, and using terms such as "party," "class," etc., J. H. Hexter has demanded a massive and rigorous revision of historical vocabulary (1962).

R. G. Collingwood saw in this relation between past and present the main object of the historian's reflection on his work: the past is an aspect or function of the present, and so it must always appear to the historian who reflects intelligently on his own work or, in other words, aims at a philosophy of history.[8] This relation between present and past in the discourse of history is in any case an essential aspect of the traditional problem of objectivity in history.

Knowledge and power: objectivity and the manipulation of the past

According to Heidegger, the past is not only man's projection of the present into the past but the projection of the most imagnary part of his present, the projection into the past of the future that he has chosen, a fiction-history or reversed desire-history. Paul Veyne is right to reject this point of view, and to say that Heidegger "only erects nineteenth-century anti-intellectual nationalist historiography into a philosophy" (1968:424). But isn't he perhaps overly optimistic when he adds: "in doing so, like Minerva's owl, he has awakened a little too late"? First of all, because there are—and I shall return to this point—at least two histories: that of collective memory and that of historians. The first appears as essentially mythic, deformed, and anachronistic. But it constitutes the lived reality of the never-completed relation between present and past. It is desirable that historical information (lavished on us by professional historians, popularized in schools, and—one could hope—by the mass media) correct this false traditional history. History must illuminate memory and help it rectify its errors. But is the historian himself immune to an illness that proceeds, if not from the past, at least from the present, or perhaps from an unconscious image of a dreamt-of future?

A preliminary distinction must be drawn between *objectivity* and *impartiality*. "Impartiality is deliberate; objectivity is unconscious. The historian does not have the right to pursue a demonstration despite contrary evidence, to defend a cause no matter what it is. He must establish and show the truth or what he believes to be the truth. But it is impossible for him to be objective, to abstract from his ideas about man, and notably when it is a question of gauging the importance of events and their causal relations" (Génicot 1980:112). But we must go further. If this distinction were sufficient, the problem of objectivity would not be, as E. H. Carr has put it, "a famous crux" which has caused much ink to flow.[9]

Let us first examine the impact of the social environment on the historian's ideas and methods. Wolfgang Mommsen has pointed out three components of this social pressure: "1) The self-image of the social group interpreted by the historian, or to which he belongs or is beholden.. 2) The historian's conception of the causes of social change. 3) The perspectives of future social changes which the historian thinks probable or possible, and which orient his historical interpretation" (1978:23). But it is not possible entirely to avoid "presentism"—the deforming influence of the present on the interpretation of the past, although one can limit its pernicious impact on objectivity. First of all—and I shall return to this important point—because there is a group of specialists who are trained to examine and judge what their colleagues produce. "Thucydides is not a colleague," Nicole Loraux has wisely said, in showing that his *History*, although it seems to us a document possessing "every mark of serious historical discourse, is not a document in the modern sense of the word, but rather a text, an ancient text, which is first of all a discourse situated within the domain of rhetoric." But I shall show later that—as Nicole Loraux is well aware—every document is a monument or a text, and it is never "pure," that is, never purely objective. It remains that the appearance of history is accompanied by that of a world of professionals who criticize the work of other historians. When a painter says about another painter's picture: "this is badly painted," or a writer says about the work of another writer, "this is badly written," everyone knows that this only means: "I don't like this." But when a historian criticizes the work of a "colleague," he may certainly be mistaken and his judgment may reflect in part his personal taste, but his criticism is based at least to a degree on "scientific" criteria. From the dawn of history the historian is judged by the yardstick of truth. Rightly or wrongly, Herodotus was long considered a "liar" (Momigliano 1986:127–42; Hartog 1980), and Polybius, setting forth his ideas about history in Book XII of his *Histories*, devotes a good deal of his energy to attacking a "colleague," Timaeus.

As Wolfgang Mommsen has said, historical works and historical judgments are "intersubjectively understandable and verifiable." This intersubjectivity is constituted through the judgment of others, and primarily that of other historians. Mommsen discerns three criteria for verification: a) Have the pertinent sources been used and has the most recent research been taken into consideration? b) To what extent have these historical judgments achieved an optimal integration of all the possible historical data? c) Are the explicit or underlying explanatory models rigorous, coherent, and noncontradictory? (p. 33). One could find other criteria, but the possibility of broad agreement on the part of specialists concerning the value of an important part of any historical work is the primary proof of the "scientific" character of history and the first touchstone of historical objectivity.

If, however, we apply to history the great journalist C. P. Scott's maxim—"Facts are sacred, opinion is free" (quoted by E. H. Carr, p. 4)—we must add two comments. The first is that if we remain within the field of scientific history, the range of opinion is less vast in history than nonprofessionals believe (I shall discuss amateur history later). The second comment is facts are often less sacred than they are supposed to be. Even if some well-established facts cannot be denied (for example, Joan of Arc's death at the stake in 1431, which only mystifiers or the misinformed care to doubt), fact itself is not the essential basis of objectivity in history. Historical facts are made and not given, and historical objectivity cannot be reduced to pure subservience to facts.

Discussions of the construction of historical fact can be found in every treatise on historical methodology (see, for exmaple, P. Salmon, pp. 46–48; E. H. Carr; pp. 1–24, J. Topolski, Part V, etc.). I shall cite only Lucien Febvre's famous inaugural lecture at the Collège de France on December 13, 1933: "Something given? No, something created by the historian, how many times? Something invented and fabricated, with the help of hypotheses and conjectures, through delicate and exciting labor. . . . To elaborate a fact is to construct it. It is, so to speak, to answer a question. And if there is no question, there is nothing at all" (pp. 7–9). Historical facts only exist within a history-problem.

Here are two more witnesses testifying that objectivity in history is not a matter of pure submission to facts. First, Max Weber: "Any attempt to understand (historical) reality without subjective hypotheses will end in nothing but a jumble of existential judgments on countless isolated events."[10] E. H. Carr humorously discusses the nineteenth-century positivist historians' "fetishism of facts":

> Ranke piously believed that divine providence would take care of the meaning of history if he took care of the facts. . . . The liberal nineteenth-century view of history had a close affinity with the economic doctrine of *laissez-faire*. . . . This was the age of innocence, and historians walked in the Garden of Eden . . . naked and unashamed before the god of history. Since then, we have known Sin and experienced a Fall; and those historians who today pretend to dispense with a philosophy of history are merely trying, vainly and self-consciously, like members of a nudist colony, to recreate the Garden of Eden in their garden suburb. (1961:13–14)

Impartiality requires no more than honesty on the part of the historian, while objectivity requires more than that. If memory is a stake in the power game, if it authorizes conscious and unconscious manipulations, if it serves individual and collective interests, history, like all sciences, takes truth as its norm. The historian engages in abuses of history only when he becomes himself a partisan, a politician or a lackey of political power (Th. Schieder, K. G. Faber, in *History and Theory*, Supplement, 1978). When Paul Valéry declares, "History is the most dangerous product the chemistry of the intellect has developed. . . . History justifies whatever one wants. Strictly speaking, it doesn't teach anything, for it contains everything and offers examples of everything" (pp. 63–64), this otherwise very acute thinker confuses human history with scientific history and shows his ignorance of historical work.

Even if he is a little optimistic, Paul Veyne is correct when he writes:

> Not to see that historical knowledge is subtended by the norm of truth is not to understand anything about it, or about science in general. To identify historical science with the national memories from which it proceeded is to confuse the essence of a thing with its origin; it is to fail to distinguish chemistry from alchemy, astronomy from astrology. . . . From the very first day . . . historians' history is defined in opposition to the social function of historical memories and bases itself on an ideal of truth and on an interest that is pure curiosity. (1968:424).

An ambitious goal, objective history is slowly constructed little by little, through the ceaseles revisions of historical work, the laborious successive rectifications, and the accumulation of partial truths. Perhaps two philosophers have best defined this slow progress of history toward objectivity.

In his *Histoire et vérité* Paul Ricoeur writes: "We expect from history a certain objectivity, the objectivity that is suited to it; the way in which history is born and reborn attests to it; it always proceeds from traditional societies' *rectification* of the official, pragmatic arrangement of their past. This rectification is not different in spirit from that of physical science in relation to the first arrangement of appearances in perception and in the cosmologies that remain dependent on it" (1955:24–25).

And Adam Schaff writes:"Knowledge necessarily takes on the character of an infinite process which—perfecting our understanding by proceeding through different approaches to reality grasped in its different aspects, accumulating partial truths—results not merely in a simple addition to what we know, in quantitative changes in our knowledge, but also in qualitative transformations of our vision of history" (pp. 338 f.).

The singular and the universal: Generalizations and regularities in history

No doubt the most flagrant contradiction in history is that while its object is singular (an event or series of events, or figures who appear only once), its goal, like that of all sciences, is the universal, general, and regular. Aristotle had already excluded history from the sciences precisely because it deals with the particular, which is not the object of scientific knowledge. Each historical fact has occurred only once, and will occur only once. In fact, this singularity constitutes for many producers or consumers of history the principal attraction of history:

Aimez ce que jamais on ne verra deux fois
(Love what you will never see again)

Historical explanation must deal with "unique" objects (Gardiner 1952 2:3, "Uniqueness in History").

The consequences of this recognition of the singularity of the historical fact can be reduced to three, each of which has played a major role in the history of history.

The first is the primacy of the event. If one thinks that historical work consists in establishing events, one has only to apply to documents a method that makes events emerge from them. Thus V. K. Dibble has distinguished four kinds of inference leading from documents to events, depending on the nature of the documents: testimony, social bookkeeping, direct indicators, or correlates.[11] The only defect of this excellent method is that it sets itself a questionable goal. It confuses events with historical facts, and we now know that the goal of history is not to establish falsely "real" data that have been given the name of events or historical facts.

The second consequence of limiting history to the singular is to privilege the role of individuals and particularly that of great men. E. H. Carr has shown how, in the Western tradition, this tendency goes back to the Greeks, who attributed their most ancient epics and their first laws to hypothetical individuals (Homer, Lycurgus, and Solon), and was renewed in the Renaissance with the vogue of Plutarch. He finds it once again in what he calls, following Isaiah Berlin, "the bad king John theory of history" (I. Berlin,"Historical Inevitability" (1954); E. H. Carr, *Society and the Individual* (1961), ch. 2. This conception, which has practically disappeared in scientific history, unfortunately continues to be retailed by too many popularizers and by the media—especially by publishers. I distinguish this popular explanation of history by reference to individuals from biography, which—in spite of its mistakes and mediocrities—is one of the major historical genres, and has produced historiographical masterpieces such as Ernst Kantorowicz's *Frederick the Second* (1927). Carr is correct to remind us of Hegel's comment on great men: "Historical individuals are those who have sought and accomplished not something imagined or presumed, but something right and necessary, and who have understood, because they have received its revelation within themselves, what is necessary and really belongs to the possibilities of the time" (Hegel 1822–30:121). As Michel de Certeau has pointed out (*L'écriture de l'histoire*, p. 99), the speciality of history is indeed the *particular*, but the particular, as G. R. Elton has shown in *The Practice of History*, is different from the individual, and "the particular specifies both historical attention and historical research, not because it is an object of thought, but on the contrary because it is the *limit of what can be thought*."

The third misleading consequence that has been drawn from the role of the particular in history is the reduction of the latter to a narrative or story. As Roland Barthes has reminded us, Augustin Thierry was one of the defenders—apparently one of the most naive ones—of this belief in the virtues of historical narrative: "It has been said that the goal of the historian was to recount, not to prove; I do not know about that, but I am sure that in history the best kind of proof, the one most capable of captivating and convincing everyone, the one that evokes the least mistrust and leaves the least doubt, is complete narration" (*Récits des temps mérovingiens*, 1851 ed., 2:227). But what does "complete" mean? Never mind the fact that a narrative, whether historical or not, is a construction, and underneath its honest and objective appearance, a whole series of implicit choices are operative. Every conception of history that identifies it with narrative seems to me unacceptable today. To be sure, the successiveness that constitutes the fabric of historical material requires us to accord narrative a role that seems to me primarily pedagogical in nature. It is the simple necessity of setting forth the *how* before inquiring into the *why* that situates narrative at the logical foundations of historical work. Narrative is thus only a preliminary phase, even if it has required prolonged preliminary work on the part of the historian. But this recognition of an indispensable rhetoric of history must not lead us to deny the scientific character of history.

In a stimulating book (*Metahistory: The Historical Imagination in Nineteenth-Century Europe*), Hayden White has recently discussed the work of the principal historians of the nineteenth century as a purely rhetorical form, a narrative discourse in prose. In order to explain, or rather to achieve an "explanatory effect," historians can choose among three strategies: explanation through formal argumentation, through emplotment, and through ideological implication. Within these three strategies, there are four possible modes of articulation for attaining the explanatory effect: for arguments, formalism, organicism, mechanism, and contextualism; for plots, romance, comedy, tragedy, and satire; and for ideological implication, anarchism, conservatism, radicalism and liberalism. The historiographical "style" of individual authors results from the specific combination of modes of articulation. This style is achieved through an essentially poetic act, to which White applies the Aristotelian categories of metaphor, metonymy, synecdoche and irony. He has applied this scheme to four historians—Michelet, Ranke, Tocqueville and Burckhardt—and to four philosophers of history—Hegel, Marx, Nietzsche, and Croce.

The result of this inquiry is first of all the observation that the works of the principal nineteenth-century philosophers of history differ only in emphasis, not in content, from those of their counterparts in "history proper." I would immediately reply that White has only discovered the relative unity of style of a period, and rediscovered what Taine had noted in an even larger perspective concerning the seventeenth century: "Between a nook in the gardens of Versailles, a philosophical argument by Malebranche, one of Boileau's rules of versification, a law made by Colbert concerning mortgages, and a maxim by Bossuet on the kingdom of God, the distance may seem infinite. The facts are so dissimilar that on first inspection they seem isolated and separate. But these facts are interconnected through the definition of the groups in which they are included" (quoted by Ehrard and Palmade, p. 72).

Next comes the characterization of the eight authors in the following manner: Michelet represents historical realism as romance, Ranke historical realism as comedy, Tocqueville historical realism as tragedy, Burckhardt historical realism as satire, Hegel the poetics of history and the path beyond irony, Marx the philosophical defense of history in the metonymic mode, Nietzsche the poetic defense of history in the metaphorical mode, and Croce the philosophical defense of history in the ironic mode.

White's seven general conclusions concerning the historical consciousness of the nineteenth century can be summed up in three ideas: (1) there is no fundamental difference between history and philosophy of history; (2) the choice among strategies of historical explanation is moral or aesthetic rather than epistemological in nature; (3) history's pretension to scientific status is only a way of disguising a preference for one or another mode of historical conceptualization.

Finally, White's most general conclusion—which goes beyond the conception of history in the nineteenth century—is that the historian's work is a force of intellectual activity that is simultaneously poetic, scientific, and philosophical.

It would be too simple to comment ironically—especially on the basis of the bare-bones outline I have given of a book full of suggestive detailed analyses—on this conception of "metahistory," its assumptions, and its simplifications. I see in it two interesting subjects for reflection. The first is that it contributes to the illumination of the crisis of historicism at the end of the nineteenth century, which I shall discuss later. The second is that it allows us to raise—on the basis of a historical example—the problem of the relations between history as a science, as an art, and as philosophy.

It seems to me that these relations are defined first of all historically, and that where White sees a kind of historical nature, there is the historical situation of a discipline. In general, one can say that history, which up until the end of the nineteenth century is intimately involved with art and philosophy, tries to be more specific, technical, scientific, and less literary and philosophical—and partially succeeds in doing so. Nevertheless, we must note that some of the greatest contemporary historians still claim for history the character of an art. Thus Georges Duby: "In my opinion, history is first of all an art, an essentially literary art. History exists only through discourse. For it to be good, the discourse has to be good" (Duby and Lardreau, p. 50). But he elsewhere asserts that "History, if it must exist, cannot be free; it may be a mode of political discourse, but it cannot be propaganda; it may be a literary genre, but it *must* not be literature" (pp. 15–16). It is thus clear that the historical work is not a work of art like others, that historical discourse has its own specific character.

The issue has been well expressed by Roland Barthes: "The narrative of past events, commonly subjected in our culture, since the Greeks, to the approval of historical 'science,' placed under the imperious guarantee of the 'real,' and justified by the principles of 'rational' exposition—does such a narrative really differ through some specific characteristic, some indubitable pertinence, from imaginary narrative, such as one finds in the epic, the novel, and drama?" (1967:65). At the time, Emile Benveniste replied, stressing the historian's intention: "The historical enunciation of events is independent of their 'objective' truth. Only the writer's 'historical' design counts" (*Problèmes de linguistique générale*, 1:240). Barthes' response, in linguistic terms, is that "in 'objective' history, the 'real' is never more than an unexpressed signified, sheltered behind the apparent omnipotence of the referent. This situation defines what could be called 'the reality effect' . . . historical discourse does not follow the real, it only signifies it, ceaselessly repeating *it happened*; but that assertion can never be anything but the signified obverse of any historical narrative" (1967:74). Barthes concludes his study by explaining the decline of narrative history today as a result of the quest for a more scientific discipline: "Thus we can see that the effacing (if not the disappearance) of narrative in current historical science, which seeks to discuss structures more than chronologies, implies, far more than a simple change from one school to another, a genuine ideological transformation. Historical narrative is dying because the sign of History is now less the real than the intelligible" (p. 75).

Paul Veyne has founded an original view of history on another ambiguity in the term "history," which in most languages denotes both historical science and an imaginary story. (Thus French distinguishes between *l'histoire* and *une histoire*, English between *history* and *story* (Gallie 1963:150–72].) For Veyne, history is indeed a story, but it is a story of *true* events (1971:16). History is interested in a particular form of singularity or individuality, which is the specific: "history is interested in individualized events none of which functions in more than one way for it, but it is not interested in individuality *per se*: it seeks to understand such events, that is, to find in them a kind of generality, or more precisely, a kind of specificity" (p. 72). And again: "history is the description of what is specific, that is, comprehensible, in human events" (p. 75). History thus resembles a novel. It is composed of *plots*. This notion has a certain interest insofar as it preserves singularity without making it degenerate into disorder, insofar as it rejects determinism but implies a certain logic, insofar as it emphasizes the role of the historian, who "builds" his historical study in the same way that a novelist builds his "story." In my view, it has the defect of suggesting that the historian has the same freedom as the novelist, and that history is not a science at all, but, despite Veyne's precautions, a literary genre, whereas it appears to me to be a science which has—and this is a banality, but it has to be said—both the characteristics of all sciences and specific characteristics.

First of all, we should note that in opposition to the defenders of positivist history, who think they can exclude all imagination—and even any "idea"—from historical work, many historians and theoreticians have demanded and still demand the right to imagination.

William Dray has even defined the "imaginative reenactment" of the past as a form of rational explanation. The "sympathy" that allows us to feel and to make others feel a historical phenomenon would therefore be only a means of exposition.[12] Gordon Leff has contrasted the historian's imaginative reconstruction with the procedures of specialists in natural science: "The historian, unlike the natural scientist, has to create his own framework in order to evluate his events; he must make an imaginative reconstruction of what, by its nature, was never actual, but was rather contained in individual events. He has to abstract the complex of attitudes, values, intentions and conventions which belong to our actions in order to grasp its meaning" (pp. 117–18).

This evaluation of the historian's imagination seems to me insufficient. There are two kinds of imagination that a historian may manifest: one that consists in enlivening what is dead in the documents, and which constitutes part of historical work, since the latter shows and explains people's actions. This capacity for imagination, which makes the past *concrete*, is a desirable quality in the historian—just as Georges Duby wished the historian to have literary talent. It is even more desirable, because it is *necessary*, for the historian to show that he possesses *scientific* imagination, which manifests itself, on the contrary, in the power of *abstraction*. Here nothing distinguishes or should distinguish the historian from other scientists. He must work on his documents with the same imagination that the mathematician brings to his calculations or the physicist and chemist to their experiments. It is a matter of a *state of mind*, and here we must agree with Huizinga when he declares that history is not only a branch of knowledge but also "an intellectual form for understanding the world" (J. Huizinga, 1936).

On the other hand, I deplore the fact that such an acute thinker as Raymond Aron, in his empirical passion, has asserted that the historian's concepts are vague because "as one approaches the concrete, one eliminates generality" (1938a:206). The historian's concepts are in fact not vague, but often metaphorical, precisely because they must refer to both the concrete and the abstract, history being—like other human or social sciences—a science less of the complex, as is often said, than of the specific, as Veyne has pointed out.

Like every science, therefore, history has to generalize and explain. It does so in a particular way. As Gordon Leff and many others have said, the method of explanation in history is essentially deductive: "there would be no history or indeed any conceptual discourse without generalization . . . historical understanding differs not in the mental processes inherent in all human reasoning but in its status as inferential rather than as demonstrable knowledge" (pp. 79–80). History is given meaning as much through making intelligible a body of originally separate data as through an internal logic of each element: "Significance in history is therefore essentially contextual" (p. 57). Finally, explanations in history are more evaluations than demonstrations, but they include the historian's opinion in a rational way that is inherent in the intellectual process of explanation: "Some form of causal analysis is clearly indispensable to any attempt to relate events; just as the historian has to distinguish between chance and necessity so he has to decide upon the long-term and short-term factors governing any situation. But, like his categories, they are ultimately conceptual. They correspond to no empirically isolable entities and so cannot be empirically confirmed or refuted. For that reason the historian's explanations come closer to evaluations" (pp. 97–99). Over the centuries, theoreticians of history have tried to establish great principles that could provide general keys to historical evolution. The two main notions that have been put forth are on one hand the *goal* or direction [*sens*] of history, and on the other, historical *laws*.

The notion of a goal or direction of history can be analyzed into three types of explanation: the belief in great cyclical movements, the idea of an end of history consisting in the perfection of this world, and the theory of a goal of history situated outside history.[13] Aztec conceptions, or in a certain way, those of Arnold Toynbee, are connected with the first opinion, Marxism with the second, and Christianity with the third.

Within Christianity a vast gap separates two groups. On one hand, there were those who, along with Saint Augustine and Catholic orthodoxy, taking as their foundation the idea of the two cities, the earthly City and the celestial City described in *The City of God*, stress the ambivalence of historical time (Marrou 1950), which is carried away both in the apparent chaos of human history (Rome is not eternal and it is not the end of history) and in the eschatological flux of Divine history. On the other hand, there are those who, with millenarians like Joachim of Floris and his disciples, seek to reconcile the second and the third conceptions of history outlined above. For this second group, history intially ends with the advent of a Third Age, the reign of the saints over the earth, before reaching its final conclusion with the resurrection of the dead and the Last Judgment. That is the opinion of Joachim of Floris and his disciples in the thirteenth century. Here we leave behind not only historical theory but even philosophy of history, as we enter into the domain of the theology of history. In the twentieth century, resurgence of religion has led certain thinkers to revive the theology of history. The Russian writer Berdyaev (1874–1948) prophesied that the contradictions of contemporary history would give way to a new "joint creation of man and God." In twentieth-century Protestantism there are various conflicting currents, for example Schweitzer's "consequent eschatology," Bultmann's "demystified eschatology," Dodd's "realized eschatology," and Cullman's "anticipated eschatology" (Le Goff 1978:712–46). Continuing Saint Augustine's analysis, the Catholic historian Henri-Irénée Marrou has developed the idea of the ambiguity of historical time: "Historical time thus appears to bear an ambiguity, a radical ambivalence: certainly it is (though not solely, as a superficial view imagines) an agent of progress, but history also has a sinister and somber side: that growth which occurs mysteriously and makes its way through suffering, death, and failure" (Marrou 1968).

I have discussed elsewhere the cyclical conception and the idea of decadence (1978:389–420), and I shall examine later an example of this conception, Spengler's philosophy of history. Concerning the idea of an end of history consisting in the perfection of this world, the most coherent law that has been advanced is that of progress.[14]

V. Gordon Childe, after having asserted that the historian's work consists in finding an order in the process of human history (1953:5) and maintained that there are no laws in history but only a "kind of order," proposed technology as an example of that order. For him, there is a technological progress "from prehistory to the age of coal" which consists in an ordered sequence of historical events. But Childe notes that in each phase this technological progress is a "social product"; if one tries to analyze it from this point of view, one finds that what seemed linear is erratic, and in order to explain "these deviations and fluctuations, we have to turn to the social, economic, political, juridical, theological, and magical institutions, to customs and beliefs—which have spurred them on or reined them in"—in short, to history in all its complexity. But is it legitimate to isolate a technological domain and to maintain that the rest of history acts on it only from the outside? Isn't technology a component of a larger whole whose parts exist only through the more or less arbitrary partitions practiced by the historian?

Bertrand Gille has recently formulated this problem in an interesting way.[15] He proposes the notion of a technical system, a coherent ensemble of structures compatible with one another. These historical technical systems reveal a "technical order." This "mode of grasping the technical phenomenon" requires a dialogue with specialists of other systems: economists, linguists, sociologists, politicians, jurists, scientists, philosophers. . . . This conception entails the necessity of a periodization, technical systems following one another, and the most important thing being to understand, if not totally explain, the passage from one technical system to another. In this way, Gille raises the problem of technical progress, in which he distinguishes "the progress of technology" from the "technical progress" which is marked by the entry of inventions into industrial or everyday life. He further observes that "the dynamics of systems, thus conceived, gives a new value to what is called, vaguely and ambiguously, industrial revolutions."

Thus is raised a problem which I shall formulate more generally as that of *revolution* in history. In historiography it is raised in the cultural domain (the print revolution: cf. M. McLuhan and E. L. Eisenstein; scientific revolutions: see Thomas Kuhn), and even in historiography itself (F. Smith Fussner, *The Historical Revolution: English Historical Writing and Thought 1560–1640*, 1962, reviewed by G. H. Nadel in *History and Theory*, 3:255–61). It is also raised in the political domain (the English revolution of 1640, the French revolution of 1789, the Russian revolution of 1917). These events and the very notion of revolution have recently been the object of intense controversy. It seems to me that the current tendency is on one hand to reformulate the problem in relation to the problematics of *longue durée* (Vovelle 1978:316 ff.), and on the other to see the controversies surrounding revolution or revolutions as a privileged area for the ideological commitments and political choices of the present. "It is one of the most 'sensitive' terrains of all historiography" (Chartier 1978:497).

My feeling is that there are in history no *laws* comparable to those which have been discovered in the natural sciences—an opinion widely shared today with the rejection of historicism and vulgar Marxism and the mistrust with regard to philosophies of history. Much depends, moreover, on the meaning accorded the words. For example, we recognize today that Marx did not formulate general laws of history but only conceptualized the historical process by unifying (critical) theory and (revolutionary) practice.[16] W. C. Runciman has observed that history, like sociology and anthropology, was "a consumer, not a producer of laws."[17]

Contrary to assertions that history is irrational, which are often more provocative than convinced, I express my conviction that the goal of historical work is to make the historical process intelligible, and that this intelligibility leads to the recognition of *regularities* in historical evolution. Open-minded Marxists acknowledge this even if they have a tendency to bend the term *regularities* in the direction of the term *laws* (Topolski 1976:275–304).

These regularities can be recognized first of all within each *series* studied by the historian, who makes it intelligible by discovering in it a logic, a *system*, a term that I prefer to *plot*, because it stresses the objective more than the subjective character of the historical operation. Such regularities must then be recognized among the series; hence the importance of the comparative method in history. A French proverb says: "*Comparaison n'est pas raison*," but the scientific character of history resides as much in noting differences as in noting resemblances, whereas the natural sciences seek to eliminate differences.

Chance obviously has its place in the process of history and does not disturb the regularities, precisely because chance is a constitutive element of the historical process and of its intelligibility.

Montesquieu declared that "if a particular cause, such as the accidental outcome of a battle, has destroyed a State, a general cause existed that created a situation in which the loss of a single battle could result in the collapse of the State," and Marx wrote in a letter: "World history would have a very mystical character if there were no room in it for chance. This chance itself naturally becomes part of the general trend of development, and is compensated by other forms of chance. But acceleration and retardation depend on such 'accidentals,' which include the 'chance' character of the individuals who are at the head of a movement at the outset" (quoted by Carr, p. 95). Attempts have recently been made to evaluate scientifically the role of chance in certain historical episodes. Jorge Basadre has studied the series of probabilities in the emancipation of Peru. He used the works of Pierre Vendryès (1952) and G. H. Bousquet (1967). Bousquet maintains that the effort to mathematicize chance excludes providentialism as well as the belief in a universal determinism. According to him, chance plays no role in either scientific progress or economic evolution, and it operates in such a way as to tend toward an equilibrium that eliminates not chance itself, but its consequences. In history, the most "efficacious" forms of chance are, in Bousquet's view, chance meteorological events, assassinations, and the birth of geniuses. Having thus outlined the issue of regularities and rationality in history, it remains for me to mention the problems of unity and diversity, of continuity and discontinuity. Since these problems are at the heart of the current crisis in history, I shall return to them at the end of this essay.

I shall limit myself here to saying that while the aim of true history has always been fundamentally to be a global or total history (*integral* and *complete*, great historians said at the end of the sixteenth century), as history establishes itself as a scientific and pedagogical discipline, it has to make use of categories which—pragmatically—fragment history. These categories depend on historical evolution itself. The twentieth century first witnessed the birth of economic and social history, and later that of the history of mentalities. Certain writers, like Chaïm Perelman, privilege periodological categories; others privilege thematic categories (Perelman, p. 13). Each has its utility and necessity. They are tools for research and exposition. They have no objective, substantial reality. In the same way, historians' aspiration to comprehend the totality of history can and must take diverse forms, which also evolve through time. The framework can be a geographical reality or a concept, as in the case of Fernand Braudel, first in *The Mediterranean and the Mediterranean World in the Age of Philip II*, and then in *Civilization and Capitalism*. Pierre Toubert and I have tried to show how the objective of a total history seems today accessible in a pertinent way through the totalizing objects constructed by the historian: for example, *incastellamento*, poverty, marginality, the idea of labor, etc. (Le Goff and Toubert).

I do not believe that the method of multiple approaches—if it does not draw on an outdated eclectic ideology—is harmful to the historian's work. It is sometimes more or less imposed on us by the state of the documentation, each kind of source requiring a different treatment within an overall problematics. In studying the development of the idea of Purgatory from the third to the fourteenth centuries, I made use of accounts of visions, *exempla*, liturgical practices, and devotional practices, and I would have made use of iconography if it had not been for the fact that for a long time Purgatory was not represented graphically. I have sometimes analyzed individuals' thoughts, sometimes collective mentalities, sometimes the level of the powerful, sometimes that of the masses. But I have always kept in mind that, with neither determinism nor fatality, with delays, losses, and turning points, the belief in Purgatory was incarnated at the heart of a system, and that this system had no meaning except through its function in an overall society (Le Goff 1981).

A monographic study limited in space and time can be an excellent historical work if it states a problem, and lends itself to comparison if it is conducted as a "case-study." Only the monograph closed in on itself, without any horizon, one of the prize offspring of positivist history and still not entirely dead, now seems to me excluded.

So far as continuity and discontinuity are concerned, I have already discussed the concept of revolution. I would like to conclude the first point of this essay by stressing the fact that the historian has to respect time, which—in various forms—is the very stuff of history, and that he must make his frameworks for chronological explanation correspond to the durations of lived experience. Dating remains and will remain one of the fundamental tasks and duties of the historian, but dating must be accompanied by another necessary manipulation of duration in order to make it historically conceivable: periodization.

Gordon Leff has forcefully reminded us that "Periodization is indispensable for every form of historical understanding" (Leff 1969:130). He pertinently adds that "Periodization, like history itself, is an empirical process shaped by the historian" (p. 150). I would add that there is no immobile history, and that history is not pure change, either, though it is the study of significant changes. Periodization is the main instrument for understanding significant changes.

The Historical Mentality: Men and the Past

I have indicated above a few examples of the way in which men construct or reconstruct their past. I now turn my attention the role of the past in societies. I welcome here the expression "historical culture" used by Bernard Guenée in his book *Histoire et culture historique dans l'Occident médiéval* (1980). Under this rubric, Guenée brings together several things: on one hand the professional baggage of historians, their library of historical works, and on the other, the public and the historian's audience. I would add to this the relationship that a society entertains, in its collective psychology, with its past. (My way of thinking is close to what English-speaking historians call "historical-mindedness.) I am aware of the risks involved in this reflection: the risk of taking for a unity a reality that is complex and structured if not by classes at least by social categories distinguished from one another by their interests and their culture, the risk of assuming that there is a "spirit of the time" or *Zeitgeist*, or even a collective unconscious—so many dangerous abstractions. Nevertheless, the research and questionnaires used in "developed" societies today show that it is possible to approach a country's feelings about its past in the same way as one approaches other phenomena and problems.[18] Since such inquiries are impossible for the past, I shall try to characterize—acknowledging the arbitrariness and simplification involved in doing so—the dominant attitude in a number of historical societies with regard to their past and to history. I shall take primarily historians as interpreters of that collective opinion, trying to distinguish what belongs to their personal ideas from what belongs to the common mentality. I recognize that I am again conflating the past with history in the collective memory. I therefore offer a few supplementary explanations that will clarify my ideas about history.

I think that the history of history must be concerned not only with professional historical production but with a whole set of phenomena which constitute the historical culture, or rather the historical mentality, of a period. A study of school history textbooks is a privileged aspect of such a study, but for all practical purposes, such textbooks have existed only since the nineteenth century. The study of literature and art can be illuminating in this respect. The role of Charlemagne in the *chansons de geste* (medieval epic songs), the birth of the romance in the twelfth century, the fact that this birth took the form of a historical romance (on ancient subjects),[19] the importance of historical plays in Shakespeare's theater, etc., all testify to the predilection of some historical societies for their past.[20] Within the framework of a recent exposition on the great French painter of the sixteenth century, Jean Fouquet, Nicole Reynaud has shown how, alongside his interest in ancient history, a sign of the Renaissance (the miniatures in the *Antiquités judaïques*, the *Histoire ancienne*, and in *Tite-Live)*, Fouquet shows a pronounced taste for the modern (the Etienne Chevalier Book of Hours, the Formigny tapestry, the *Grandes Chroniques de France*, etc.).[21] We should add the study of first names, guides for pilgrims and tourists, engravings, popular literature sold by peddlers, etc., etc. Marc Ferro has shown how cinema has added an important new source for history: the film, explaining, correctly, that cinema was the "agent and source of history" (M. Ferro, 1977). This is true of all the modern media, and would suffice to explain why, with the advent of mass journalism, cinema, radio, and television, the relationship between men and history has enjoyed a considerable revival. Santo Mazzarino has attempted such an enlargement of the notion of history (in the sense of historiography) in his great study *Il pensiero storico classico* (1966/67:206–19). Mazzarino is especially concerned to trace historical mentality in ethnic, religious, and irrational elements, in myths, poetic fantasies, cosmological theories, etc. A new conception of the historian results, which Arnaldo Momigliano has well defined: "For Mazzarino, the historian is not essentially a professional searcher for the truth of the past, but rather a sorcerer, a 'prophetic' interpreter of the past conditioned by his political opinions, his religious faith, his ethnic characteristics, and finally, but not exclusively, by the social situation. Every fantastic evocation of the past, whether poetic, mythical, utopian, or in any other mode, depends on historiography."

Here again we should draw a distinction. The object of history is indeed this diffuse sense of the past which recognizes in the productions of the imagination one of the principal expressions of historical reality, and notably of the way people react to their past. But this indirect history is not the history of historians, which is the only one with a scientific vocation.

The same is true of memory. Just as the past is not history but the object of history, so memory is not history, but both one of its objects and an elementary level of its development. The journal *Dialectiques* has published (no. 30, 1980) a special issue devoted to the relations between memory and history, *"Sous l'histoire la mémoire."* In this issue, the British historian Ralph Samuel, one of the main founders of the "History Workshops" which I shall discuss later, makes some ambiguous statements under the no less ambiguous title, "Deprofessionalizing History." If he means thereby that considering oral history, autobiographies, and subjective history enlarges the basis for scientific work, modifies the image of the past, or allows the forgotten people of history to speak, he is entirely correct and stresses one of the great advances in contemporary historical scholarship. But when he puts "autobiographical writing" on the same level as "professional writing," and adds that "professional practice establishes neither a monopoly nor a guarantee" (*Dialectiques* 30:16), the danger seems great. What is true—and I shall return to this point—is that the historian's traditional sources are often no more "objective"—and in any case not as "historical"—as the historian believes them to be. The criticism of traditional sources is insufficient but the historian's work must be done on the newer sources as well. A self-governing historical science would not be merely a disaster, but nonsensical as well. For even if history only distantly approaches scientific status, it is a science that depends on knowledge that is professionally acquired. Certainly, history is not as technical as the physical or biological sciences, and I do not think it should be, so that it may remain more easily comprehensible and even verifiable by the majority of people. Alone among the sciences, history has the good (or bad) luck to be practicable by amateurs. In fact, it needs popularizers. Professional historians are often not willing to perform this function, which is nevertheless necessary and worthy of respect; sometimes they are simply not good at performing it. The era of the new media increases the need and the opportunities for semiprofessional mediators.

I should perhaps add that I often take pleasure in historical novels—when they are well done and well-written—and that I willingly grant their authors the freedom of imagination that belongs to them, so long as I am in turn allowed, when I am asked my opinion as a historian, to point out the liberties they have taken with history. And why should there not be a literary area of history, fictions in which, while respecting the basic givens of history—customs, institutions, mentalities—history would be rewritten by exploiting the role of chance and of particular events? I would find in such fictions the double pleasure of surprise and of respect for what is most important in history. Thus I have admired a novel by Jean d'Ormesson, *La gloire de l'empire*, which rewrites Byzantine history with talent and knowledge. Not a story slipping between the interstices of history, like *Ivanhoe*, *The Last Days of Pompeii*, *Quo Vadis*, *The Three Musketeers*, etc., but the invention of a new course of political events on the basis of the fundamental structures of a society.

This kind of work is often well done and useful. But is everyone to become a historian? I do not claim power for historians outside their own territory, that is, outside historical work and its echo in the general society—and particularly in education. What should be over and finished is historical imperialism in the domain of science and politics. At the beginning of the nineteenth century history was almost nothing. Historicism, in its various guises, wanted to be everything. History should not rule over other sciences, and even less over society. But like the physicist, the mathematician, the biologist (and, in another way, specialists in the human and social sciences), the historian must be listened to, for history is a fundamental branch of knowledge.

The relations between the present and the past should not lead to confusion or skepticism any more than the relations between memory and history. We now know that the past depends partly on the present. All history is contemporary insofar as the past is grasped in the present, and thus responds to the latter's interests. This is not only inevitable but legitimate. Since history is lived time (*durée*), the past is both past and present. It is the historian's task to make an "objective" study of the past in its double form. To be sure, since he is himself implicated within history, he cannot attain a true "objectivity," but no other history is possible. The historian will make further progress in understanding history by putting himself in question in the course of his analysis, just as a scientific observer takes into account the modifications he may make in the object he is observing.

We know very well, for example, that the progress of democracy leads us to inquire more fully into the role of the "little people" in history, to place ourselves at the level of everyday life—and that affects, in different ways, all historians. We also know that the evolution of the world leads us to conceive the analysis of societies in terms of *power*, and thus that problematic has entered into history. We also know that history is written, generally speaking, in the same way in the three major groups of countries that exist today: the Western world, the Communist world, and the third world. It is true that the relations of historical scholarship in these three areas depend on power relations and international political strategies, but they also depend on the dialogue between specialists, between professionals, which develops in a common scientific perspective. This professional framework is not purely scientific, or rather, as for all scientists and professionals, it requires a moral code, what Georges Duby calls an *ethic* (Duby and Lardreau 1980:15–16), and what I shall call more "objectively" a *deontology*. I shall not dwell on this, but it is essential, and I observe that, in spite of a few deviations, this deontology exists and functions rather well.

Historical culture (or mentality) does not depend solely on the relations between memory and history, or between present and past. History is a science of time. It is closely linked to the different conceptions of time that exist in a society and are an essential element of the mental equipment of its historians. I shall come back to the conception of a confrontation in Antiquity between societies faced with processes of acculturation and in the thought of historians, between a circular conception and a linear conception of time. Historians have been correctly reminded that their propensity to envisage only a "chronological" historical time has to give way to more uncertainty if they take into account philosophical questions about time, of which Augustine's acknowledgment is representative: "What, then, is time? I know well enough what it is, provided that nobody asks me; but if I am asked what it is and try to explain, I am baffled" (*Confessions*, XI, 14; Starr 1966:24–25). Reflecting on Marshall McLuhan's famous book, *The Gutenberg Galaxy* (1962), Elizabeth Eisenstein emphasizes the dependence of conceptions of time on the technical means of recording and transmitting historical facts. She sees in printing the birth of a new kind of time, that of books, which marks a break in the relations between Clio and Cronus (1966:36–64). This conception rests on the opposition between oral and written. Historians and ethnologists have drawn attention to the importance of the passage from oral to written. Jack Goody has also shown how cultures depend on their means of translation, the advent of literacy being linked to a profound mutation of a society (1977b). He has moreover corrected certain received ideas about the "progress" that marks the passage from oral to written. The written is supposed to provide more freedom, orality leading to a mechanical knowledge, learned by heart and intangible. The study of tradition in oral cultures shows, however, that the specialists in tradition can innovate whereas the written text may on the contrary have a "magical" character that makes it more or less untouchable. We should therefore not oppose an oral history presumed to be faithful and immobile to a written history presumed to be malleable and perfectible. In an important book, M. T. Clanchy, studying the passage from memorized remembrance to the written document in medieval England, has also shown that the essential thing is less the use of writing than the change in the nature and function of writing, the transition from writing as a sacred technique to writing as a utilitarian practice, the conversion of an elitist, memorized production into written production available to everyone, a phenomenon that became general in Western countries only in the nineteenth century, but whose origins are in the twelfth and thirteenth centuries.

Concerning the oral/written pair, which is also fundamental for history, I should like to make two remarks. It is clear that the passage from oral to written is very important for memory and also for history. But we must not forget that (1) orality and writing generally coexist in societies, and this coexistence is very important for history; (2) history, while it enters a decisive stage with writing, is not coeval with it, for there is no society without history.

Apropos of "societies without history," I shall offer two examples. On one hand, that of a "historical" society that some people consider as resistant to time and not susceptible of being analyzed and understood in terms of history: India. On the other, "prehistoric" or "primitive" societies.

Louis Dumont has most brilliantly defended the ahistorical thesis concerning India. Dumont observes that Hegel and Marx accorded India a separate destiny, putting it practically outside history, Hegel by making the Hindu castes the foundation of an "unshakable differentiation," Marx by maintaining that in contrast with Western development, India experienced "a stagnation, the stagnation of a 'natural' economy—as opposed to a mercantile economy—on which 'despotism' is superimposed (1964:49). Dumont's analysis leads to conclusions very close to those of Marx, but through different and more precise considerations. After having easily refuted the opinion of vulgar Marxists who want to reduce the case of India to the simplistic image of a unilinear evolution, he shows that "Indian development, which was extraordinarily precocious, stops early on, and does not break out of its own framework; the form of interaction is not the one which, rightly or wrongly, we identify with our own history" (p. 64). Dumont sees the cause of this blockage in two phenomena in India's distant past, the precocious secularization of the royal function and the assertion—also very early—of the individual. Thus the "politico-economic sphere, cut off from values by the initial secularization of the royal function, has remained subordinated to religion" (p. 63). India has remained in an immobile caste structure in which hierarchical man is radically differentiated from the man of Western societies (1966:), whom I shall call by contrast "historical man." Finally, Dumont turns his attention to the "contemporary transformation" of India, noting that it cannot be interpreted in the light of concepts valid in the West, and that India has succeeded in throwing off foreign domination "while realizing the minimum of modernization" (p. 72). I lack competence to discuss Dumont's ideas. I shall limit myself to observing that his thesis does not deny the existence of an Indian history, but affirms its specificity. I see in this, beyond the now rather banal rejection of a unilinear conception of history, the indication of long periods during which no significant evolution takes place in some societies, and of a resistance to change in certain kinds of society.

The same is true, it seems to me, of "prehistoric" or "primitive" societies. Concerning prehistoric societies, a great specialist like André Leroi-Gourhan has emphasized that the uncertainties concerning their history arise primarily from the inadequacy of the investigations. "It is clear that if for a half-century we had exhaustively analyzed only fifty well-chosen sites, we would have today, for a certain number of stages in human culture, the materials for a substantial history" (1974:104). Henri Moniot observed in 1974 that "There was Europe, and that was all of history. Far back, there were a few 'great civilizations,' whose texts, ruins, and sometimes connections based on kinship, exchanges, or heritage with our maternal classical antiquity, or the size of the human masses that they opposed to the European powers and European inspection, caused them to be admitted at the frontiers of Clio's empire. The rest were—by the common accord of the man in the street, textbooks, and universities—just so many tribes without history." And he adds: "All that has changed for us. For the last ten or fifteen years, for example, black Africa has been invading the historians' field" (p. 160). Moniot explains and defines this African history which remains to be written.

Decolonization allows it, since the new relations of inequality between the former colonizers and colonized "no longer destroy history," and the formerly dominated societies are attempting a "repossession of themselves" which "calls for the recognition of their heritages." This is a history that benefits from the new methods of the human sciences (history, ethnology, sociology), and which has the advantage of being "on site," making use of all sorts of documents and particularly oral documents.

A final opposition presents itself in the field of historical culture which I shall try to illuminate: the opposition between myth and history. It will be helpful to distinguish two cases here. In historical societies we can study the birth of new historical curiosities whose beginnings are often rooted in myth. Thus in the medieval West, when noble families, nations, or urban communities become interested in giving themselves a history, they often begin with mythical ancestors who inaugurate the genealogies, with their legendary founding heroes. Thus the Franks claimed to descend from the Trojans, the Lusignan family claimed to descend from the fairy Mélusine, and the monks of Saint-Denis attributed the foundation of their abbey to Denis the Areopagite, the Athenian converted by Saint Paul. In these cases we see very clearly the historical conditions under which these myths are born and hence become part of history.

The problem is more difficult when it is a matter of the origins of human societies or of so-called primitive societies. Most of the latter have explained their origins through myths, and it has generally been thought that a decisive phase in the their evolution consisted in passing from myth to history.

Daniel Fabre has shown how myth, which seems "resistant to historical analysis," can be recuperated by the historian, for "it was constituted somewhere in a precise historical period."[22] Either, as Lévi-Strauss has put it, myth recuperates and restructures the outmoded leftovers of "earlier social systems," or the long cultural life of myths allows us, through literature, to make them the "historian's meat," as J.-P. Vernant and P. Vidal-Nacquet have done for Hellenic myths by studying the tragic theater of ancient Greece. Marcel Détienne has observed that "In contrast to the event-oriented history of the antiquarian and the ragpicker who work their way through mythology, trying to dig up a scrap of archaism or the fossilized memory of some 'real' event, the structural analysis of myths, isolating certain forms that remain constant despite differences in content, proposes a general history inscribed in a *longue durée*, diving underneath conscious expressions and locating under the apparent fluidity of things the great internal currents that silently traverse it."[23]

Thus from the points of view of the new historical problematics, myth is not only an object of history, but pushes historical time back toward the origins, enriches the historian's methods, and underpins a new level of history, "slow" history.

Writers have rightly stressed the relationship between the expression of time in linguistic systems and the conception of history held by the people who use them. A model study of this kind is Emile Benveniste's "Les relations de temps dans le verbe français" (1959: 237–50). A precise study of the grammatical expression of time in the documents used by the historian and in historical narrative itself yields valuable information for historical analysis. André Miquel gives a remarkable example of this in his study of a story from the *Arabian Nights*, in which he was able to show that the underlying framework of the story was nostalgic longing for the original Arabic Islam.[24] It remains that the evolution of conceptions of time is of great importance to history. Christianity marked a turning point in history and in the way in which history was written because it combined at least three conceptions of time: (1) the circular time of the liturgy linked to the seasons and recuperating the pagan calendar; (2) chronological time, homogeneous and neutral, calculated by computation; and (3) linear, teleological time or eschatological time. The Enlightenment and evolutionism sketched out the idea of an irreversible progress that had enormous influence on nineteenth-century historical science, and particularly on historicism. In the twentieth century, the works of sociologists, philosophers, artists, and literary critics have had considerable impact on new conceptions of time that have been accepted by historical science. Thus the idea of the multiplicity of social times, elaborated by Maurice Halbwachs (1925), served as a starting point for Fernand Braudel's reflections, which were given concrete form in his fundamental article on "*la longue durée*" (1958). In this article, Braudel proposes that the historian should distinguish among three historical speeds, those of "individual time," "social time," and "geographical time"; that is, the rapid and agitated time of events and politics, an intermediary time of economic cycles that determines the rhythm of societies' evolution, and the very slow, "almost immobile" time of structures. Or again, the sense of lived time expressed in a literary work like that of Marcel Proust, which some philosophers and critics have urged historians to consider (e.g., Jauss 1955; Kracauer 1966). This latter orientation subtends one of the current tendencies in history, which is concerned with a history of *lived experience*.

As Georges Lefebvre has pointed out, "for us as Western people, history was created, as was virtually all our thought, by the Greeks" (p. 36). Nevertheless, to limit ourselves to written documents, the most ancient vestiges of an interest in transmitting to posterity testimony about the past extend from the beginning of the fourth millennium to the beginning of the first millennium B.C., and concern on the one hand, the Middle East (Iran, Mesopotamia, Asia Minor) and on the other, China. In the Middle East, this preoccupation with perpetuating dated events seems to be particularly linked with political structures, with the existence of a government and more particularly of a monarchical government. Inscriptions detailing the military campaigns and victories of the sovereigns, a Sumerian list of kings (c. 2000 B.C.), annals of the Assyrian kings, accounts of the high deeds of the kings of ancient Iran found in the royal legends of the ancient Medo-Persian tradition:[25] the royal archives of Mari (nineteenth century B.C.), of Ugarit in Ras-Shamra, of Hattousha in Bogazköy (fifteenth to the thirteenth centuries B.C.).[26] Thus the themes of royal glory and of the royal model have often played a decisive role at the origins of different peoples' and civilizations' histories. Pierre Gibert has maintained that in the Bible, history appears along with royalty, letting us moreover glimpse, around Samuel, Saul, and David, promonarchical and antimonarchical trends.[27] When the Christians later create a Christian history, they insist on the image of a model king, the emperor Theodosius the younger, whose *topos* will be imposed on the Middle Ages by, for example, Edward the Confessor and Saint Louis.[28]

More generally, the idea of history is often attached to the State's structures and to its image, and to this is opposed—positively or negatively—the idea of a society without government and without history. Isn't an avatar of that ideology of history to be found in Carlo Levi's autobiographical novel, *Christ Stopped at Eboli* (1945)? This Piedmontese, antifascist intellectual, in exile at Mezzogiorno, discovers that he shares a common hatred of Rome with the peasants abandoned by the government, and slips into a state of ahistoricity, of immobile memory: "Shut up in a room, and in a closed world, it pleases me to return in memory to that other world, closed in on pain and customs, outside the reach of History and the State, eternally patient, in this land of mine, with neither consolation nor sweetness, where the peasant lives his immobile civilization, in poverty and isolation, on an arid soil, in the presence of death."

I shall not discuss at length non-Western mentalities, and I do not want to reduce them to stereotypes and give the impression that just like the Indian mentality (and even then, as we have seen, it would have to be granted that Indian civilization is "outside of history"), they would be enclosed within a sclerotic tradition hostile to the historical spirit. Let us consider instead the Hebraic mentality. It is clear that for historical reasons, no other people has experienced history as destiny so much as the Jews have, no other people has experienced the world as a drama of their collective identity. Nevertheless, the sense of history has suffered significant vicissitudes among the Jews, and the creation of the state of Israel has led the Jews to reevaluate their history (see Ferro 1981). To limit ourselves to the past, consider H. Butterfield's opinion:

> No country—not even England with its Magna Carta—has ever been so obsessed with history, and it is not strange that the ancient Hebrews showed powerful narrative gifts, and were the first to produce anything like a national history—the first to sketch out the history of mankind from the time of the Creation. They reached high quality in the construction of their narrative, especially in the recording of fairly recent events, as in the case of the death of David and the succession to his throne. After the Exile they concentrated more on the Law than on history, and they turned their attention to speculation about the future and in particular about the end of the mundane order. In a sense they lost touch with the hard earth. But they did not quickly lose their gift for historical narrating, as is seen in I Maccabees before the Christian era and the writings of Josephus in the first century A.D. (1973 2:466)

But if this retreat into the law and eschatology is undeniable, we must still add a qualification. For example, here is what Robert R. Geis says about the image of history in the Talmud:

> The third century marks a turning point in the teaching of history. The causes are on one hand the improvement in the Jews' situation as a result of their being granted in 212 the right to become Roman citizens and of the ensuing peacefulness, and on the other, the still powerful influence of the Babylonian schools that separates the representation of the end of history from its terrestrial nature. Nevertheless, the Biblical belief in this world remains recognizable, as we can see from the image of history in the first masters, the Tannaïm. The

> renunciation of history will not be definitive. What Rabbi Meir (130–60 A.D.) says in his interpretation of Rome is never abandoned: "A day will come when the supremacy will be returned to its possessor (Koh. r. 1) for the realization of the kingdom of God on this earth." (1955:124)

Like India, and like the Jewish people, and as we shall see, like Islam, China seems to have had a precocious sense of history which was fairly rapidly blocked. But Jacques Gernet has contested the view that the cultural phenomena that have led people to believe in a very ancient historical culture derive from a sense of history. As early as the first half of the first millennium B.C., collections of documents classified in chronological order appeared, such as the *Annals of Lu* and the *Chou King*. Starting with Sima Qian (145?–85 B.C.), who has been called the "Chinese Herodotus," dynastic histories develop according to the same schema: they are collections of public documents brought together in chronological order: "Chinese history is a patchwork of documents." One therefore has the impression that the Chinese very early accomplished two conscious acts of historical procedure: the collection of archives, and the dating of documents. If one examines the nature and function of these texts and the attributions of the persons who are their producers or guardians, however, another image appears. In China, history is closely linked to the written document: "There is no history in the Chinese sense of the word other than what is written." These writings do not have a memory function, however, but rather a ritual, sacred, magic function. They are a means of communication with the divine powers. They are written down "so that the gods may observe them," so that in this way they may become efficacious in an eternal present. The document is not intended to serve as a proof, but to be a magic object, a talisman. It is not produced for men but for the gods. The date has no other purpose than to indicate the auspicious or inauspicious character of the time in which the document was produced: "It does not indicate a moment in time but an aspect." The annals are not historical documents but ritual writings; "far from implying the notion of human development, they note correspondences that are eternally valid." The Great Scribe who preserves them is not an archivist but a priest of symbolic time whose duties include maintaining the calendar. In the Han dynasty (c. 200 B.C.–A.D. 220) the court historian is a magician, an astronomer who precisely establishes the calendar.[29] Nevertheless the use made by modern sinologists of these false archives is not merely an instance of the "cunning of history" showing that the past is a constant creation of history. The Chinese documents reveal a different meaning and function of history according to the various civilizations, and the evolution of Chinese historiography under the Sung dynasty (eleventh–twelfth century), for example, and its renewal in the Qianlong period (1736–1795), to which the very original work of Zhang Xuecheng (1738–1801) testifies, shows that Chinese historical culture was not unchanging (see C. S. Gardner; G. Hölscher).

Islam at first favored a kind of history strongly linked to religion (and more particularly to the period of its founder, Mohammed) and to the Koran. The cradle of Arab history is Medina, and its motivation is the collection of memories of the origins destined to become "a sacred and untouchable repository." With the conquest history acquires a double nature: that of an annalistic history of the caliphate, and that of a universal history, of which the great example is the history by Tabarî (d. 310/923) and Mas'ûdî (d. 345/956), written in Arabic and Shiîte in inspiration.[30] However, in the great collection of the works of ancient cultures (Indian, Iranian, Greek) in Baghdad, in the time of the Abassids, the Greek historians were forgotten. In the domains of the Zangids and the Ayyubids (Syria, Palestine, Egypt) in the twelfth century, history (especially biography) dominates literary production. History flourishes as well at the Mongolian court, and among the Mamluks, under Turkish domination. I discuss the solitary genius Ibn Khaldoun separately (see pp. 000–000}. Nevertheless, in the Islamic world history never took the leading role it won in Europe and the West. It remained "so powerfully centered on the Koran's revelation, and its career over the centuries and the numberless problems it poses, that today it seems to lend itself with difficulty, if not with reticence, to a type of historical study and methods inspired by the West."[31] Whereas for the Jews history was an essential factor in collective identity—playing the same role that was played by religion in Islam—among the Arabs and Muslims history was above all "nostalgia for the past," the art and science of regret (see Rosenthal and the texts he presents). However, Islam had a different sense of history than the West had, and it did not experience the same methodological developments in history; Ibn Khaldoun is a special case (see Spuler).

Western learning thus maintains that history was born with the Greeks. It is linked to two main motivations. The first is ethnic in character. It is a question of distinguishing the Greeks from the Barbarians. The idea of civilization is united with the conception of history. Herodotus considers the Libyans, the Egyptians, and especially the Scythians and the Persians, in an ethnographic perspective. The Scythians, for example, are nomads—and nomadism is difficult to conceive. At the center of this geohistory is the notion of a frontier: civilization is within, the barbarians outside. The Scythians who crossed the frontier and tried to hellenize themselves—to civilize themselves—were killed by their own people because the two worlds could not be mixed. The Scythians are merely a mirror in which the Greeks see themselves reversed (Hartog 1980).

The other force driving the development of Greek historiography is the politics linked to social structures. M. I. Finley remarks that there is no history in Greece before the fifth century B.C. No annals comparable to those of the Assyrian kings, no interest in history on the part of poets and philosophers, no archives. It is the epoch of myths, outside of time, transmitted orally. In the fifth century, memory is born out of the interests of aristocratic (and royal) families and the priests of temples such as those at Delphi, Eleusis, and Delos.

For his part, Santo Mazzarino is of the opinion that historical thought first arose in Athenian Orphic circles, in the middle of a democratic reaction against the old aristocracy and particularly against the family of the Alcmeonids:

> History was born in an Athenian religious sect, and not among the freethinkers of Ionia. . . . Orphism had been spread by Phylos, in the *genos* most hostile to the Alcmeonids, the *genos* from which Themistocles, the commander of the Athenian fleet, was later born. . . . The Athenian revolution against the conservative party of the old landed aristocracy had certainly already begun, around 630 B.C., as a result of the new requirements of the commercial and maritime world that dominated the city. . . . "Prophecy regarding the past" was the principal weapon in the political struggle. (Mazzarino 1966 1:32–33)

History thus appears as a political weapon. This motivation finally absorbs Greek historical culture, for opposition to the Barbarians is only another way of exalting the city. This praise of civilization inspires in the Greeks, moreover, the idea of a certain technical progress: "The orphism that had given the first impetus to historical thought had also 'discovered' the very idea of technical progress, in the form that the Greeks could conceive. Epic poetry had already spoken of the dwarfs that lived on Mount Ida, the inventors of metallurgy or 'the art of Hephaistos,' and described them as spirits who were more or less goldsmiths" (Mazzarino, p. 240).

Thus when the idea of the city disappeared, the consciousness of historicity disappeared along with it. The sophists, while retaining the idea of technical progress, rejected any notion of moral progress, reduced historical development to individual violence, and dispersed it in a collection of "scabrous anecdotes." This is an affirmation of an anti-history that no longer considers development as history, but as a collection of contingent acts produced by individuals or isolated groups (Châtelet 21:9–86).

This Roman historical mentality was not very different from the Greek one; in any case, the latter shaped the former. Polybius, the Romans' Greek mentor in thinking about history, saw in Roman imperialism the dilation of the city's spirit. Confronting the barbarians, Roman historians celebrated the civilization incarnated by Rome, which Sallust lauds by contrast with Jugurtha, the African who borrowed from Rome only the means of warring against it; which Livy illustrates by contrast with the savage races of Italy and the Carthaginians, foreigners who sought to reduce the Romans to slaves as the Persians had tried to do with the Greeks; which Caesar incarnates against the Gauls; which Tacitus seems to admire in the good Breton and German savages, and finally sees as exemplified by the ancient, virtuous Romans who lived before decadence set in. Roman historical mentality is in fact—as the Islamic historical mentality will later be—dominated by a longing for origins, the myth of the ancients' virtues, the nostalgia for ancestral ways of life, for the *mos maiorum*. The identification of history with Greco-Roman civilization is tempered only by the belief in decadence which Polybius erected into a theory based on the resemblance between human societies and individuals. Constitutions develop, decline and die as individuals do, because like individuals, they are subject to the "laws of nature," and even Roman grandeur will pass away—a theory that Montesquieu will remember later on. The lesson of history for the Ancients amounts, in the end, to a negation of history. Its positive legacy consists in the great deeds of the ancestors, heroes and great men. Decadence must be resisted by reproducing at the individual level the ancestors' great deeds, by repeating the eternal models of the past. History, as a source of *exempla*, is not far from the rhetoric of persuasive techniques. It will therefore turn with predilection to harangues and discourses. At the end of the fourth century, Ammien Marcellin sums up, in his baroque style and with his taste for the extravagant and tragic, the essential characteristics of the ancient historical mentality. This Syrian idealizes the past, evokes Roman history through literary *exempla* and has as his sole horizon—even though he had traveled over most of the Roman empire, with the exception of Britain, Spain, and North Africa west of Egypt—eternal Rome, *Roma eterna* (Momigliano 1977:127–40).

Christianity has been seen as constituting a break, a revolution in historical mentality. By giving history three fixed points—the Creation, the absolute beginning of history; the Incarnation, the beginning of Christian history and of the history of salvation; and the Last Judgment, the end of history—Christianity is supposed to have substituted for ancient conceptions of cyclical time the notion of a linear time, to have oriented history and given it *a meaning*. Sensitive to dates, Christianity tries to date the Creation, the principal landmarks in the Old Testament, and the birth and death of Jesus as precisely as it can. A historical religion anchored in history, Christianity is supposed to have lent a decisive impetus to history in the West. Guy Lardreau and Georges Duby have again emphasized the link between Christianity and the development of history in the West. Lardreau recalls Marc Bloch's remark, "Christianity is a historians' religion," and he adds, "I am quite simply convinced that we practice history because we are Christians." To which Georges Duby responds: "You are right: there is a Christian way of thinking, which is history. What is history in China, in India, in black Africa? Islam has had admirable geographers, but historians?" (Duby and Lardreau, pp. 138–39).

Christianity has certainly promoted a certain propensity to reason in historical terms characteristic of Western habits of thought, but the establishment of an intimate link between Christianity and history seems to me to need qualification. First of all, recent studies have shown that we should not reduce the ancient historical mentality—and particularly the Greek historical mentality—to the idea of cyclical time (Momigliano 1977:179–204; Vidal-Naquet 1960:55–80). Neither can Christianity be reduced to the conception of linear time; a type of cyclical time, liturgical time, plays a major role in Christianity. Christianity's primacy long led it to date only the day and month without mentioning the year—so as to integrate the event into the liturgical calendar. Moreover, teleological, eschatological time does not necessarily lead to a valorization of history. It may be thought that salvation will occur outside of history as well as through history. These two tendencies have existed, and still exist, within Christianity (see the article "*escatologia*" by J. Le Goff, *Enciclopedia Einaudi* [1978], 5:712–46). If the West has accorded special attention to history, and has particularly developed historical mentality and granted history an important role, it is in proportion to social and political evolution. Very early on, certain social groups and the ideologists for political systems had an interest in thinking of themselves in historical terms and in imposing the frameworks of historical thought. As we have seen, this interest first appeared in the Middle East and in Egypt, among the Hebrews, and then among the Greeks. It is only because it was for a long time the dominant occidental ideology that Christianity provided the West with certain forms of historical thought. As for other civilizations, if they seem to grant a lesser role to the historical spirit, it is on one hand because we reserve the word "history" for Western conceptions and do not recognize as historical other ways of thinking about history, and on the other, because the social and political conditions that have favored the development of history in the West have not always obtained elsewhere.

It remains that Christianity has contributed important elements to historical mentality even beyond the Augustinian conception of history, which had such a great influence on the Middle Ages and later periods. Christian historians in the Middle East in the fourth and fifth centuries also had an important influence not only in the Orient, but also, indirectly, on the West. That is the case for Eusebius of Caesarea, Socrates Scholasticus, Evagrius, Sozomen, and Theodoret of Cyrrhus. They all believed in free will (Eusebius and Socrates Scholasticus were even followers of Origen), and therefore believed that fate (*fatum*) played no role in history, in contrast to what the Greco-Roman historians believed. For the latter, the world was governed by the *Logos* or *Divine Reason* (otherwise called *Providence*) which constituted the structure of all nature and all history. "In this way history could be analyzed and the internal structure of its series of events considered."[32] Drawing on ancient culture, this Christian historical humanism had accepted the notion of Fortune in order to explain the "accidents" of history. The fortuitous character of human life revealed itself again in history and gave birth to the idea of the wheel of fortune, which was so popular in the Middle Ages, and which introduced another cyclical element into the conception of history. Christians also preserved two essential ideas of pagan historical thought, but profoundly transformed them: the idea of the emperor, but on the model of Theodosius the Younger, it was an image of an emperor who was half warrior, half monk, and the idea of Rome, while rejecting both the notion of Rome's decline and that of its eternity. In the Middle Ages the theme of Rome became either the concept of a Holy Roman Empire which was both Christian and universal (see F. Galco, *La Santa Romana Repubblica*, 1942), or the utopia of a Kingdom of the Last Days, the chiliastic dreams of an emperor of the end of time.

The West was indebted to Christian historical thought for two other ideas that had a great career in the Middle Ages—the framework, borrowed from the Jews, of a universal chronicle; and the idea of privileged types of history—biblical history and ecclesiastical history.[33]

I shall now mention a few types of historical mentality and practice that are linked to certain social and political interests in various periods of Western history.

The great social and political structures of the Middle Ages—feudalism and cities—are linked to two phenomena of historical mentality: genealogies and urban historiography. To these can be added—in the service of a national monarchical history—the royal chronicles, the most important of which were, from the end of the twelfth century, the *Grandes Chroniques de France*, "in which the French believed as much as they did in the Bible" (Guenée 1980:339).

The interest that important families in a society have in establishing their genealogies when the social and political structures of that society reach a certain stage is well-known. The first books of the Bible already recite the litany of the patriarchs' genealogies. In so-called "primitive" societies, genealogies are often the first form taken by history, the result of a moment when memory has a tendency to organize itself in chronological series. Georges Duby has shown how in the eleventh and especially the twelfth centuries, the lords, both greater and lesser, patronized—in the West, and particularly in France—an abundant genealogical literature "in order to enhance the reputation of their lineage, and more precisely to aid their matrimonial strategy and to enable them to contract more advantageous alliances" (Guenée 1980:64, cited after Duby). Reigning dynasties went a step further, establishing imaginary or manipulated genealogies to strengthen their prestige and authority. Thus in the twelfth century the Capetian kings of France succeeded in connecting themselves with the Carolingians (Guenée 1978:450–77). And thus the interests of princes and nobles led to a memory organized around the lineage of great families (see Génicot 1975). Diachronic family relationship becomes a organizing principle of history. A particular case: the papacy feels the need, when it asserts the pontifical monarchy, to have its own history, which obviously cannot be dynastic, but which the papacy wants to be different from that of the Church itself.[34]

On the other hand, the cities, when they established themselves as political organisms conscious of their power and prestige, also wanted to *enhance* this prestige by boasting about their antiquity, the glory of their origins and founders, the exploits of their former citizens, and the exceptional moments when they enjoyed the protection of God, the Virgin, or their patron saints. It is true that these histories acquired an official, authentic character. Thus, on April 3, 1262, the chronicle of the notary Rolandio was publicly read in the cloister of Saint Urban of Padua, before the professors and students of the University that conferred on that chronicle the title of the true history of the city and of the urban community.[35] Florence drew attention to its foundation by Julius Caesar.[36] Genoa had its own authentic history as early as the twelfth century.[37] It is to be expected that Lombardy, an area with strong cities, should have had a powerful urban historiography.[38] It is natural that no city in the Middle Ages aroused more interest in its own history than Venice. But medieval Venetian autohistoriography experienced many revealing vicissitudes. First, there is a striking contrast between the earlier historiography that reflected the city's internal divisions and struggles more than the unity and serenity that it finally achieved: "The historiography reflects a reality in movement, the struggles and partial conquests that mark it, one or more forces that are active within it—and not the satisfied serenity of someone who is contemplating a finished process" (G. Gracco, in Petusi, p. 45). On the other hand, in the middle of the fourteenth century, the Annals of the Doge Andrea Dandolo acquired such a reputation that they obliterated earlier Venetian historiography (G. Fasoli, in Pertusi, pp. 11–12). This is the beginning of "public historiography" or "commissioned historiography" which reaches a culmination at the beginning of the sixteenth century with Marino Sanudo il Giovane's *Diarii*.

The Renaissance is a great period for the historical mentality. It is marked by the idea of a new, global history, a *complete* history, and by important advances in methodology and historical criticism. From its ambiguous relations with Antiquity (which is both a paralyzing model and an inspiring pretext), the humanist history of the Renaissance derives a twofold, contradictory attitude toward history. On the other hand, it has a sense of differences and of the past, of the relativity of civilizations, but also the search for man, for a humanism and an ethic in which history paradoxically becomes the *magistra vitae* (the "teacher of life") by denying itself and by providing eternally valid examples and lessons (see Landfester). No one has expressed this ambiguous taste for history more clearly than Montaigne: "the historians come right to my forehand. They are pleasant and easy . . . man in general, the knowledge of whom I seek, appears in them more alive and entire than in any other place—the diversity and truth of his inner qualities in the mass and in detail, the variety of the ways he is put together, and the accidents that threaten him."[39]

In this context it is not surprising that Montaigne should declare that in history "his man" is Plutarch, whom we consider more a moralist than a historian. On the other hand, history then makes an alliance with the law, and this alliance culminates in the work of the Protestant François Baudouin, who studied with the great jurist Dumoulin: *De Institutione historiae universae et eius cum jurisprudentia conjunctione* (1561). The goal of this alliance is to unite the real and the ideal, customs and morality. Baudouin agrees with the theoreticians who dream of a "complete" history, but his vision of history remains "utilitarian" (Kelley 1970).

I should like to discuss here the reactions, in the sixteenth century and at the beginning of the seventeenth century, to one of the most important phenomena of that period—the discovery of the New World. I shall mention two examples, one concerning the colonized peoples, the other concerning the colonizers. In a pioneering book, *La Vision des vaincus*, Nathan Wachtel has studied the reactions of the Indian memory to the Spanish conquest of Peru. Wachtel first reminds us that the conquest did not affect a society without history: "One should not imagine that this is produced by an evil genius; in history, every event is produced in a field that is already constituted, composed of institutions, customs, practices, meanings, and multiple traces, which both resist and offer a purchase to human action" (1971:300). The result of the conquest seems to be a loss of identity on the part of the Indians. The death of the Gods and of the Inca, along with the destruction of the idols, constitute for the Incas "a collective trauma"—a very important notion in history, which should take its place among the principal forms of historical discontinuity: the great events (revolutions, conquests, defeats) are experienced as "collective traumas." The vanquished react to this destructuration by inventing a "restructuring praxis" whose principal expression is in this case "the dance of conquest"; this is a "danced restructuration, in the imaginary mode, for the other forms of praxis have proven ineffective" (pp. 305–6). Here Wachtel makes an important remark concerning historical rationality: "When we speak of a logic or rationality of history, these terms do not imply that we claim to define mathematical, necessary laws valid for all societies, as if history were subject to some natural determinism; but the combination of factors that make up the non-eventual character of the event outline an original, distinct area that supports a group of mechanisms and regularities—that is, a coherence, which is often not consciously recognized by contemporaries—whose reconstitution proves in turn indispensable for understanding the event" (p. 307). This conception allows Wachtel to define the historical consciousness of the conquerors and the conquered: "History appears rational only to the conquerors, while the vanquished people experience it as irrationality and alienation" (p. 309). However, a final example of the cunning of history appears: the vanquished people constitute for themselves, instead of a history, a "tradition as a means of rejection." The vanquished's slow history is thus a form of resistance to the conquerors' quick-moving history. And paradoxically, "to the degree that the debris of the ancient Incan civilization have crossed the centuries up to our own time, we can say that even this kind of revolt, this impossible praxis, has in a certain way triumphed in the end" (p. 314). This offers the historian a twofold lesson: on one hand, tradition is indeed a kind of history, and often, even if it carries along the flotsam and jetsam of a distant past, it is a relatively recent historical construction, a reaction to a political or cultural trauma, and usually both at once; on the other hand, this slow history, which one finds again in "popular" culture, is in fact a kind of anti-history insofar as it opposes the ostentatious and lively history promoted by the dominant groups.

Through a study of the iconography of the collection *Les Grands Voyages*, published and illustrated by the Bry family between 1590 and 1634, Bernadette Bucher has defined the relations that Westerners established between history and the ritual symbolism according to which they represented and interpreted the Indian/American society they had discovered. They projected their European and Protestant ideas and values into the symbolic structures of the images of the Indians. In this way the cultural differences between the Indians and the Europeans—and particularly differences in culinary customs—appeared to the Bry family at a certain moment "as the sign that the Indian is rejected by God."[40] Bucher's conclusion is that "the symbolic structures are the work of a system of recombination (a *combinatoire*) in which the adaptation to environment and events, and thus human initiative in general come constantly into play by means of a dialectic between structure and event" (pp. 229–30). Thus the Europeans of the Renaissance rediscover the historical procedure of Herodotus, and make the Indians into a mirror in which they can contemplate themselves. Thus do cultural encounters give rise to diverse historiographical responses to the same event.

Nevertheless, despite its efforts in the direction of a new, independent history, Renaissance history remains highly dependent on the dominant social and political interests, and in this case, particularly those of the state. From the twelfth to the fourteenth centuries, the protagonist of historical production had been a seigneurial, monarchical milieu: the protegés of the great men, like Geoffrey of Monmouth and William of Malmsbury, who dedicated their works to Robert of Gloucester, the monks of Saint-Denis, working for the greater glory of the kings of France who protected their abbey, Froissart writing for Philip of Hainault and the queen of England, et al., or, finally, in the urban milieu, the notary-chronicler.[41]

From then on, in the urban milieu, the historian is a member of the *haute bourgeoisie* in power, such as Leonardo Bruni, the chancellor of Florence from 1437 to 1444, or high officials in the government, such as Machiavelli, the secretary of the Florentine chancellery (although he wrote his great works after he was dismissed from the chancellery in 1512 upon the return of the Medici), and Guiccardini, the ambassador of the republic of Florence and afterward, the servant of Pope Leo X and then of Alessandro, Duke of Tuscany.

It is in France that one can best trace the monarchy's effort to domesticate history—notably in the seventeenth century, when the defenders of Catholic orthodoxy and the supporters of royal absolutism condemn as "libertinism" the historical criticism of the historians of the sixteenth century and of the reign of Henry IV (Huppert 1970: 178–80). This effort is manifested by the appointment of official historians from the sixteenth century to the Revolution.

If the expression "royal historian" is used for the first time in referring to Alain Chartier's role at the court of Charles VI, it is at that time "an honor rather than a precise function." The first true royal historiographer is Pierre Paschal, named to this office in 1554. From then on, the historiographer is an apologist. He occupies, moreover, only a modest role, even though in 1646 Charles Sorel tried, in his preface to Charles Bernard's *Histoire du roi Louis XIII*, to define the office of royal historiographer in such a way as to give it more importance and prestige. He emphasizes the utility and function of his office: to prove the rights of the king and the kingdom, to praise good acts, to give examples for posterity, and all this for the greater glory of the king and the kingdom. Nevertheless the office remained relatively obscure, and Boileau and Racine's effort to change this, in 1677, failed. Philosophers strongly criticized the office, and the program for reforming it set forth by Jacob Nicolas Moreau in a letter of August 22, 1774 to the President of the Cour des Comptes of Provence, J. B. D'Albertas, arrived too late. The French Revolution abolished the office of historiographer (Fossier 1977 258:73–92).

The spirit of the Enlightenment, in somewhat the same way as the Renaissance, had an ambiguous attitude toward history. Philosophical history—and especially in the case of Voltaire (mainly in the *Essai sur les moeurs et l'esprit des nations*, which was conceived in 1740, and of which the definitive edition was published in 1769)—contributed to the development of history "a considerable broadening of curiosity and especially a progress of the critical spirit" (Ehrard and Palmade, p. 37). But "the rationalism of the *philosophes* inhibited the development of the sense of history. Is it better to rationalize the irrational, as Montesquieu tries to do, or to drown it in sarcasm, as Voltaire does? In both cases history is put through the sieve of an atemporal reason" (p. 36). History is a weapon against "fanaticism," and the periods in which "fanatacism" was dominant, notably the Middle Ages, are worthy only of scorn and oblivion: "We need to know the history of these times only in order to scorn it,"MDSU wrote Voltaire. On the eve of the French Revolution, the Abbé Raynal's *Histoire philosophique et politique des établissements et du commerce des Européens dans les deux Indes* (1770) enjoyed a great success: "For Raynal, as for the *philosophes* and their followers in general, history is the duelling ground on which reason and prejudice do battle" (p. 36).

Paradoxically, the French Revolution did not stimulate historical reflection in its time. Georges Lefebvre (*La naissance . . .*, pp. 154–60) has proposed several reasons for this indifference to history: the revolutionaries were not interested in history, they were making it, they wanted to destroy a detested past and were not concerned with devoting time to it that would be better employed in creative tasks. Just as youth was drawn to the present and the future, "the public that under the old Regime had been interested in history had now been dispersed, had disappeared, or had gone bankrupt."

Nevertheless, Jean Ehrard and Guy Palmade have rightly reminded us of what the Revolution did to promote history in the domain of institutions, documentation, and education. I shall return to this. In the same way, if Napoleon tried to put history at his service, he continued and developed, in this domain as in many others, what the Revolution had begun.

The Revolution's main achievement in the domain of historical mentality was to have effected a break and given to many people in France and in Europe generally the feeling that it had not only begun a new era, but that history began with this era, in any case French history: "We have, strictly speaking, a history of France only since the Revolution," the periodical *La Décade philosophique* writes in the month of Germinal of the Revolutionary year X. Michelet will later exclaim: "Before Europe, let it be known that France will have only a single, inexpiable name, which is its true, eternal name: Revolution." Thus is established a major historical trauma, which is positive for some and negative for others (the counterrevolutionaries and reactionaries): the myth of the French Revolution (Le Goff 1978).

I shall discuss later the ideological climate and the atmosphere of Romantic sensibility in which the hypertrophy of the historical sense known as historicism was born and developed. Here I shall mention only two currents, two ideas that contributed in an important way to the promotion of the nineteenth-century passion for history: the bourgeois inspiration then linked to the notions of class and democracy, and national feeling. The great historian of the bourgeoisie is Guizot. In the communal movement of the twelfth century, he already sees the victory of the bourgeois and the birth of the bourgeoisie: "The formation of a great social class, of the bourgeoisie, was the necessary result of the local liberation of the bourgeois."[42] Whence the class struggle, the driving force of history: "the third great result of the liberation of the communes was class struggle, a struggle that fills modern history. Modern Europe was born from the struggle between different classes in society" (Ehrard and Palmade, p. 212). Guizot and Augustin Thierry (the latter particularly in his *Essai sur l'histoire de la formation et des progrès du Tiers Etat*, 1850) had an attentive reader, Karl Marx: "Long before I, bourgeois historians had described the historical development of this class struggle, and the bourgeois economists had expressed its economic anatomy."[43] The democracy that resulted from bourgeois victories had an acute observer in the person of the Comte de Tocqueville: "I have an intellectual taste for democratic institutions, but by instinct I am an aristocrat, that is, I despise and fear the crowd. I love liberty, legality and respect for rights passionately, but not democracy" (p. 61). At the beginning of the nineteenth century, De Tocqueville studies the progress of democracy in ancien régime France (as it heads toward explosion in the Revolution, which is thus not a cataclysm or a sudden schism, but the outcome of a long history) and in America, with a mixture of attraction and repulsion,[44] expressed in formulas that go almost further than Guizot's: "One is first a member of his class, before being of a certain opinion," or "One can no doubt cite individual cases against me; I am talking about classes; they alone should occupy the historian's attention" (Ehrard and Palmade, p. 61).

The other current is the national feeling that sweeps across Europe in the nineteenth century and contributes powerfully to the expansion of the historical sense. For example, Michelet exclaims: "Frenchmen of every condition, of every class, remember one thing: you have only one sure friend on this earth, and it is France!" Federico Chabod points out that if the idea of a nation goes back to the Middle Ages, what is new is the religion of the fatherland, which dates from the French Revolution: "The *nation* becomes the *fatherland*: and the fatherland becomes the new divinity of the modern world" (my opinion is exactly the reverse: the Middle Ages discovered the fatherland, and the nation dates from the Revolution)—a new divinity, and as such, *sacred.* There is the great novelty that flows from the period of the French Revolution and the Napoleonic empire. Rouget de Lisle was the first to say it in the next to the last stanza of *La Marseillaise*:

> Sacred love for the fatherland
> Lead us, support our avenging arms.

And Foscolo repeats it fifteen years later at the end of the *Sepolcri*:

> Where the blood spilled for the fatherland
> Becomes *holy* and is mourned.
>
> [Ove fia *santo* e lagrimato il sangue
> Per la patria versato.]
>
> (Chabod 1943–47:51)

He goes on to add that this feeling was especially strong in nations and among peoples that had never before been able to realize their national unity: "It is evident that the idea of a nation will be particularly dear to peoples who are not yet politically united. . . . Thus it will be especially in Italy and Germany that the national idea will find enthusiastic and persistent supporters; and behind them, other divided and dispersed peoples, above all the Poles" (p. 55).

In reality, France is no less affected by this influence of nationalism on history. It is national feeling that inspires a great classical work, the *Histoire de France* published under the direction of Ernest Lavisse from 1900 to 1912, on the eve of the First World War. Here is the program that Lavisse assigned for education in history:

> To historical education falls the glorious duty of making our fatherland loved and understood . . . our ancestors the Gauls and the forests of the druids, Charles Martel at Poitiers, Roland at Roncevaux, Godefroy de Bouillon in Jerusalem, Joan of Arc, all the heroes of our past, even those enveloped in legend. . . . If the schoolboy does not carry away with him the living memory of our national glories, if he does not know that our ancestors have fought on countless battlefields for noble causes, if he has not learned how much blood and how many efforts it has taken to make the unity of our fatherland and later to bring out of the chaos of our outdated institutions the sacred laws that made us free, if he does not become a citizen imbued with his duties and a soldier who loves his flag, the teacher will have wasted his time. (see Nora 1962)

I have not yet emphasized that up until the nineteenth century an essential element in the formation of a historical mentality is lacking. History is not an object of education. Aristotle had excluded it from the sciences. The medieval universities did not put it among the subjects to be taught (see Grundmann). The Jesuits and the Oratorians gave it a certain place in their schools (see de Dainville). But it is the French Revolution that gives the impetus, and it is the advances in education at the primary, secondary, and university levels in the nineteenth century that ensure the diffusion of a historical culture among the masses. Henceforth one of the best sources for studying the historical mentality will be school textbooks (Amalvi 1979).

Philosophies of History

As I have said, I share with most historians a certain mistrust arising from the feeling that mixing genres is harmful, and from the misdeeds of all ideologies that tend to make historical reflection draw back from the difficult path of science. I should gladly say with Fustel de Coulanges: "There is philosophy, and there is history, but there is no philosophy of history," and with Lucien Febvre: "Philosophizing . . . which signifies, when the historian says it . . . the worst kind of crime" (1933:433). But I should also say with Febvre: "Two spirits, the philosophical and the historical; that much we agree on. Two spirits, neither of which can be reduced to the other. But it is precisely not a question of 'reducing' them to one another. It is a question of proceeding in such a way that, while both remain in their respective positions, each is not ignorant of its neighbor to the point of remaining, if not hostile, then at least foreign to it" (p. 282).

I shall go further: the study of philosophies of history is not only part of any reflection on history, but necessary for any study of historiography. This is true, first, to the extent that the ambiguity (revealed by the vocabulary) resulting from the double meaning of history as the unfolding of the time of men and societies and as the science of this unfolding remains fundamental. Second, it is true insofar as the philosophy of history has often been motivated by a desire to fill—probably inadequately—a gap left by a regrettable lack of interest in theoretical problems on the part of "positivist" historians, who wanted to be thought of as pure scholars, and who refused to acknowledge the "philosophical" prejudices underlying their work, which they claimed was purely "scientific." ("Historians who refuse to judge do not succeed in abstaining from judgment. They succeed only in concealing from themselves the principles that are the basis for their judgments.")[45]

However, here, even more than in other parts of this essay, I shall not try to be comprehensive. I shall place myself resolutely within the discontinuity of the doctrines, for it is the intellectual models and not the evolution of thought that interests me, even if the way the selected examples fit into their historical context will require my attention. I shall choose examples among individual thinkers (Thucydides, Augustine, Bossuet, Vico, Hegel, Marx, Croce, Gramsci), among schools (Augustinianism, historical materialism), or trends (historicism, Marxism, positivism). I shall take two examples of theoreticians who were both historians and philosophers of history, without having attained a very high level in either of these disciplines, but who aroused revealing reactions in the twentieth century: Spengler and Toynbee. I set aside the case of a great non-Western mind, Ibn Khaldun, and the case of a great contemporary intellectual who was both a great historian and a great philosopher, and who played a major role in the renewal of history: Michel Foucault.

It seems to me that E. H. Carr is generally right in writing that "The classical civilization of Greece and Rome was basically unhistorical. . . . Herodotus as the father of history had few children; and the writers of classical antiquity were on the whole as little concerned with the future as with the past. Thucydides believed that nothing significant had happened in time before the events which he described, and that nothing significant was likely to happen thereafter" (1961:103–8). Perhaps it would be desirable to examine more closely the summary of Greek history (the *Archeologia*) and the principal events since the Median wars (the *Pentecontaetia*) that precedes the *History of the Peloponnesian War*.

Thucydides (c.460–c.400 B.C.) wrote a history of the Peloponnesian War from its beginning in 431 to about 411. "He thinks of himself as a positivist,"[46] setting forth "the facts in order, without commentaries." His philosophy is thus incomplete. "The Peloponnesian war is itself *stylized*, and so to speak, *idealized*" (Aron 1961:164). The great motor of history is human nature. J. de Romilly has pointed out the passages in which Thucydides indicates that his work will be "a permanent acquisition" because it will be valid "so long as human nature remains the same," and because it illuminates not only the events in Greece in the fifth century but also "those which, in the future, by virtue of their human character, will be similar or analogous." Thus history is supposed to be immobile, eternal, or rather it is likely to be the eternal repetition of a single model of change. This model of change is war: "After Thucydides there was no longer any doubt that wars represented the most obvious factor in change" (Momigliano 1977:165). War is "a historical category" (Châtelet 1962 1:216 ff.). It is brought about by the other Greeks' reactions of fear and jealousy when confronted by Athenian imperialism. Events are the products of a rationality that the historian must make intelligible: "Thucydides, at the same time that he gradually extends the intelligibility of a voluntary individual act to events that no one has willed, raises the event, whether or not it was in conformity with the actors' intentions, above historical particularity by explaining it through the use of abstract sociological or psychological terms" (ibid.). Thucydides, like virtually all ancient historians, believes that history, in his writing, is closely associated with rhetoric. He therefore accords particular significance to *discourses* (Pericles' funeral oration on the Athenian soldiers, the dialogue between the Athenians and the Melians) and the role he attributes—with deep pessimism—to the conflict between individual ethics and politics makes him a precursor of Machiavelli, one of the most influential thinkers in Western philosophy of history. Ranke devoted his first historical work—his "thesis"—to him.

Even if we exaggerate the contrast between a pagan history that is supposed to turn on a cyclical conception of history and a Christian history that is supposed to direct it along a linear trajectory toward a goal, the dominant tendency of Judeo-Christian thought brings about a radical change in thinking—and writing—about history. "It was the Jews, and after them the Christians, who introduced an entirely new element by postulating a goal towards which the historical process is moving—the teleological view of history. History thus acquired a meaning and purpose, but at the expense of losing its secular character ... history itself became a theodicy" (Carr, p. 104). Saint Augustine was, even more than the ancient Christian historians, and in spite of himself, the great theoretician of Christian history. Events and the work of his apostleship led him to deal with history. He had first to refute the neoplatonic philosopher Porphyry (234–305), "the most learned man of his time," who had asserted that "the universal path to salvation" as Christians understood it "was not supported by historical knowledge" (Brown 1967:374). He then tried to refute the accusations made by the pagans, after the sack of Rome by Alaric and his Goths in 410, against Christianity, which according to them had undermined the traditions and strength of the Roman world, the incarnation of civilization. Augustine rejected the idea that the ideal of humanity was to oppose change. Men's salvation was not tied to the permanence of things Roman. There were two historical schemas at work in human history. Their prototypes were Cain and Abel. The former was the origin of a human history that served the devil, the latter the source of a history that tried to return to God, that "longed for Heaven"; the former was Babylon, the latter, Jerusalem and Zion. In human history, the two cities have been inextricably linked; in them, men are foreigners, "pilgrims" (Brown, ch. 27, *civitas peregrina*) until the end of time, when God will separate the two cities. Human history was first a chain of events without meaning, "this time in the course of which those who die give way to those who are born to succeed them" (*The City of God*, IX, 1,1) until the Incarnation occurs to give these events a meaning: "Past centuries in history would have remained like empty jars had not Christ come to fill them" (*Tractatus in Johannem*, 9, 6). The history of the terrestrial city is similar to the evolution of a unique organism, the individual body. It passes through the six ages of life and with the Incarnation, it enters old age; the world is getting old (*mundus senescit*), but humanity has discovered the sense of the immense concert that carries it along until "the splendor of the centuries all together" shall be revealed. The "precision of history" shows nothing but the solemn succession of events, whereas a few privileged moments allow us to glimpse in a "prophetic prevision" the possibility of salvation. Such is the picture that the *City of God* (413–427) finally paints, mixing the joyous hope of salvation with the tragic sense of life (Marrou 1950).

The ambiguities of Augustinian historical thought gave rise later on, and particularly in the Middle Ages, to a whole series of deformations and simplifications: "One can follow from century to century the metamorphoses, which are usually mere caricatures of the Augustinian schema set out in *The City of God*" (Marrou 1961:20). The first caricature was a work by a Spanish priest, Orose, whose *History Against the Pagans* (415–417), inspired directly by Augustine's teaching at Hipponeum, had a major influence on the Middle Ages. In this way the mystical notion of the Church, the prefiguration of the Divine City and the ecclesiastical institution which claimed to have authority over earthly society, was bound together with the pseudo-explanation of history by reference to a Providence that was unforeseeable but always well-directed, the belief in a progressive decadence of humanity, otherwise infallibly led toward the end willed by God, and the duty to convert non-Christians at any price, in order to cause them to enter into this history of salvation reserved for Christians alone.

While Western history in the Middle Ages slowly and humbly, in the shadow of this "Augustinian" theory of history, pursued the tasks of the historian's craft, Islam was belatedly producing a work of genius in the realm of the philosophy of history, Ibn Khaldun's *Muqqaddima*. But unlike *The City of God*, it prefigured, without directly influencing, some of the procedures and attitudes of modern scientific history. Specialists agree in considering Ibn Khaldun to be "an exceptional critical mind for his time," "a genius, that is, a person with peerless intuition," "ahead of his time in his ideas and his method" (V. Monteil in his Preface to Ibn Khaldun). Arnold Toynbee sees in *Al-Muqqaddima* "without doubt the greatest work of its kind that has ever been created by anyone, in any time or any place."

Without being able to analyze the *Muqqaddima* in its time, I shall discuss it here as being henceforth part of humanity's overall historical production, and moreover capable of directly influencing current historical reflection in the Islamic world and in the third world. Here is the opinion of an Algerian intellectual, a physician imprisoned by the French during the Algerian war who read Ibn Khaldun in his cell: "I have been especially struck by the subtlety and insightfulness of his remarks concerning the State and its role, on History and its definition. He has opened up perspectives unknown to psychology . . . as well as to political sociology, for example, by accenting the opposition between city-dwellers and rural people, or the role of *esprit de corps* in the constitution of empires and the role of luxury in their decadence."[47] The French geographer Yves Lacoste sees in the *Muqqaddima* "a fundamental contribution to the history of under-development. It marks the birth of History as a science, and it introduces us to an essential stage in the past of what we call today the third world."

Ibn Khaldun was born in Tunis in 1332 and died in Cairo in 1406. He wrote the *Muqqaddima* in his retreat in Algeria, near Biskra, in 1377, before going to spend the rest of his life in Cairo as a *cadi* (judge), from 1382 to 1406. His work is an *Introduction* (*Muqqaddima*) to Universal History. In this regard, he takes his place in a great Muslim tradition and overtly proclaims that affiliation. The beginning of the *Muqqaddima* reminds a modern Western reader of what was written in the West a century or two later, during the Renaissance, and of what certain historians of classical antiquity had written.

> History is a noble science. It has many useful aspects. It seeks to attain a noble end. It causes us to know the peculiar natures of ancient nations, as they are expressed in their national character. It transmits to us the biographies of the prophets, the chronicles of the kings, their dynasties, and their policies. In this way, anyone who desires it may obtain a felicitous result, by imitating historical models in religious or profane matters. To write historical works, one must have at one's disposal many sources and various kinds of knowledge. One must also have a reflective, profound mind which can guide the seeker after truth and protect him against error. (Ibn Khaldun 1:13)

Ibn Khaldun presents his work as "a commentary on civilization" (*'umrah*). Change and its explanation are what matter to him. He differs from historians who limit themselves to speaking of events and dynasties without explaining them. Ibn Khaldun, on the contrary, "gives the causes of events," and believes that he therefore includes "the philosophy (*hikma*) of history." He has been seen as the first sociologist. It seems to me that he is rather a mixture of a historical anthropologist and a philosopher of history. He takes a certain distance on tradition: "Historical research closely links error with credulity. Blind faith in tradition (*taqlid*) is congenital." Thanks to his book "we need no longer believe blindly in tradition." What is particularly remarkable about his explanations is his reference to society and civilization, which are for him the essential structures and domains even though he neglects neither technology nor economics. Here, for example, is the kind of testimony that the edifices built by a dynasty constitute for the historian:

> All these works of the ancients were possible only through technology and the concerted effort of an enormous labor-force. . . . We must not adhere to the popular belief according to which the ancients were bigger and stronger than we. . . . The error of the storytellers arises here from the fact that they admire the vast proportions of antique monuments, without understanding the different conditions of social organization (*itgima*) and cooperation. They do not see that everything had to do with social organization and technology (*hindam*). As a result, they wrongly imagine that the ancient monuments are due to the strength and energy of larger beings. (1:346–48)

As is natural for a Muslim, on the basis of what he sees and what he thinks about Islam's past, he accords major importance to the opposition between nomadic and sedentary peoples, bedouins and city-dwellers. A man from the urbanized Maghreb, he is particularly interested in urban civilization. The dynastic and monarchical phenomenon interests him as well, and he observes that it is not a product of urbanization: "The dynasty precedes the city" (2:ch.4). Where he appears to us as a philosopher of history is in his theory of the influence of climates (which anticipates Montesquieu, but which was already traditional among the Muslim historians and geographers of his period, and which is not free of racism—with respect to black people), and especially his theory of decline (Le Goff 1978 4:389–420). Every social and political organization lasts only a certain time, and goes more or less rapidly into decline: for example, the prestige of a family lineage lasts only four generations. This mechanism is particularly striking in the case of monarchies, where the dynastic value of lineage lasts no more than three generations: by nature, the monarchy wants glory, luxury, and peace, but when it has become glorious, luxurious, and peaceful, a monarchy is in decline. Ibn Khaldun does not distinguish moral and social aspects in this process:

> A dynasty lasts, generally, not more than three generations. The first retains the bedouin virtues, the roughness and savagery of the desert . . . it therefore also retains its clan spirit, its members are decisive and feared, and their people obey them. . . . Under the influence of the monarchy and their well-being, the second generation passes from a bedouin life to sedentary life, from privation to luxury and abundance, from common, shared glory to the glory of an individual. . . . The vigor of the tribal spirit is partly broken. People get used to servility and obedience. The third generation has completely forgotten the taste for glory and blood ties, because it is governed by force . . . its members depend on the dynasty that protects them, like women and children. The clan spirit disappears altogether. . . . The sovereign must then appeal to his clients, to his followers. But one day God allows the monarchy to be destroyed. (I, 3, 22, pp. 334–35)

What underpins this theory is the analogy between a sociopolitical form and a human individual, an organicist, biological model of history. It remains nonetheless that the *Muqqaddima* is one of the great classics of historical knowledge. As Jacques Berque has put it: "It is a North African, Islamic, and worldwide thought. . . . For this man living in disgrace, the bitter joy of the intelligible has marked history, which was at a turning point, and he had the merit of being the first to situate it in such a vast perspective."

Let us return to the West. Greco-Roman antiquity did not have a genuine sense of history. It advanced as general explanatory schemas only human nature (that is, immutability), destiny and fortune (that is, irrationality), and organic development (that is, biologism). It situated the historical genre in the domain of literary art and assigned it the functions of amusement and moral utility. But it prefigured a "scientific" conception and a practice of history by emphasizing testimony (Herodotus), intelligibility (Thucydides), the search for causes (Polybius), and the search for and respect for truth (all of the above and Cicero as well). Christianity gave a meaning to history but subordinated it to theology. The eighteenth and especially the nineteenth centuries ensured the triumph of history by giving it a meaning secularized by the idea of *progress*, and by fusing its knowledge-function with its wisdom-function by means of scientific conceptions (and practices) which assimilated it either to *reality* (and no longer only to truth, as in historicism) or to *praxis* (Marxism).

But the middle ground, which separates the medieval theology of history from the triumphant historicism of the nineteenth century, is not without interest from the point of view of the philosophy of history. According to Georges Nadel, the golden age of the philosophy of history was the period from about 1550 to 1750 (19xx 3:291–315). He takes as his point of departure Polybius' statement (I,2): "The best education and the best apprenticeship for active political life is the study of history."

I introduce one remark at this point. One can in fact see here the influence of Machiavelli and Guicciardini. But only if we note the original position of each of these thinkers concerning the relations between history and politics. Here I am basing my comments on the work of Félix Gilbert. For Machiavelli, the essential idea is the specificity of politics, and in a certain way, since politics has to be a search for stability in society, it must be opposed to history, which is a perpetual flux, subject to the caprices of Fortune, as indeed Polybius and other ancient historians thought. For Machiavelli men must realize "the impossibility of establishing a permanent social order, which respects God's will, or in which justice would be distributed in such a way as to respond to all human requirements." As a result, "Machiavelli holds firmly to the idea that politics has its own laws, and consequently is or should be a science; his goal is to keep a society alive in the perpetual flux of history." The consequences of this conception were "the recognition of the necessity of political cohesiveness and the thesis of the autonomy of politics, which experienced a later development with the concept of the State" (1965:171).

Guicciardini, on the other hand, desires and realizes the autonomy of history on the basis of the same observation of change (about which people said jocularly that it was the only *law* discernible in history). A specialist in the study of change, "the historian thus acquired his specific function, and history assumed an autonomous existence in the world of knowledge; the meaning of history was to be sought nowhere but in history itself. The historian became a registrar and interpreter at once. Guicciardini's *Storia d'Italia* is the last great historical work conducted in accordance with the classical model, but it is also the first great work of modern historiography" (1965:255).

Returning to Nadel, his idea is that from the Renaissance to the Enlightenment the dominant conception of history was that of an exemplary history, didactic in intent, inductive in method, and founded on the commonplaces of the Roman Stoics, rhetoricians, and historians. History had once again become a means of educating the governing classes, as it had been in Polybius' time. This conception of history as *magistra vitae* inspired either particular studies, *Artes Historicae* (one collection of such treatises, the *Artis Historicae Penus*, in two volumes, was published in Basel in 1579), of which the most important were, in the sixteenth century, the *Methodus ad facilem historiarum cognitionem*, by Jean Bodin (1560); in the seventeenth century, the *Ars Historica* (1623) by Vossius, for whom history was the knowledge of particularities whose remembrance is useful "ad bene beateque vivendum" (for living well and happily); in the eighteenth century, the *Méthode pour étudier l'Histoire* by Lenglet du Fresnoy—the first edition of this work, which was followed by several other editions, was published in 1713.

The history of the philosophers of the Enlightenment, which tried to make history rational and open to ideas of civility and progress, did not replace the conception of exemplary history, and history escaped the great scientific revolution of the seventeenth and eighteenth centuries. This conception survived until it was replaced by historicism. This new dominant conception of history was born in Germany, and more particularly in Göttingen. At the end of the eighteenth century and at the beginning of the nineteenth, university professors, who had not been interested in a public for which history was supposed to be an ethical science, transformed history into a matter for professionals and specialists. "The struggle between antiquarian history and philosophical history, between the learned pedant and the well-bred gentleman ended with the victory of the *scholar* over the *philosopher*" (Nadel, p. 315). Savigny had already said in 1815 that "History is not a mere collection of examples, but the only path to true knowledge about our particular condition."[48] The clearest declaration, which has become famous, is Ranke's: "To history has been attributed the function of judging the past and instructing the present in order to make the future useful; my efforts do not aim at such lofty functions—they tend only to show how things really happened."[49]

Before examining the new conceptions of German scholarly history in the nineteenth century, that is, historicism, I should like to amend Nadel's interesting idea on two points. The first is that the ideas of the principal historians of the end of the sixteenth century cannot be reduced to the idea of exemplary history; the theory of a *complete* or *integral* history goes far beyond such a concept. The second—to which

Nadel himself alludes—is that the Christian providentialist theory of history still has followers in the seventeenth century, its most remarkable expression being Bossuet's *Discours sur l'histoire universelle* (1681).

In the second half of the sixteenth century, a certain number of French historians expressed a very ambitious view of a realized *integral* or *complete* history. This conception is encountered in Bodin, in Nicolas Vignier (*Sommaire de l'histoire des François*, 1579, and *Bibliothèque historiale*, 1588), in Louis le Roy (*De la vicissitude ou variété des choses en l'univers* . . . , 1575), and especially in Lancelot de la Popelinière, in a volume containing three treatises: *L'Histoire des histoires*, *L'Idée de l'histoire accomplie*, and *Le Dessein de l'Histoire nouvelle des François* (1599). Bodin is known particularly for his idea of the influence of climate on history, which anticipates Montesquieu and historical sociology. But his *Méthode* (1566) is no more than an introduction to his great treatise *La République* (1576). He is a philosopher of history and of politics and not a historian. His conception of history is still based on the humanist idea of *utility*. All these learned men have in common three ideas that are best expressed by La Popelinière. The first is that history is not pure narrative, not a literary work. It must seek causes. The second, the newest and most important, is that the object of history is both particular *civilizations* and *civilization* in general. This begins even before writing. "In its most primitive form," Georges Huppert writes, "the thesis La Popelinière defends is that history is to be sought everywhere, in songs and dances, in symbols, and in other mnemonic devices" (1970:143). This is the history of the time when men were "rural and not civilized." The third idea is that history should be universal, in the most complete sense: "History worthy of the name must be *general*." Myriam Yardeni has correctly emphasized that this history was very new, and that La Popelinière had precisely stressed its *novelty*. But he was handicapped by his Christian pessimism (1964:109–26).

The historical Augustinianism that still weighs on La Popelinière produced his final masterpiece, as well as Bossuet's *Discours sur l'Histoire universelle de France* (1681). Bossuet, who had written an *Abrégé de l'Histoire de France* for his pupil, the Dauphin, the son of Louis XIV, and composed his *Discours* for his disciple as well: the first part, a panorama of history up to Charlemagne, is a genuine *discourse*, while the second, a "demonstration of the truth of the Catholic religion in its relation to history, is a *sermon*" (G. Lefebvre, p. 97). The third part, an examination of the destiny of empires, is the most interesting. In reality, beneath the general assertion of the unforeseeable reign of Providence over history, there appears a rationality of History which results from the fact that particular events participate in general systems determined by overall causes, God intervening (rarely) only through the intermediary of secondary causes. But although Bossuet has read scholarly works, and frequently oscillates between apologetics and polemics, the idea of a truth that develops through time is foreign to him. "For him, change is always a sign of error. What this historian, the prisoner of a certain theology, most lacks is the sense of time and development" (Ehrard and Palmade 1964:33).

I should also mention an original philosophy of history that was isolated in its own time, but which has had an astonishing later career, that of Giambattista Vico, a professor at the University of Naples (1668–1744), whose main work, *La scienza nuova* (or more precisely, *Principi d'una scienza nuova d'intorno alla commune natura delle nazioni*) was republished several times between 1725 and 1740.

Vico is a Catholic, but also a rationalist. He "introduces a special kind of dualism between sacred and profane history. He placed all morality and rationality on the side of sacred history, and saw in profane history the development of irrational instincts, a truculent imagination, and a violent injustice" (Mamigliano 1977:255–56). Human passions lead nations and peoples into decadence. A kind of class struggle between the conservative "eroi" (heroes) on the one hand, and on the other, plebeian "bestioni" (brutes) and partisans of change generally results in the victory of the *bestioni*, decadence after the apogee, and the transfer of power to another people which rises and declines (*corso* and *ricorso*) in its turn: man makes the historical world.

This philosophy of history inspired various kinds of admiration. Michelet translated the *Scienza nuova* into French in 1826, asserting that "The key to the *Scienza nuova* is this: *humanity is its own product*." Croce shaped his historical thought in part through reading and commenting on Vico (*La Filosofia di Giambattista Vico*, 1911). There is a Marxist interpretation of Vico, which Marx recommended to Lasalle in 1861, and which was developed by Georges Sorel,[50] Antonio Labriola, Paul Lafargue, and by Trotsky's quotation of Vico on the first page of the *History of the Russian Revolution*, which inspired Nicola Badaloni's *Introduzione a Giambattista Vico* (1961). Ernst Bloch wrote: "In Vico we find for the first time since Augustine's *City of God* a philosophy of history without a history of salvation, but supported by the affirmation, applicable to all of history, that there would be no human community without the tie of religion" (*La Philosophie de la Renaissance*, p. 179).

Nadel has defined historicism as follows:

> Its foundation is the recognition that historical events must no longer be studied as illustrations of morals or politics, but as historical phenomena. In practice, this is marked by the appearance of history as an independent university discipline, in fact as well as in name. In theory, this is expressed by two propositions: 1) what has happened must be explained in relation to the moment at which it occurs, and 2) a specific science exists for the purpose of explaining what has happened, a science that makes use of logical processes: the science of history. Neither of these propositions was new, but the emphasis on them was new, and led to their doctrinal exaggeration. The conclusion was drawn from the first proposition that to write the history of something was to give a sufficient explanation of it, and those who saw a logical order in the chronological order of events regarded historical science as capable of predicting the future. (p. 291)

Historicism should be situated among the other philosophical currents of the nineteenth century, as Maurice Mandelbaum has done. He notes that historicism has two distinct and perhaps opposed sources. The first is the Romantic revolt against the Enlightenment, while the other was, in some respects, the continuation of the Enlightenment tradition. The first tendency appeared at the end of the eighteenth century, especially in Germany, and it considered historical development on the model of the growth of living creatures. Hegel was influenced by this tendency, and went much further. The second tendency tried to establish a science of society based on the laws of social development; its chief proponents were Saint-Simon and Comte. Marxism also belonged to this tendency. In reality, in the nineteenth century historicism set its mark on every school of thought, and what caused it finally to triumph was Darwin's theory of *The Origin of Species* (1859), evolutionism. The central concept is *development*, often associated with *progress*. But historicism found an obstacle in the problem of the existence in history of meaningful laws, and in the idea of a single model of historical development.

Following Georg Iggers, I shall mention here—briefly—the theoretical foundations of German historicism in Wilhelm von Humboldt and Leopold von Ranke, the summit of historicist optimism in the Prussian school, and the crisis of historicism in Dilthey's and Max Weber's critical philosophies of history, along with the historical relativism of Troeltsch and Meinecke.

Wilhelm von Humboldt (1767–1835), a philosopher of language and a diplomat who founded the University of Berlin in 1810, wrote numerous historical works. He summed up his thoughts on history in his treatise *Über die Aufgabe des Geschichtschreibers* (The Historian's Task), written in 1821, but only published in 1882. Humboldt was often very close to Romanticism and was influenced (both positively and negatively) by the French Revolution. He was the creator of the "theory of historical ideas, and emphasized the central importance of politics in history; he saw in these the keystones of the philosophy and the history that inspired German historical science from Ranke to Meinecke" (Iggers 1971:84–86). His *ideas* are not metaphysical or platonic; they are historically incarnated in an individual, a people ("the spirit of the people," *Volksgeist*), or a period ("the spirit of the times," *Zeitgeist*), but they remain vague. Although he is "neither a nihilist nor a relativist," he has a fundamentally "irrational" conception of history.

Leopold von Ranke (1795–1886, made a noble in 1865) was the greatest and the most important of the nineteenth-century German historians and theorists of history. His work as a historian concerns mainly European history of the sixteenth and seventeenth centuries and Prussian history of the eighteenth and nineteenth centuries. Toward the end of his life he wrote a *Weltgeschichte* (World History), which remained unfinished. Ranke was more a methodologist than a philosopher of history. He was the "master of the critical-philological method" (Fueter 1911:173). Struggling against anachronism, he denounced the false historical romance of Romanticism (for example, the novels of Sir Walter Scott) and asserted that the historian's great task was to tell "how things really happened." Ranke impoverished historical thought by granting an excessive importance to political and diplomatic history. But his thought has been distorted in two ways: one positivist, the other idealist. French historians (e.g., Langlois and Seignobos) and especially American historians have seen in him the "father of history," of a history that limits itself to "the strict observation of facts, the absence of moralizing and ornament, pure historical truth."[51]

Like Humboldt, Ranke was in fact a (prudent) supporter of the doctrine of historical ideas. He believed in the progress of culture as the content of history, and accorded historical psychology great importance, as he showed in his *History of the Roman Popes* (1834–36). But although much has been made of the phrase in which he said that "every people is in immediate contact with God," he was an "adversary of national historical theories" (Fueter, p. 169).

Historicist optimism reaches its apogee in the Prussian school, whose most remarkable figures were Johann Gustav Droysen (1808–1884), who expressed his theories in his *Grundriss der Historik* (Leipzig, 1868), and Heinrich von Sybel (1817–1895). Droysen sees no conflict between morals and history or politics. If a government is not based on force alone, but also on an ethics, it reaches the supreme stage of ethico-historical achievement, the State. In the nineteenth century the Prussian state was the model of that success, which had also been realized in antiquity by Alexander. Within the state, there was no more conflict between individual freedom and common good. Sybel emphasized even more the state's mission and the reality of the general progress of humanity. For him, the state's interest was preeminent, since if a conflict arose between them, might had to win out over right.

This brief summary should be complemented by a study of the close connections between these views of history and German and European history in the nineteenth century, and by a study of other domains of science in which German historicism was victoriously implanted, for example, in historical studies of law and economics, historical linguistics, etc. (Iggers, p. 173).

German historicism ebbed at the end of the century, while it triumphed elsewhere in positivist guises (in France and the United States) or idealist guises (Italy: Croce). As Iggers has clearly shown, the critique of historicism had already been made before the First World War, especially as a critique of idealism, and later as a critique of the idea of progress. I shall distinguish the philosophers' critique from that of the historians.

Concerning the former, I refer to Raymond Aron's great book, *La philosophie critique de l'histoire* (1938b) and to the fine studies by Pietro Rossi, *Lo storicismo tedesco contemporaneo* (1956), and by Carlo Antoni, *Lo storicismo* (1957). I shall discuss the two principal figures in the philosophical critique of historicism: Dilthey and Max Weber.

Dilthey (1833–1911) began by criticizing the fundamental concepts of Humboldt's and Ranke's historicism: the popular soul (*Volksseele*) and the soul of the nation (*Volksgeist*), a social organism. He considers these "mystical" concepts useless for historians (Iggers, p. 180). Later he thought knowledge was possible in sciences of the spirit (*Geisteswissen-*

shaften)—including history—because life "objectifies itself" in institutions such as the family, bourgeois society, the state, law, art, religion, and philosophy (p. 188).

The whole critique of historicism at the end of the nineteenth century and the beginning of the twentieth is ambiguous. As we have just seen in Dilthey, its goal is more to transcend historicism than to reject it.

Max Weber (1864–1920) was not only a great philosopher but also a great historian and sociologist. Raymond Aron has summed up Weber's theory of history this way:

> All Weber's polemics are designed to demonstrate his own theory indirectly by refuting the conceptions that might threaten it. *History is a positive science*: this proposition puts into question a) the metaphysicians, whether conscious or unconscious, avowed or ashamed, who use a transcendental concept (freedom) in the logic of history, and b) the aesthetes or positivists who start out from the prejudice that sciences and concepts necessarily concern the general, the individual being comprehensible only intuitively. *History is always partial*, because the real is infinite, because the inspiration of historical research changes with history itself. These propositions put into question a) the "naturalists" who proclaim that laws are the only goal of science or who think they can exhaust the content of reality by means of a system of abstract relations, b) the naive historians who, unconscious of their own values, imagine that the selection of the important and the accidental can be discovered in the historical world itself, and c) all the metaphysicians who imagine that they have grasped in a positive manner the essence of phenomena, the deep forces, the general laws that control change, over the heads of men who think and believe that they act. (1938b:279)

One can see that Max Weber opposed historicism of both the idealistic and positivistic tendencies, the two trends in German historical thought of the nineteenth century.

The period of historicism and its critique closes with the last two great German historians of the nineteenth and twentieth centuries, Ernst Troeltsch (1865–1922) and Friedrich Meinecke (1862–1954). Toward the end of their careers they published two works on historicism: Troeltsch, *Der Historismus und Seine Probleme* (1922), and Meinecke, *Der Historismus und seine Überwindung* (*Historicism and Its Triumph*, 1924).

Troeltsch and Meinecke are the first to use the term *historicism* to describe the German historical movement of the nineteenth century, whose central figure was Ranke. An interminable polemic ensued about whether *Historismus* was better translated as "historism" or "historicism," and eventually about the possibility of drawing a distinction between the two terms (Iggers 1973). The two works are in fact both a critique of historicism and a tribute to its glory. Troeltsch, who thought, like Ranke, that there was not *a* history, but rather *histories*, tried to overcome the fundamental dualism of historicism: the conflict between nature and mind, between action under the impulsion of force (*Kratos*) and action in accord with a moral justification (*Ethos*), between historicist consciousness and the need for absolute values. Meinecke accepted this dualism.[52] He defined historicism as "the highest degree attained in the understanding of human affairs." As Carlo Antoni has observed, Meinecke stopped short of the disslution of reason and of faith in thought, the unifying principle of human nature, because of the very humanism that Ranke had maintained. But Delio Cantimori thinks Croce was right in seeing in Meinecke's historicism a certain "irrational" betrayal of "true historicism."

> "Historicism" in the scientific sense of the term is the assertion that life and reality are historical, and nothing but historical. This assertion has as its corollary the negation of the theory that maintains that reality is divided into a superhistory and a history, into a world of ideas and values and a lower world that reflects it, or has reflected it up to now, in a fleeting and imperfect way, and over which we must once and for all take control by making imperfect history or history pure and simple, give way to rational, perfect reality. . . . Meinecke, on the other hand, makes historicism consist in the admission of the irrational element in human life, in holding fast to the individual without neglecting the typical and the general which is linked to the individual, and in the projection of this vision of the individual on the background of religious faith or mystery. But true historicism, insofar as it criticizes and surpasses the abstract rationalism of the Enlightenment, is more profoundly rationalist than the latter. (Croce, quoted by Cantimori 1945:500)

On the eve of Nazism, Troeltsch's and Meinecke's works are the celebratory funeral monuments of historicism.

Let us now go back to examine the ideas of Georg Wilhelm Friedrich Hegel (1770–1831), who was the first philosopher to put history at the center of his thought. Under the influence of the French Revolution, he was the first to see "the essence of reality in historical change and in the development of man's consciousness of himself" (Carr 1961:131). Affirming that "everything that is rational is real, and everything that is real is rational," he claims that history is governed by reason: "The only idea that philosophy contributes is this simple idea of reason, the idea that reason governs the world and that consequently universal history has developed rationally" (Hegel 1822–30:47). History itself is caught up in a system, which is that of Spirit (*Geist*). History is not identical with logic. Hélène Védrine has drawn attention to a passage in Hegel's *Encyclopedia of the Philosophical Sciences*: "But the spirit thinking the history of the world, by throwing off these limitations of the spirits of particular peoples and its own worldliness, grasps its concrete universality and elevates itself to the knowledge of absolute spirit, as an eternally real truth, in which knowing reason is free for itself, and in which necessity, nature, and history are only at the service of the revelation of this spirit, and the vessels of its honor" (p. 470). Védrine correctly remarks that this text does prove Hegel's idealism, but also sees especially manifest in it "the paradox of all philosophies of history: in order to grasp the meaning of development, it is necessary to find the focal point where events are abolished in their singularity and where they become significant in accordance with a framework which permits them to be interpreted. In its totalization, the system produces a concept of its object such that the object becomes rational and thereby escapes unpredictability and a temporality in which chance could still play its role" (Védrine, p. 21). Concerning the historical process, Hegel thinks that "only peoples who form a State can be known to us" (*Lessons on the Philosophy of History*, 1837), and in the *Philosophy of Right* (1821) he portrays the modern, postrevolutionary state formed of three classes, the substantial or peasant class, the industrial class, and the universal (i.e., bureaucratic) class, as representing perfection in history. Or rather, no doubt Hegel does not stop history at that point; he thinks that prehistory is over, and that History, which is no longer dialectical change but the rational functioning of Spirit, is beginning.

It is true that Ranke strongly criticized Hegel,[53] and his model of a single process of linear development, but it can be maintained that "from the point of view of understanding no less than from the point of view of value, Hegel represents a complete historicism, systematically applied" (Mandelbaum, p. 60).

Historical materialism can be considered under the rubric of historicism only by taking the latter term in a very broad sense. (See Althusser's critique of this idea, pp. 00–00.) For Marx (1818–1882),[54] the "materialist conception of history" (an expression he never used) has a twofold character: (1) as a general principle of historical research in a form of conceptualization that is simply outlined, and (2) as a theory of the real historical process, an application—the study of bourgeois society, which leads to a historical outline of the development of capitalism in Western Europe. Marx's principal texts concerning history are found in *The German Ideology* (1844–46), which allows us to "grasp historical materialism in its genesis and in its nuances" (Vilar), in the 1859 "Preface" to the *Contribution to Political Economy* (but here we should be wary of quotations taken out of context and commentaries that distort or impoverish Marx's thought), and finally, in *Capital* (1867–99).

Marx's fundamental thesis is that the *mode of production* of material life conditions the social, political, and intellectual process in general. It is not men's consciousness that determines their existence, but on the contrary, it is their social being that determines their consciousness.

Against Hegel, Marx rejected all philosophy of history that is assimilated to a theology. In the *Communist Manifesto* he wrote with Engels in 1848, he postulated that the history of every existing society is the history of class struggle.

On a certain number of particularly contestable and dangerous theses of historical materialism Marx, without being responsible for misleading interpretations and illegitimate consequences that others drew during his lifetime or after his death, always either accepted excessive and simplifying formulations or left important concepts vague or ambiguous.

Marx did not formulate general laws of history, he only conceptualized the historical process; but he sometimes used the dangerous term "law" himself, or allowed his thought to be formulated in this way. For example, he did not object when, in a review of the first volume of *Capital*, A. Sieber, a professor at the University of Kiev, used the word "laws" in referring to his ideas (Mandelbaum, pp. 172–73). He let Engels set forth in his *Anti-Dühring* (1878) a crude conception of the mode of production and the class struggle. As has been observed, his historical documentation (and that of Engels) was insufficient, and he did not write true historical works, but pamphlets. He left the most dangerous of his concepts vague, namely, the distinction between infrastructure and superstructure, although he never expressed a crudely economic conception of the infrastructure, nor designated as a superstructure anything but the political construction that was the state (here he is in complete opposition to most German historians of his time and to several defenders of what would later be called historicism) and ideology, which was for him a pejorative term. Neither did he make clear just how critical theory and revolutionary practice were supposed to be combined in the historian's life and work. He provided theoretical but not practical bases for posing the problem of the relation between history and politics. Although he discussed the history of Asia, for all practical purposes his argument is based only on European history, and he was unfamiliar with the concept of civilization. Concerning his rejection of mechanical laws in history, we can quote a letter of 1877, in which he declares that "Events strikingly similar, but occurring in a different historical milieu, lead to completely dissimilar results. By studying each of these evolutions separately and then comparing them, it is easy to find the key to the understanding of this phenomenon; but it is never possible to arrive at this understanding by using the *passe-partout* of some historical-philosophical theory whose great virtue is to stand above history" (quoted by Carr, p. 59).

Marx criticized the "event-oriented" conception of history: "One sees how much the earlier conception of history was an absurdity which ignored real relations, and limited itself to the great, resounding political and historical events" (quoted by Vilar, p. 372). As Vilar puts it, "He wrote few 'history books,' but he always wrote historian's books; the 'concept of history' is in his practice" (p. 374). We know that in his youth, Benedetto Croce (1856–1952) was attracted by Marxism, and Gramsci thought Croce was later obsessed by historical materialism.[55] For Croce, as for historical materialism, "the identity of history and philosophy is immanent in historical materialism" (Gramsci, p. 217). But Croce refused to follow this identity to its ultimate conclusion, that is, to conceive it "as a historical foreshadowing of a phase yet to come"; he especially refused to identify *history* with *politics*, that is, *ideology* with *philosophy* (pp. 217–18). He forgot that "reality in movement and the concept of reality, even if they are logically distinct, must be conceived historically as an inseparable unity" (p. 216). Thus he fell into "idealist" *sociologism*, according to Gramsci, and his *historicism* was only a kind of reformism, not "*true*" *historicism*, but *an ideology in the pejorative sense of the word*. It seems to me that Gramsci is largely right in contrasting Croce's philosophy of history with that of historical materialism. If Gramsci sees a common root, I think it is because he returned (as did Croce) past Marx to Hegel, because he interprets historical materialism as a kind of historicism (Marx did not think it was), and perhaps because he was unable completely to escape the influence of Croce, whom he called in 1917 "the greatest contemporary European thinker."

Concerning Croce's historical idealism, there can be no doubt. In the *Teoria e storia della storiografia* (*Theory and History of Historiography*, 1915), he defined the idealist conception this way:

> It is not a question of establishing, alongside others, an abstract individualist and pragmatic historiography, an abstract history of Spirit, of the abstract universal, but rather of understanding that the individual and the idea, taken separately, are two equivalent abstractions, that both are incapable of providing the subject of history, and that true history is the history of the individual as universal and of the universal as individual. The point is not to sacrifice Pericles in favor of Politics, or Plato in favor of Philosophy, or Sophocles in favor of Tragedy; it is rather to think and represent Politics, Philosophy, and Tragedy as Pericles, Plato, and Sophocles, and the latter as Politics, Philosophy, and Tragedy in particular moments. For if, outside the relation with Spirit the individual is the shadow of a dream, Spirit outside its individuations is also the shadow of a dream; and to attain universality in historical conception is at the same time to obtain individuality, and to make both of them solid thanks to the solidity that each confers on the other. If the existence of Pericles, Sophocles, and Plato were indifferent, wouldn't we have to proclaim that the Idea is indifferent as well? (1915:92–93)

And in his *Storia come pensiero e come azione* (History as Thought and as Action, 1938), after having criticized the rationalistic positivism of Ranke's "precisely what happened," he goes so far as to claim that "there is no unity other than that of thought itself, which distinguishes and unifies." As F. Chabod comments, "There is not unity *in itself*, but only in critical thought" (1927:511).

Arnaldo Momigliano has pointed out that Croce had little influence on philosophers: "No one can foresee whether Croce's philosophy will provide a starting point for future philosophers. He currently has few disciples in Italy, and perhaps none in other countries. Even Collingwood had ceased to be his disciple before his premature death" (1977:355).

Delio Cantimori has observed that professional historians have not considered most of Croce's work as history, even the works that bear the title *History of*... This was true of Federico Chabod, whom Croce had nevertheless made the director of the Istituto per gli Studi Storici (The Institute for Historical Studies) that he founded in Naples (1945:402).

I admit that I share Chabod's view, although it must be emphasized that Croce, unlike many philosophers of history who were "pure" philosophers, was also a genuine historian. On the other hand, I think Cantimori is right to stress a major advance in thinking about history that is largely due to Croce: the distinction between history and historiography.

> In the course of his multiple and diverse historiographical experiments and his reflections on historiographical work, Croce rediscovered and clearly transmitted to studies on history and historical questions, through the distinction between *res gestae* and *historia rerum gestarum*, the result of the great, fundamental, and in substance irreversible critical experiment of modern philosophy, which is knowledge of the known and not of the unknown. This does not mean that for Croce we should not do research in archives or on hitherto unknown materials, but on the contrary, that we must do so, and that only through the direct study of documents or a series of documents can we evaluate the importance and meaning of these materials.

Having discussed in detail the whole spectrum of the professional historian's procedures, Cantimori concludes, concerning Croce:

> We must not give up criticism (*historia rerum*), having the illusion that we can grasp the substance or essence of things as they actually occur and that we can know them once and for all (*res gestae*); for only such a critical distinction allows us to maintain a viewpoint from which we can follow the movement and the progress of societies and individuals, of men and things—and to know them as living and concrete, and not in the abstract and generically. (1945:406)

To this fundamental distinction we should add the fact that Croce also insisted on the importance of the history of historiography: "By taking an interest in the history of historiography, Croce indicated the necessity and the possibility of this second critical insight for historians, as a scale and a graduated measure, to attain, through the recognition of interpretations of their general cultural and social environment, an exposition and judgment that are well-informed and autonomous, that is, free from repetitions and tributes to metaphysics and to methods deriving not from technique and experience, but from philosophical and scholastic principles" (p. 407).

Antonio Gramsci (1891–1937) is said to have preached a flexible Marxism, and it is true that in his writings as in his political action we find considerable flexibility. But I do not think that his conceptions of history represent a progress in historical materialism. I see in them rather a certain return to Hegelianism, on the one hand, and a slipping into vulgar Marxism on the other. He recognizes, to be sure, that history does not function as a science, and that one cannot apply to it a mechanical conception of causality. But his famous theory of the "*historical unit*" (*bloco storico*) seems to me dangerous for historical science. The claim that infrastructure and superstructure form a historical unit, in other words, his statement that "the complex, contradictory, and discordant whole of the superstructure is the reflection of the whole of social relations" ("Materialismo storico," p. 39) has been generally understood as introducing more flexibility into the doctrine of the relations between infrastructure and superstructure that Marx had left relatively vague, and which seems to be the falsest, weakest, and most dangerous tenet of historical materialism, even if Marx did not reduce the infrastructure to economics. What Gramsci seems to abandon is the pejorative conception of ideology, but since he leaves ideology in the superstructure, the rehabilitation of ideology only increases the threat to the independence of the intellectual sector (but not to its autonomy, which clearly does not exist). Gramsci doubly reinforces the subordination of intellectual work. On one hand, alongside traditional intellectuals and organic intellectuals Gramsci recognizes as valid only those intellectuals who identify science and praxis, thus going beyond the links that Marx had outlined. Moreover, he includes science in the superstructure. At the origin of these modifications, one can see the Gramscian conception of historical materialism as an "absolute historicism."

Louis Althusser protested vehemently against the "historicist" interpretation of Marxism, which he linked to his "humanist" interpretation. He sees the historicist interpretation as arising from "the vital reaction against the mechanism and the economy of the Second International, in the period that preceded the revolution of 1917 and especially in the years that followed it."[56] This conception is both historicist and humanist (the two characteristics were discovered, according to Althusser, through historical contingency, but are not necessarily contingent from a theoretical point of view), and it was initially that of the German left, of Rosa Luxemburg and Mehring, and later, after the revolution of 1917, that of Lukács and especially of Gramsci, before being taken up again, in a certain way, by Sartre in his *Critique de la raison dialectique*. It is in the Italian Marxist tradition where Gramsci is the heir of Labriola and of Croce (Althusser tends to minimize the opposition between Gramsci and Croce) that Althusser finds the most prominent expressions of Marxism as "absolute historicism." He quotes the famous passage in Gramsci's note on Croce: "We have forgotten in the very common expression [of historical materialism] that we must put the accent on the first term, 'historical,' and not on the second, which is metaphysical in origin. The philosophy of praxis is absolute 'historicism,' the absolute bringing-down-to-earth and 'terrestriality' of thought, an absolute humanism of history" (1931/32:159). To be sure, Althusser recognizes the role of polemics in this text, but since he is not blackballing Gramsci, whose sincerity and revolutionary honesty seem to him above suspicion, he simply wants to deprive some of these occasional writings of any theoretical value. For him, it is an error to identify "the speculative genesis of the concept" with "the genesis of concrete reality itself," that is, with the process of "empirical" history. Gramsci was wrong to formulate "a truly 'historicist' conception of Marx, a 'historicist' conception of the relation between Marx's theory and real history." Althusser thinks we must distinguish between *historical materialism*, which can be seen as a theory of history, from dialectical materialism, which is a philosophy that escapes historicity. He is no doubt correct, as an interpreter of Marx, to make this distinction, but when he reproaches the "historicist" conception of Marxism with forgetting the absolute novelty, the "break" that Marxism is supposed to constitute because it is a science, "an ideology which this time is based on a science—*and that has never been seen before*," it is no longer clear if he is speaking of historical materialism or dialectical materialism, or both (19 2:73–108). It seems to me that by partially cutting Marxism off from history, Althusser makes it move toward metaphysics, toward belief rather than science. It is only through a constant oscillation between praxis and science, each nourishing the other while remaining carefully distinct, that scientific history could disengage itself from lived history, an indispensable condition for the historical discipline's achievement of scientific status. Where Althusser's critique of Gramsci seems to me particularly pertinent is when, in discussing "Gramsci's amazing pages on science" ("Science is also a superstructure, an ideology," Gramsci, "Materialismo storico," p. 56), he reminds us that Marx rejects a broad application of the concept of superstructure, which is valid only for the juridico-political superstructure and the ideological superstructure (the corresponding "forms of social consciousness"), and that in particular "Marx *never includes . . . scientific knowledge in it*" (2:92). Thus what might be positive about the

Gramscian interpretation of historical materialism as historicism—in spite of the dangers of the various kinds of fetishization that it implies—is negated by his conception of science as superstructural. History—the two senses of the word being conflated—also becomes "organic," the expression and instrument of the group in power. The philosophy of history is pushed to its culmination: history and philosophy are conflated, thus forming another kind of "historical unit": "The philosophy of a historical epoch is therefore nothing other than 'the history' of that same epoch, which the mass of variations that the group in power has succeeded in determining in the preceding reality: in this sense history and philosophy are indivisible, and form a 'unit'" ("Materialismo storico," p. 21).

It seems to me that Galvano della Volpe's "historical" rather than "historicist" interpretation of the Marxian and Marxist dialectic is closer to the relations that Marx established between history and the theory of the historical process: "The only contradictions (or rather the contraries) that interest Marx, from the point of view of resolving them or transcending them in their unity, are the *real* ones; they are precisely historical, or rather, historically determined or specific contradictions"[57]

I shall now briefly discuss two conceptions of history that I mention only for the impact they have had in the recent past—particularly among the general public.

Oswald Spengler (1880–1936) reacted against the ideology of progress, and in *The Decline of the West* (1916–1920) he presents a biological theory of history, constituted by civilizations that are "living entities of the highest rank," whereas individuals exist only insofar as they participate in these living entities. There are two phases in the life of societies: the cultural phase which corresponds to their rise and apogee, and the civilization phase that corresponds to their decline and death (see Le Goff 1978 4:389–420). Spengler thus rediscovers the cyclical conceptions of history. Arnold Toynbee (1889–1978), on the other hand, was a historian. In *A Study of History*, he starts out from Spengler hoping to succeed where his predecessor had failed. He distinguishes twenty-one civilizations that have attained a stage of full development in the course of history from cultures that have achieved only a lesser level of development. All these civilizations pass through four phases: a brief genesis during which the new civilization is subject to a *challenge* (usually from the outside) and gives its *response*, a long period of growth, then a halt—marked by an accident, and finally a phase of disintegration which may be very long.[58] This schema is "progressive," "open," at the level of humanity. In reality, alongside this history consisting in a succession of cycles another history exists, a "Providential" history, in which humanity as a whole is proceeding toward a *transfiguration* that reveals "the historian's theology." Thus Toynbee combines a Spenglerian theory with an Augustinian conception of history. Critics have rightly objected not only to the "metaphysical" aspect of this conception, but also to its arbitrary and confused distinction between civilizations and cultures, Toynbee's imperfect knowledge of several of these civilizations and cultures, the illegitimate nature of the comparisons made between them, and so on. Raymond Aron has nevertheless emphasized Toynbee's chief merit: the desire to escape a Eurocentric, Westernizing history. "Spengler tried to refute the rationalist optimism of the West, on the basis of a biological philosophy and a Nietzschean conception of heroism; Toynbee tried to refute the provincial pride of Western peoples" (p. 76).

Michel Foucault plays an exceptional role in the history of history, for three reasons.

First, because he was one of the greatest of the new historians: the historian of madness, of psychiatry, of penology and prisons, and finally of sexuality, he introduced some of the most "provocative" new objects of history and revealed one of the great turning points in Western history at the end of the Middle Ages and in the nineteenth century: the sequestering (*le grand renfermement*) of "deviants."

Second, because he offered the most perspicacious diagnosis of this renovation of history, which he sees as taking four forms:

1. "The questioning of the document": "History in its traditional form undertook to 'memorize' the *monuments* of the past, to transform them into *documents* and to make these traces speak, although they are often not verbal, or silently express something other than what they say; in our time history is what transforms *documents* into *monuments*, and in the place where one used to decipher the traces left by men, where one tried to recognize the image of what they had been, it now deploys a mass of elements that it tries to isolate, group, make pertinent, to put into relationships, and to constitute as wholes" (1969:13–15).
2. "The notion of discontinuity takes on a major role in the historical disciplines" (p. 16).

3. The theme of the possibility of a complete, global history begins to fade away, and one sees emerging the very different design of what might be called a *general* history determining "what form of relationship between the differing series can legitimately be described" (pp. 17–18).
4. New methods. "The new history encounters a certain number of methodological problems, several of which no doubt considerably precede it, but which as a group now characterize it. Among them, we may mention: the constitution of coherent and homogenous collections of documents (open or closed collections, delimited or indefinite), the establishment of a principle for choosing (according to whether one is attempting to deal exhaustively with the body of documents, to sample it using statistical methods, or to determine in advance the most representative elements); the definition of the level of analysis and of the elements that are pertinent to it (in the materials studied, one may note numerical indications; references—explicit or not—to events, to institutions, to practices; the words used, with the rules governing their use and the semantic fields that they outline, or the formal structure of the propositions and the ways they are linked to each other); the specification of a method of analysis (quantitative treatment of the data, their breakdown in accordance with assignable traits whose correlations may be studied, interpretive deciphering, analysis of frequencies and distributions); the delimitation of the units and subunits that articulate the material studied (regions, periods, unitary processes); the determination of the relations that allow us to characterize a unit (it can be a matter of numerical or logical relations; of functional, causal, or analogical relations; or of the relation of the signifier to the signified. (pp. 19–20)

Foucault proposed an original philosophy of history closely linked with practice and with the methodology of the historical discipline. I leave the task of characterizing it to Paul Veyne:

> For Foucault, the interest of history does not lie in the elaboration of invariants, whether the latter are philosophical or organized in human sciences, but rather in using the invariants, whatever they might be, to dissolve the constantly recurring forms of rationalism. History is a Nietzschean genealogy. That is why for Foucault, history is a kind of philosophy (which is neither true nor false); in any case, it is very far

> from the positivist vocation traditionally attributed to history. "Let no one enter here who is not, or is not becoming, a philosopher." A history written in abstract words rather than in the language of the period, still bearing local color; a history that seems to find partial analogies everywhere, to outline typologies, for a history written in a network of abstract words presents less picturesque diversity than an anecdotal narrative. (1978:378)

Foucauldian genealogical history thus completely fulfills the program of traditional history; it does not neglect society, economy, etc., but it structures this material differently: not in terms of periods, peoples, or civilizations, but in terms of practices; the plots that are recounted are the history of practices in which people have seen truths, and of their struggles concerning these truths. This new model history, this "archeology," as its inventor calls it, "is deployed in the dimension of a general history" (*L'Archéologie du savoir*, p. 215); "It does not specialize in practice, discourse, the hidden part of the iceberg, or rather, the hidden part of discourse and of practice is inseparable from the visible part" (Veyne 1978:284–385). "Every history is archeological by nature and not by choice: explaining and clarifying history consists in seeing it first as a whole, in relating the so-called natural objects to the dated and rare practices that objectivize them, and in explaining these practices, not on the basis of a single source or motor, but on the basis of all the neighboring practices in which they are anchored" (p. 385).

History as a Science: The Historian's Craft

The best proof that history is and must be a science is that it needs techniques and methods, and that it can be taught. Lucien Febvre said more restrictively: "I describe history as a scientifically conducted study, not a science." The strictest theoreticians of so-called positivist history, Charles V. Langlois and Charles Seignobos, expressed in a striking formula that constitutes history's fundamental creed, what is at the basis of historical science: "No documents, no history" (p. 2).

However, the difficulty begins here. If the document is easier to define and to locate than the historical fact, which is never given as such but constructed, it nevertheless poses serious problems for the historian. First, it becomes a document only as the result of an investigation and a choice. The investigation is in general not the historian's own task, but that of auxiliaries that bring together the collection of documents in which the historian finds his documentation: archives, archeological excavations, museums, libraries, etc. The losses, the choices made by the collectors of documents, the quality of the documentation, are the objective but constraining conditions of the historian's craft. More delicate are the problems that are posed for the historian himself on the basis of this documentation.

The historian has first of all to decide what he will consider as a document and what he will reject. For a long time, historians thought that the true historical documents were those that illuminated that part of human history which was worthy of being preserved, reported, and studied, the history of great events (the lives of great men, military and diplomatic events: battles and treaties), political and institutional history. On the other hand, the idea that the birth of history was linked to that of writing led to a privileging of the written document. No one magnified the text as the historical document more than Fustel de Coulanges did. In 1888, in *La Monarchie franque*, the third volume of his *Histoire des Institutions politiques de l'ancienne France*, he wrote:

> Laws, charters, formulas, chronicles and histories—we have to read all these categories of documents, without omitting a single one.... [The historian] has no other ambition than to see the facts clearly and understand them correctly. He does not seek them in his imagination or in his logic; he seeks and finds them through the careful, detailed observation of texts, just as the chemist finds his in carefully conducted experiments. His only special ability consists in drawing from the documents everything that they contain and in not adding anything to them that they do not contain. The best of all historians is the one who keeps closest to the texts, who interprets them the most judiciously, who does not write or even think except in accordance with them.

In 1862, however, in a lecture at the University of Strasbourg, Fustel had declared:

> Where written documents are lacking in history, history has to ask dead languages to reveal their secrets, and in their forms and words it has to divine the thoughts of the people who spoke them. History has to examine fables, myths, the dreams of the imagination, all those old falsehoods underneath which it must discover something very real, human beliefs. Where man has passed, where he has left some imprint of his life and his intelligence, there is history.[59]

The whole renewal of history we are currently living through was directed against Fustel's ideas of 1888. I shall not discuss here the dangerous naivete which led to passivity with respect to documents. Documents respond only to the historian's questions; he must not approach them, of course, with prejudices and fixed ideas, but rather with working hypotheses. Let us be grateful that Fustel, the great historian that he was, did not in fact work according to the method that he himself recommended in 1888. I shall not emphasize again the necessity of historical imagination.

What I want to stress here is the multiform character of historical documentation. In 1949, replying to Fustel de Coulanges, Lucien Febvre asserted:

> History is written with written documents; that is clear. When there are any. But it can be written, it has to be written, without written documents, if there are none. With everything the historian's ingenuity can find to make his honey, lacking the usual flowers. Thus, with words, signs, landscapes, and tiles. With kinds and shapes of fields and weeds. With lunar eclipses and horse collars. With geologists' expertise in stones and chemists' analyses of metal swords. In a word, with everything which, belonging to man, depends on man, serves man, expresses man, signifies man's presence, activity, tastes, and ways of being. (1933: 428)

And Marc Bloch also declared: "The diversity of historical testimony is almost infinite. Everything that man says or writes, everything he makes, everything he touches can and must teach us about him" (p. 63).

I shall come back to the enormous expansion of historical documentation today, which has come about especially through the increase in audiovisual documentation, the use of graphic or properly iconographic documents, etc. Here I want to stress two particular aspects of this extension of documentary research.

The first concerns archeology. I am not concerned here with the question as to whether it is a science auxiliary to history or an independent science. I note only how much its development has contributed to the renewal of history. When it made its first advances in the eighteenth century, it immediately conquered for history the vast territory of prehistory and protohistory, and renewed ancient history. Intimately connected with the history of art and of technology, it is a key part of the broadening of historical culture expressed in *L'Encyclopédie*. Pierre Duval points out that "It is in France that the 'antiquarians' accord, for the first time, the archeological document, the *objet d'art*, the tool or vestige of a construction, an intense as well as objective and disinterested attention."[60] Duval emphasizes the role of Peiresc (1580–1637), a councilor at the Parlement of Aix, but it was the English who founded in London the first scientific society in which archeology played an essential role, the Society of Antiquaries (1707); in Italy, the first excavations were begun that concern the archeological discovery of the past, at Herculaneum (1738) and at Pompeii (1748); it was a German and a Frenchman who published the two most important eighteenth-century works concerning the use of archeological evidence in history: Winckelmann in his *History of Ancient Art* (1764) and the Comte de Caylus in his *Recueil d'antiquités égyptiennes, étrusques, grecques, romaines et gauloises* (1752–1767). In France, the Musée des Monuments Français, of which Alexandre Lenoir was the first conservator in 1796, awakened a taste for archeology and contributed to the overturning of the negative view of the Middle Ages. Archeology is one of the areas of historical science that has been most fully renovated in recent decades: interest shifted first from the object and the monument to the overall site, whether urban or rural, and then to the landscape, rural and industrial archeology, quantitative methods, etc.[61] Archeology has also developed toward the constitution of a history of material culture, which is first of all "the history of the great mass and of the majority of men,"[62] which has already inspired a masterpiece of contemporary historiography: Fernand Braudel's *Civilisation matérielle et capitalisme* (1980).

I also note that historical reflection today is just as interested in the lack of documents, in the silences of history. Michel de Certeau has subtly analyzed the historian's "deviations" toward these "zones of silence"; the examples he gives are "sorcery, madness, the festival, popular literature, the forgotten world of the peasant, Occitania, etc." (1974:27). But he is speaking here about the silences of traditional historiography, whereas we must go further, I believe, to question historical documentation itself concerning its lacunae, and to ask ourselves about the holes and blank spots in history, the things it has forgotten. We have to inventory the archives of silence, and write history on the basis of documents and the absence of documents.

History has become scientific by carrying out a critique of the documents that are known as "sources." Paul Veyne is perfectly correct in saying that history must be "a struggle against the perspective imposed by the sources," and that "true problems of historical epistemology are problems of criticism and the center of all reflection on historical knowledge should be this: historical knowledge is what sources make of it" (1971:265–66). Veyne adds to this observation the remark that "the historian cannot improvise . . . one has to know what questions to ask himself, and what problematics are outdated; one cannot write political, social or religious history with the respectable, realistic, or advanced ideas that one may have on these subjects as a private individual."

Historians have, especially from the seventeenth to the nineteenth centuries, developed a criticism of documents that is today established and remains necessary, but which reveals itself to be insufficient (see Salmon 1969 2:85–140). Traditionally, an external criticism or criticism of authenticity is distinguished from an internal criticism or criticism of credibility.

The goal of external criticism is essentially to find the *original* and to determine whether the document one is examining is authentic or false. It is a fundamental procedure. It nevertheless requires us to make two complementary observations. The first is that a "false" document is also a historical document that can provide valuable testimony regarding the period in which it was forged and concerning the period during which it was considered to be authentic and used. The second is that a document, and particularly a text, may over the course of time undergo apparently scientific manipulations that have in reality obliterated the original. For example, it has been brilliantly demonstrated that the letter from Epicurus to Herodotus that is preserved in Diogenes Laertius' *Lives, Teachings, and Apophthegms of the Famous Philosophers* was reworked by a secular tradition that buried the letter of the text under the annotations and corrections which, whether intentionally or not, finally stifled and distorted the letter of the text through "a reading that was uncomprehending, indifferent, or partisan."[63]

Internal criticism is supposed to interpret the meaning of the document, to assess the competence of its author, determine his sincerity, measure the exactness of the document, and test it against other evidence. Here again, and here especially, the program is insufficient. Whether we are concerned with documents that are conscious or unconscious (traces left by men without any intention to leave a message for posterity) the conditions under which the document was *produced* must be carefully studied. In fact, the structures of power in a society include the power of certain social categories and dominant groups to voluntarily or involuntarily leave behind them testimony that can orient historiography in one direction or another. Power over future memory, the power to perpetuate, must be recognized and defused by the historian. No document is innocent. It must be judged. Every document is testimony or evidence (*monument*) which we have to know how to destructure, to take apart. The historian must be able, not simply to discern a fake, to judge the credibility of a document, but also to demystify it. Documents become historical sources only after having undergone a treatment whose purpose is to transform their mendacious function into a confession of the truth.[64]

Jean Bazin, analyzing the production of a "historical narrative"—the story of the advent of a famous king of Segou (Mali) at the beginning of the nineteenth century, told by a Muslim man of letters passionately interested in history—warns that "because it presents itself as not being fiction, a historical narrative is always a trap: it can easily be believed that its object takes the place of meaning, that it says nothing besides what it recounts," whereas in reality "one historical lesson conceals another, political or ethical lesson, which remains, so to speak, to be realized" (1979:446). Therefore it is necessary to study, with the aid of a "sociology of narrative production," the "conditions of historicization." It is necessary on one hand to know the status of the storytellers (and this remark is valid for the various types of producers of documents and for the historians themselves in the different kinds of societies), and on the other to recognize the signs of power, for "this kind of story depends rather on a metaphysics of power." Concerning the first point, Bazin observes that "the specialists in narrative occupy, between the sovereign and his dependents, a sort of third position of illusory neutrality: they are constantly invited by both sides to construct the image which the sovereign's dependents have of him as well as that which the sovereign has of his dependents" (p. 456). Bazin compares his work with Louis Marin's analysis of the "Projet de l'Histoire de Louis XIV" by means of which Pellisson tried to obtain the office of official historiographer: "The king needs the historian, because political power cannot be complete, cannot be absolute, unless a certain use of force is the point on which the force of *narrative* power is brought to bear" (Marin 1979:26; cf. Marin 1978).

The development of methods making history a craft and a science was a long process and is still going on. It has experienced, in the West, pauses, delays, and accelerations, sometimes regressions; it has not progressed at the same speed in all areas, and has not always given the same meaning to the terms used to define its objectives, even the apparently most "objective" term, "truth." I shall follow the main lines of its evolution from the double point of view of conceptions and methods on one hand, and instruments of research on the other. The essential stages seem to me to be the Greco-Roman period from the sixth to the fifth centuries B.C., which invented "historical discourse," the concept of testimony, and the logic of history, and founded history on truth; the fourth century A.D., in which Christianity eliminates the idea of blind chance, gives a meaning and direction to history, disseminates a concept of time and a periodization of history; the Renaissance, which begins by outlining a critique of documents based on philology and ends with the conception of a complete history; the seventeenth century, which, with the Bollandists and the Benedictines of Saint-Maur, lays the foundations for modern scholarship; the eighteenth century, which creates the first institutions devoted to history and broadens the field of historical curiosity. The nineteenth century perfects the methods of scholarship, establishes the bases of historical documentation, and spreads history into every domain; in the second half of the twentieth century, from the 1930s onward, history is both fashionable and in crisis, the historian's territory is considerably expanded, and there is a revolution in documentation. I shall devote the last part of this essay to this recent phase in historical science.

It should moreover not be thought that during the long stretches of time in which historical science made no qualitative advance the development of the historian's craft was equally stagnant (for a brilliant study of this problem in the Middle Ages, see Bernard Guenée, 1979 and 1980). With Herodotus, the importance of testimony makes its entry into historical narrative. For him, testimony *par excellence* is personal testimony, the kind in which the historian can say: "I saw, I heard." This is particularly true for the part of his investigation devoted to the barbarians, through whose territory he traveled on his voyages (see F. Hartog). It is also true for the narrative of the Median wars, events that occurred during the generation that preceded his, and about which he was able to collect hearsay testimony. This primacy accorded oral and eyewitness testimony remained in history; it retreated more or less into the background when the critique of written documents from the distant past took the center of the stage, but had several important later revivals. Thus in the thirteenth century members of the new mendicant orders, the Dominicans and the Franciscans, in their desire to "adhere" to the new society, privileged personal oral testimony, contemporary or very recent, preferring, for example, to insert into their sermons *exempla* whose subject matter was drawn from their own experience (*audivi*, I have heard it said) rather than from their bookish learning (*legimus*, we read). *Memoirs* nevertheless gradually became neighbors of history rather than history itself, the authors' complacency with regard to themselves, their quest for literary effect, and the taste for pure narration, all making them different from history and making historians regard this material as relatively suspect. Jean Ehrard and Guy Palmade acknowledge that "It is possible to group historians and memorialists together in a purely literary perspective," but they exclude the genre of *Memoirs* from their excellent study and collection of texts on *History* (p.7). Testimony tends to reenter the historical domain, and in any case poses problems for the historian, with the development of the "media": in journalism, the rise of "immediate history," and the "return of the event" (Lacouture 1978:270–93; Nora 1984 1:210–28).

Arnaldo Momigliano has emphasized that the "great" historians of Greco-Roman antiquity dealt exclusively or preferentially with the recent past. After Herodotus, Thucydides wrote the history of the Peloponnesian War, a contemporary event, Xenophon dealt with the Spartan and Theban hegemonies, which he had witnessed first hand (404–362 B.C.), Polybius devoted his *Histories* chiefly to the period from the Second Punic War (218 B.C.) to his own time (c. 145 B.C.), Sallust and Livy did the same, Tacitus went back to the century preceding his own and Ammianus Marcellinus was interested especially in the second half of the fourth century. Nevertheless, from the fifth century B.C. onward, ancient historians were capable of collecting good documentation on the past, but that did not prevent them from being primarily interested in contemporary or recent events (1977:161—63).

The primacy accorded eyewitness or directly recorded testimony did not keep ancient historians from trying to criticize such testimony. Thus Thucydides:

> As for the narrative of the events of the war, in writing it I have not felt obligated to trust either the information provided by the first person who came along or my own personal conjectures; I speak only as an eyewitness or after making a critique as attentive and as complete as possible of my information. That was not achieved without difficulty, since for each event, the testimony diverges according to the sympathies and the memory of each individual. In listening to me one may well miss myth and its charms. But for anyone who wants to

> clearly understand the history of the past and to recognize in the future the resemblances and the analogies that proceed from the human condition, it will suffice if he thinks he has derived some profit from it. It is a permanent acquisition rather than a work designed to please an audience of the moment. (*Peloponnesian War*, 1:22)

With Polybius, it is more than a logic of history that is the historian's goal. It is the search for causes. Concerned about method, Polybius devotes the whole of the twelfth book of his *Histories* to defining the work of the historian through a critique of Timaeus. He had already defined his objective: to write, instead of a monographic history, a general, synthetic, and comparatist history. "No one, at least to my knowledge, has tried to verify the general and total structure of past facts.... It is only by starting from the relation and the comparison of all the facts with each other, from their resemblances and differences, that one can, after examination, draw profit and pleasure from history" (1:4). And we should especially note the essential assertion that "One must attach less importance, when writing or reading history, to the narrative of the facts in themselves, than to what has preceded, accompanied, and followed the events; for if one takes away from history the 'why,' the 'how,' the reason why the act was accomplished and its logical end, what remains is no more than a piece of bravado and cannot become an object of study; it may amuse us at the moment, but it is absolutely useless in the future.... I affirm that the most necessary elements of history are the consequences, the accompaniments of facts, and especially the causes" (Polybius, III, 31, 11–13, and 32, 6). That said, it must not be forgotten that Polybius places the notion of Fortune in the first rank of historical causality, that his chief criterion for judging testimony or sources is moral in character, and that discourses play an important role in his work (see Pedech). Above all, the ancient historians founded history on truth. "The historian's essential task is to recount history in accordance with the truth," Polybius assures us. And Cicero gives the definitions that remained valid during the Middle Ages and the Renaissance. Particularly this one: "Who does not know that the first law of history is not to say anything false? and next, to say everything that is true?"[65] And it is often forgotten that in the celebrated apostrophe (generally not quoted in full) where he claims for the orator the privilege of being the best interpreter of history, of being the one who ensures his immortality, and where he launches his famous definition of history as "the teacher of life" (*magistra vitae*), Cicero calls history the "light of truth."[66]

Although Momigliano has correctly stressed the ancient historians' predilection for recent history, we should not exaggerate as Collingwood does: "Their method tied them on a tether whose length was the length of living memory" (1932:26). Tacitus, for example, praises the moderns—and this runs counter to the Roman tradition—but shows his knowledge and chronological mastery of the past, of a past that in fact he flattens out and brings into relation with the present:

> When I hear people talk about the ancients, I think of people of a distant past, born long before we were, and Ulysses and Nestor present themselves before my eyes, though they lived thirteen hundred years before our age; you quote Demosthenes and Hyperides to me; now it is certain that they were contemporaries of Philip and Alexander, whom they both even outlived. From this we can conclude that not much more than three hundred years have passed between our period and that of Demosthenes. This interval, compared with the weakness of our bodies, no doubt seems long; compared with the true duration of the centuries and with the consideration of time which has no limits, it is very short and puts Demosthenes very near us. In fact, if, as Cicero has written in his *Hortensius*, the great, the true year is the one in which the precise present position of the heavens and the stars will reoccur, and if that year comprises twelve thousand nine hundred fifty-four of the divisions we call years, it follows that your Demosthenes, whom you put in the past and among the ancients, has lived in the same year, and I should say, even the same month, as we. (*Dialogue des orateurs*, XV)

More than the goal given to history, what seems to me important about Christian historiography, from the point of view of the historian's equipment and methods, is its impact on chronology. Of course, the latter was first elaborated by the ancient historians—in general, those who are not considered to be among the greatest—that the Christian historians used. Diodorus Siculus (first century B.C.) made a concordance of the consular years and the Olympiads. Trogus Pompeius (first century A.D.), known through Justinian's summary (second or third century A.D.), presented the theme of the four successive empires. But the first Christian historians had a decisive influence on historical work and on the chronological framework of history.

Eusebius of Caesarea, the author of a *Chronicle* at the beginning of the fourth century, then of an *Ecclesiastical History*, was "the first ancient historian to show the same attention as a modern historian in faithfully quoting the copied material and in correctly identifying his sources."[67]

This critical way of using documents allowed Eusebius and his successors safely to go back beyond the memory of living witnesses. More generally, Eusebius, whose work is a patient, scrupulous, and above all profoundly human attempt to deal with the relations between Christianity and the temporal world (Sirinelli 1961:495), did not seek to privilege a properly Christian chronology; Hebraic-Christian history, which he makes begin with Moses, was for him only one history among others (pp. 59–61), and "his somewhat ambiguous project of a synchronic history is situated between an ecumenical view and a simple improvement in scholarship" (p. 63).

The Christian historians borrow from the Old Testament (Daniel's dream, Daniel 7) and from Justinian the theme of the succession of the four empires: Babylonian, Persian, Macedonian, and Roman. Eusebius, whose chronicle was taken up and completed by Saint Jerome and Saint Augustine, set forth a periodization of history according to biblical history, which distinguished six ages (up to Noah, up to Abraham, up to David, up the Babylonian captivity, up to Christ, after Christ), which Isidore of Seville, at the beginning of the seventh century,[68] and Bede, at the beginning of the eighth century, sought to calculate.

The problems of dating and chronology are essential for the historian. Here again ancient historians and societies had laid the foundations. The Babylonian and Egyptian lists of kings had provided the first chronological frameworks. The practice of conceiving time in terms of the years of a reign had made its appearance in Babylon around 2000 B.C. In 776 B.C. the computation by the Olympiads begins: in 754 the list of the Spartan ephors, in 686–685 that of the eponymous archons of Athens, in 508 the consular computation in Rome. In 45 B.C., Caesar instituted the Julian calendar in Rome. Christian ecclesiastical computation of time focuses particularly on the dating of Easter. Some doubts remained for a long time, for example, concerning the establishment of the beginning of the chronology and the beginning of the year. The acts of the Nicean Council are dated both by the names of the consuls and by the years of the era of the Seleucidae (312–311 B.C.). The Latin Christians in general first adopted the era of Diocletian or of the martyrs (A.D. 284). But in the sixth century the Roman monk Denis the Little proposed to adopt the age of the Incarnation, and to establish the birth of Christ as the beginning of chronology.[69] This was not definitively adopted until the eleventh century. But all the research on ecclesiastical computation, whose most remarkable expression was Bede's treatise *De temporum ra-*

tione (725), despite its hesitations and failures, constituted an important stage on the way toward mastery over time (see Le Goff, "Calendario," in *Enciclopedia Einaudi* (1977), 2:501–534; Cordoliani 1961; Guenée 1980:147–65).

Bernard Guenée has shown that the Western Middle Ages had "historians determined to reconstruct their past and possessed of a lucid erudition." These historians, who until the twelfth century were usually monks, first of all benefited from a growth in documentation. We have seen that archives are a very ancient phenomenon, but the Middle Ages accumulated titles and documents in monasteries, churches, and the royal administration, and founded numerous libraries. Dossiers were established, the system of references designating book and chapter became general, notably under the influence of Gratian, the author of a compilation of canon law, the *Concordia Discordantium Canonorum*, also known as the *Decretum Gratiani*, in Bologna (c. 1140), and of the theologian Pierre Lombard, the Bishop of Paris, who died in 1160. It can be said that the end of the eleventh century and most of the twelfth century were "the time of a triumphant erudition." Scholasticism and the universities, which were indifferent and even hostile to history, which was not taught (Borst 1969) marked a certain regression of historical culture. However, "a vast lay public continued to love history," and at the end of the Middle Ages these enthusiasts, knights or merchants, became more numerous and the taste for national history came to the fore at the same time that states and nations were asserting themselves. All the same, the place of history in the realm of knowledge remained a modest one; up until the fifteenth century it was considered only a science auxiliary to morals, law, and especially theology (see W. Lammers), although Hugh of St. Victor, in the first half of the twelfth century, said in a remarkable text that it was "the foundation of all science."[70] But the Middle Ages did not represent a hiatus in the evolution of historical science; on the contrary, it is characterized by "the continuity of the historical effort" (Guenée, p. 367).

The Renaissance historians rendered a few eminent services to historical science: they began the critique of documents with the help of philology, they began to "secularize" history and to rid it of myths and legends, and they laid the foundations of the sciences auxiliary to history and cemented the alliance of history with erudition.

Scientific criticism of texts has been traced back to Lorenzo Valla (1405–1457), who proved, in *De falso credita e ementita Constantini dona-*

tione desclaratio (1440), written at the behest of the Aragonese king of Naples battling against the Holy See, that the "Donation of Constantine" was a forgery, since the language of the text was not that of the fourth century but dated from four or five centuries later. Thus the pope's claims to the Papal States founded on Constantine's alleged donation to Pope Silvester were based on a Carolingian forgery. "In this way history as philology, or as the conscious critique of oneself and of others, was born" (Garin, p. 115). Valla also applied textual criticism to ancient historians (Livy, Herodotus, Thucydides, Sallust) and even to the New Testament, in his *Annotationes*; Erasmus wrote a preface for the 1505 Paris edition of this work. But Valla's biography of the father of his protector, the *History of Ferdinand the First, King of Aragon*, completed in 1445 and published in Paris in 1521, is no more than a series of anecdotes dealing primarily with the king's private life (Gaeta 1958).

It has been written that "just as Biondo is the chief scholar among the humanist historians, so Valla is the chief critic." I am not sure—after Bernard Guenée's work—that one can defend such a summary formulation. Biondo, in his manuals on ancient Rome (*Roma instaurata*, 1446, printed in 1471; *Roma triumphans*, 1459, printed c. 1472) and in his *Decades*, a history of the Middle Ages from 412 to 1440, was a great collector of sources, but in these works there is neither a critique of sources nor a sense of history. The documents are published alongside each other, at most (in the *Decades*) in chronological order, but Biondo, the pope's secretary, was the first to include archeology in historical documentation.

As early as the fifteenth century the humanist historians inaugurated a secular historical science disencumbered of fables and supernatural interventions. The great name here is that of Leonardo Bruni (1369–1444), the chancellor of Florence, whose *History of Florence* (up to 1404) does not mention the legends concerning the city's foundation, and never speaks of Providential intervention. "With him the way is opened toward a natural explanation of history" (Fueter 1:20), and Hans Baron has described this as the "profanation" (*Profanierung*) of history.

The rejection of pseudo-historical myths gave rise to a long polemic concerning the alleged Trojan origin of the Franks. By turns, Étienne Pasquier, in his *Recherches de la France* (Book I, 1560; ten books in the posthumous edition of 1621), François Hotman in his *Franco-Gallia* (1573), Claude Fauchet in his *Antiquités gauloises et françaises jusqu'à Clovis* (1599), and Lancelot de la Popelinière in his *Dessein de l'histoire nouvelle des François* (1599), all question the Trojan origin of the Franks, and Hotman maintains persuasively that they were of Germanic origin.

The role of the Reformation in these advances in historical method should be emphasized. By arousing spirited debates on the history of Christianity, and by freeing themselves from the ecclesiastical authoritarian tradition, the Reformers contributed to the evolution of historical science.

Sixteenth-century historians, and especially the French historians of the second half of the century, bore forward the torch of scholarship passed on to them by the Italian humanists of the Quattrocento. Guillaume Budé made an important contribution to numismatics with his treatise on Roman coins (*De asse*, 1514). Joseph Juste Scaliger (1540–1609) dealt with chronology in his *De emendatione temporum* (1583). The Protestant Isaac Casaubon (1559–1614), the "phoenix of scholars," responded to *Annales ecclésiastiques* of the very Catholic Cardinal Caesar Baronius (1538–1607) in his *Emendationes* (1612), the Fleming Justus Lipsius (1547–1606) also enriched historical scholarship, notably in the areas of philology and numismatics. Numerous dictionaries were published, including Robert Estienne's *Thesaurus linguæ latinæ* (1531) and his son Henri's *Thesaurus linguæ graecæ* (1572), the Fleming Grüter (1560–1627) published the first *Corpus* of inscriptions, for which Scaliger made the index. Finally, we must not forget that the sixteenth century contributed the concept of *century* to historical periodization (Le Goff 1978).

Whereas the humanists—emulating Antiquity—had kept history, despite the advances in scholarship, within the domain of literature, a few of the great historians of the sixteenth and the beginning of the seventeenth centuries explicitly distinguish themselves from men of letters. Many of these are jurists (Bodin, Vignier, Hotman, et al.), and these "learned men of the robe" anticipate the history of the "philosophes" of the eighteenth century (Huppert 1970:188). Donald Kelley has shown that the history of the origins and nature of feudalism does not date from Montesquieu but from scholarly debates in the sixteenth century.[71]

The new history that the great humanists of the end of the sixteenth and beginning of the seventeenth centuries wanted to promote was bitterly opposed in the first part of the sixteenth century, and ranked among the manifestations of libertinism. The result was the growing gap between scholarship and history (in the sense of historiography) noted by Paul Hazard.[72] Scholarship made decisive advances during the century of Louis XIV, whereas history underwent a near-total eclipse.

"The scholars of the seventeenth century were not interested in the great questions of general history. They compiled glossaries, like the great royal officer Du Cange (1610–1688). Like Mabillon, they wrote lives of the saints. They published sources on medieval history, like Baluze (1630–1718). They studied coins, like Vaillant (1632–1706). In short, they tended toward antiquarian research much more than toward historical research" (Huppert, p. 185).

Two projects took on particular importance. They are situated in the framework of a *collective* investigation: "the great novelty is that under the reign of Louis XIV, scholarship began to be pursued collectively" (G. Lefebvre, p. 101). This was in fact one of the conditions required by scholarship.

The first of these projects was produced by Jesuits; its initiator was Father Heribert Rosweyde (d. Antwerp, 1629), who had established a sort of repertory of manuscripts of saints' lives preserved in Belgian libraries. On the basis of these papers, Father Jean Bolland persuaded his superiors to approve a plan to publish saints' lives and hagiographic documents in calendrical order. Thus a group of Jesuits specializing in hagiography was established; they were known as "Bollandists" and in the month of January 1643 they published the first two volumes in the *Acta Sanctorum*. The Bollandists are still very active today in an area that has never ceased to be in the forefront of scholarship and historical research. In April 1675, a Bollandist, Father Daniel Van Papebroch, published in the second volume of the *Acta Sanctorum* a dissertation "on the discernment of the true and the false in old parchments." Papebroch's application of his method was not successful. It remained for a French Benedictine, Jean Mabillon, to be the true founder of "diplomatics."

Mabillon belonged to the other team that gave scholarship its aristocratic status, that of the Benedictines of the reformed congregation of Saint-Maur, who made Saint-Germain-des-Prés in Paris the "citadel of French scholarship." Their research program had been laid out in 1648 by Luc d'Achery. Their domain included the Greek and Latin Church Fathers, Church history, and the history of the Benedictine order. To refute Papebroch, Mabillon published in 1681 his *De re diplomatica*, which laid down the rules of diplomatics (the study of "diplomas") and the criteria that allow one to discern the authenticity of public or private documents. Marc Bloch, not without a certain exaggeration, sees in "1681, the year of the publication of *De re diplomatica*, a great date in the history of the human spirit" (p. 77). Mabillon's work teaches notably that the agreement of two independent sources establishes the truth, and taking his inspiration from Descartes, he applies the principle of "everywhere making enumerations so complete and so general" that one can be "sure of not having omitted anything."[73]

Two anecdotes have been recorded that show how profound the divorce between history and scholarship had become by the turn of the eighteenth century. When Father Daniel, the official historiographer of Louis XIV, whom Fueter nevertheless calls a "conscientious worker," was preparing to write his *History of the French militia* (1721), he was taken to the royal library and shown 1200 works that might prove useful to him. He looked through a certain number of them for an hour or so, and then declared that "all these documents were so many useless scribblings which he did not need to write his history." The abbé de Vertot (1655–1735) was about to finish a work on the Turks' siege of Rhodes. New documents were brought to him. He refused to take them, saying, "My siege is done."

This scholarly work went on and extended into the eighteenth century. Historical research, having become drowsy, awakened, notably on the occasion of the debate concerning the origins—whether Germanic or Roman—of French society and institutions. Historians began once again to search for causes, but they combined concern for scholarship with this intellectual reflection. This alliance justifies—although it is somewhat unjust concerning the sixteenth century—Collingwood's opinion: "In the strict sense in which Gibbon and Mommsen are historians, there are no historians before the eighteenth century," that is, no author of a "study both critical and constructive, that takes as its field the whole of the human past, and whose method is to reconstruct the past on the basis of written and nonwritten documents, analyzed and interpreted critically."[74] Henri Marrou has emphasized that "The great merit of Gibbon . . . is precisely to have achieved a synthesis between the contribution of classical scholarship as it had gradually been formulated from the first humanists up to the Benedictines of Saint-Maur and their imitators, and a sense of the great human problems envisaged in a high, broad perspective, such as might have been developed in him through his familiarity with philosophers" (1961:27).

With philosophical rationalism (which had, as we have seen, bad consequences as well as good for history), the final rejection of Providence, and the search for natural causes, the horizons of history were enlarged to include all aspects of society and all civilizations. In his *Projet d'un*

Traité sur l'Histoire (1714), Fénelon urges the historian to study "the customs and state of the whole body of the nation," and to show truth and originality—what painters call *il costume*—at the same time as changes: "Every nation has its way of life, which is very different from that of its neighbors; each people often changes for its own customs." Voltaire, in his "Nouvelles considérations sur l'histoire" (1744), had asked for "an economic, demographic history, a history of technology and customs, and not only a political, military, diplomatic history—a history of men and not only of kings and great men. A history of structures, and not only of events. A history in movement, a history of evolutions and transformations, and not a static history, a tableau-history. An explanatory history, and not a purely narrative, descriptive, or dogmatic history. In short, a total history" (quoted in Le Goff 1978:223).

In the service of this program—or of less ambitious programs—the historian henceforth had a concern for scholarship which more and more numerous enterprises and—this is a new element—institutions sought to satisfy. In this century of Academies and Learned Societies, history and allied subjects were not forgotten.

On the level of institutions, I shall choose as my example the French Academy of Inscriptions and Belles-Lettres. The "little academy" founded by Colbert in 1663 at first included only four members, and its mission was purely utilitarian: to write mottos for medals and inscriptions for monuments which would perpetuate the glory of the Sun-King. In 1701, its membership was raised to forty, and it became autonomous. It was rebaptized with its present name in 1716, and as early as 1717 it began regular publication of papers devoted to history, archeology, and linguistics, and undertook the preparation of the *Receuil des Ordonnances des Rois de France.*

On the level of the historian's tools, I shall cite on the one hand *L'art de vérifier les dates*, which the Maurists first published in 1750, and on the other the establishment between about 1717 and 1720 of the royal archives in Turin (whose regulations are the best archivistic expression of the period), and the printing of the catalog of the royal library in Paris from 1739 to 1753.

As representing scholarly activity in the service of history, I shall mention Ludovico Antonio Muratori (b. 1672), who became librarian of the Ambrosian Library in Milan in 1694, the librarian and archivist of the Duke of Este in Modena in 1700, and who died in 1750. Between 1744 and 1749, he published the *Annali d'Italia*, which had been preceded by the *Antiquitates Italiae Medii Ævi.* He was in correspondence with Leibnitz, among others.[75]

Muratori took Mabillon as his model, but like the Renaissance humanists he disencumbered history of miracles and omens. He pushed the critique of sources further than Mabillon did, but he is also not a true historian. There is no historical elaboration of the documentation and history is reduced to political history. Everything that concerns institutions, customs, and mentalities is put into the *Antiquitates.* "His *Annali* should be regarded more as chronologically ordered studies for Italian history than as a historical work" (Fueter 1:384).

From the point of view that concerns me here, the nineteenth century is decisive, because it achieves a definitive development of the critical method of dealing with documents that had occupied historians since the Renaissance, disseminates that method and its results through teaching and publishing, and unites history and scholarship.

Concerning the historian's scholarly equipment, I shall take the example of France. The Revolution and the empire created the National Archives which, put under the authority of the minister of the Interior in 1800, were put under the authority of the minister of Public Instruction in 1883. The Restoration created the École des Chartes in 1821 to train a team of specialized archivists who were supposed to be more historians than administrators, and who from 1850 onward were given the direction of the Departmental Archives. Archeological research on the principal sites of Antiquity was encouraged by the establishment of the École d'Athènes (1846) and the École de Rome (1874), historical scholarship in general by the foundation of the École Pratique des Hautes Études (1868). In 1804 the Académie Celtique was established to study the French national past. In 1884 it became the Société des Antiquaires de France. In 1834 the historian Guizot, having become a minister, instituted a Comité des Travaux historiques charged with the publication of a collection of *Documents inédits sur l'histoire de France.* In 1835, the Société française d'Archéologie founded in 1833 held its first meeting. The Commission des Monuments historiques was founded in 1837. The Société de l'Histoire de France was established in 1835. Henceforth, "an armature" for history exists: university chairs, university centers, learned societies, collections of documents, libraries, journals. After the monks of Middle Ages, the humanists and royal officers of the Renaissance, the philosophers of the eighteenth century, the bourgeois professors established history at the heart of Europe and through its influence, in the United States, where the Library of Congress was founded in Washington in 1800.

The movement was European, and strongly colored by the national spirit, if not by nationalism. A striking sign of this is the rapid creation, in most European countries, of a (national) historical journal. In Denmark the *Historisk Tidsskrift* (1840), in Italy the *Archivio storico italiano* (1842), followed by the *Rivista storica italiana* (1884), in Germany the *Historische Zeitschrift*, in Hungary *Szazadok* (*The Centuries*, 1866), in Norway *Historisk Tidsskrift* (1870), in France *La Revue historique* (1876), which had been preceded in 1839 by the *Bibliothèque de l'École des Chartes*, in Sweden the *Historisk Tidsskrift* (1881), in England the *English Historical Review* (1886), in the Netherlands the *Tijdschrift voor Geschiedenis* (1867), in Poland the *Kwartalnik Historyczny* (1887), and in the United States *The American Historical Review* (1895).

But Prussia was the great center, beacon, or model of nineteenth-century scholarly history. Not only did Prussian scholarship create institutions and prestigious collections such as the *Monumenta Germaniae Historica* (starting in 1826), but historical production succeeded better there than anywhere else in combining historical thought and scholarship with teaching in the form of the *seminar*, and thereby ensured the continuity of scholarly effort and historical research. A few great names emerge: the German-Dane Niebuhr (1776–1831) for Roman history (*Römische Geschichte*, 1811–1832); the scholar Waitz (1813–1886), a student of Ranke's, the author of a *Deutsche Verfassungsgeschichte* (1844–1878) and from 1875 on the director of the *Monumenta Germaniae Historica*; Mommsen (1817–1903), who dominated ancient history, where he put epigraphy in the service of political and juridical history (*Römische Geschichte*, beginning in 1849); Droysen (1808–1884), the founder of the Prussian school, a specialist in Greek history, and the author of a manual of historiography, *Grundriss der Historik* (written in 1858, published in 1868); the school known as "national-liberal" with Sybel (1817–1895), the founder of the *Historische Zeitschrift* (1859); Häusser (1818–1867), the author of a *History of Germany in the Nineteenth Century*; Treitschke (1834–1896), et al. The greatest name in the greatest German historical school of the nineteenth century is that of Ranke (1795–1886), whose ideological role in historicism I have already discussed. I mention him here as the founder in 1840 of the first *seminar* on history in which teacher and students engaged together in the criticism of texts.

German scholarship exercised a strong attraction on nineteenth-century European historians, including the French, who were almost prepared to believe that the war of 1870–71 had been won by the Prussian teachers and German scholars. Historians like Monod, Jullian, and Seignobos, for example, went to Germany to complete their training in the seminars offered there. Marc Bloch went to polish up his learning among the German scholars in Leipzig. At the University of Liège, one of Ranke's students, Godefroid Kurth (1847–1916), began a seminar in which the great Belgian historian Henri Pirenne (1862–1935), who contributed to the founding of economic history in the twentieth century, did his apprenticeship.

Nevertheless, by the end of the nineteenth century the dangers of German scholarship were recognized, especially outside Germany. In 1896, Camille Jullian observed that "History in Germany is becoming scattered and fragmented"; sometimes it "gradually dwindles into a kind of philological scholasticism: the great names are disappearing one after the other; let us hope that we do not see the epigones of Alexander or the grandchildren of Charlemagne reappear before our eyes." In Germany and elsewhere in Europe, German scholarly historicism degenerated into two opposed tendencies: an idealist philosophy of history, and a "positivist" ideal of scholarship that avoided ideas and excluded the search for causes from history.

It was for French professors to give this positivist history its charter: the *Introduction aux Études historiques* (1898) by C.V. Langlois and Charles Seignobos, which, presenting itself as a "breviary of the new methods," simultaneously disseminated the benefits of a progressive, necessary scholarship and the seeds of a sterilization of the spirit and methods of history.

It remains to discuss the positive side of nineteenth-century scholarly history, as Marc Bloch has done in his *Apologie pour l'histoire* (pp. 80–83). "The conscientious effort made in the nineteenth century" made it possible for "the techniques of criticism" to cease being the monopoly of "a handful of scholars, exegetes, and antiquarians," and "the historian has been brought back to the workbench." It was to ensure the triumph of "the most elementary precepts of an ethics of the intelligence" and "the forces of reason . . . that our humble notes, our niggling little references were written—these notes and references that today so many wits deride without understanding them" (Ehrard and Palmade, p. 78).

Thus, firmly supported by its servants, the auxiliary sciences (archeology, numismatics, sigillography, philology, epigraphy, papyrology, diplomatics, onomastics, genealogy, heraldics), history has taken its seat on the throne of scholarship.

History Today

I should now like to outline the renewal of history today as a scientific practice and to mention the role of difference and the Other in societies.

On the first point, I may be permitted to be relatively brief, and to refer to another study in which I have presented the genesis and the principal aspects of the renewal of historical science over the past half-century (Le Goff 1978:210–41). This tendency seems to me to be primarily French, but it has also manifested itself elsewhere, notably in Great Britain and in Italy, especially in connection with the journals *Past and Present* (since 1952) and *Quaderni Storici* (since 1966).

One of its oldest manifestations being the development of social and economic history, we should mention here the role of German historical science associated with the journal *Vierteljahrschrift für Sozial-und-Wirtschaftsgeschichte* founded in 1903, and the journal founded by Henri Pirenne, who developed a theory of the economic origin of cities in medieval Europe. As for the important role played by sociology and anthropology in the mutation of history in the twentieth century, the influence of a great mind like Max Weber and the influence of Anglo-Saxon sociologists and anthropologists are well known.

"Oral history" has enjoyed a great and precocious success in the English-speaking countries. The vogue of quantitative history has been considerable more or less everywhere, except perhaps in the Mediterranean countries.

Ruggiero Romano, who has offered an image—explosive in its intelligence and its partisanship—of *Storiografia italiana oggi* (*Italian Historiography Today*), has indicated a group of countries in which history and historians actively participate in social and political life—and not only in cultural life: Italy, France, Spain, Latin America, and Poland, whereas this is not the case in English- , Russian- , and German-speaking countries.

Historical research and reflection on history today develop in a climate of criticism and disenchantment with the ideology of progress and, more recently, in the West, in a climate colored by the repudiation of Marxism, in any case of vulgar Marxism. A whole body of work with no scientific value which was able to delude people only under the pressure of fashion and a certain politico-intellectual terrorism has lost all credibility. Let us point out that the anti-Marxist pseudo-history that seems to have taken the worn-out theme of irrationality as its banner has flourished.

Since Marxism has been the only coherent theory of history in the twentieth century apart from that of Max Weber, it is important to see what happens in light of the disaffection with Marxist theory and the renewal of historical practice in the West (begun some time ago, not against Marxism but outside it)—if one agrees with Michel Foucault that certain problems that are capital for the historian can be formulated only on the basis of Marxism. In the West a certain number of good historians have tried to show that Marxism could not only get along with the "new history," but also that Marxism was one of the fathers of this new history through its interest in structures, its conception of a total history, and its interest in the area of techniques and material activities.

Pierre Vilar and Guy Bois have expressed the wish that "the renewal pass by way of a certain return to the sources," and collective anthologies like *Aujourd'hui l'Histoire* and *Éthnologie et histoire*, published in Paris in 1984 and 1975 by Les Éditions Sociales, reveal a desire for openness.[76] An interesting series of texts published a few years ago by a certain number of Italian Marxist historians has shown the vitality and the evolution of this research.[77] A work like Alain Guerreau's *Le féodalisme, un horizon théorique* manifests, despite its exaggerations, the existence of a new and powerful Marxist thought. The historical production of Eastern countries is little-known in the West. With the exception of Poland and Hungary, what we do know is not very encouraging. There may be interesting works and trends in East Germany (see Guerreau 1980).

I have designated a few great historians of the past as the ancestors of the new history through their interest in the search for causes, their curiosity with regard to civilizations, their interest in the material, the quotidian, and psychology. From La Popelinière, at the end of the sixteenth century, to Michelet, passing by way of Fénelon, Montesquieu, Voltaire, Chateaubriand, and Guizot, it is a lineage impressive in its diversity. We must add the name of the Dutch historian Johann Huizinga

(d. 1945), whose masterpiece, *The Waning of the Middle Ages* (Haarlem, 1919) brought sensibility and collective psychology into history.

Marc Bloch and Lucien Febvre's foundation in 1929 of the journal *Annales* (first called *Annales d'histoire économique et sociale*, known since 1945 as *Annales. Economies. Sociétés. Civilisations*) is considered the birth certificate of the new history.[78] The ideas of the journal inspired the foundation in 1947 by Lucien Febvre (d. 1956; Bloch, a member of the French Resistance, was shot by the Germans in 1944) of an institution devoted to research and to the teaching of research in the human and social sciences, the Sixth Section (economic and social sciences) of the École Pratique des Hautes Études en Sciences Sociales. Such an institution had been envisioned by Victor Duruy when the École was founded in 1868 but it had never materialized. This establishment, which in 1975 became the École des Hautes Études en Sciences Sociales, and in which history had an eminent place alongside geography, economics, sociology, anthropology, psychology, linguistics, and semiology, ensured the diffusion in France and abroad of the ideas that were at the origin of the "Annales."

These ideas can be summarized as (1) the critique of historical fact and event-oriented history, in particular political history; (2) the quest for collaboration with other social sciences (the sociologist Emile Durkheim, the sociologist/anthropologist Marcel Mauss, and the economist François Simiand—who had published in 1903 in the *Revue de synthèse historique* (a pioneering journal in the new history, under the direction of Henri Berr, 1863–1954) an article titled "Méthode historique et science sociale," denouncing the "political," "individual," and "chronological" "idols" the *Annales* program inspired—all shaped the outlook of the *Annales*); (3) the replacement of history-as-narrative by history-as-problem; and (4) attention to the present.

Fernand Braudel (1902–1985) was the author of a revolutionary "thesis" on *La Méditerranée et le monde méditerranéen à l'époque de Philippe II*, in which history was divided into three superimposed levels, "geographical time," "social time," and "individual time"—the time of events being taken up only in the third part. In 1958 he published in the *Annales* the article on *la longue durée* ("Histoire et sciences sociales, la longue durée"), which was later to inspire an important part of historical research.

Almost everywhere in the 1970s colloquia and works, most of them collective, defined the new orientations of history. In 1974 a collective work titled *Faire de l'Histoire* (Le Goff and Nora, eds.) presented the "new problems," "new approaches," and "new objects" of history. Among the new problems are the quantitative in history, conceptualizing history, history before writing, the history of people without history, acculturation, ideological history, Marxist history, and the new event-oriented history. The new approaches concern archeology, economics, demography, religious anthropology, new methods in the history of literature, art, the sciences, and politics. The new problems discussed included climate, the unconscious, myth, mentalities, language, the book, youth, the body, cooking, public opinion, film, and the festival.

Four years later, in 1978, a *Dictionnaire de la Nouvelle Histoire* (Le Goff, Chartier, and Revel, eds.), by addressing a still broader public, bore witness to the progress in popularizing the new history and to the rapid shifts in interest within its field, and at the same time to its focus on certain themes: historical anthropology, material culture, the imaginary, immediate history, *longue durée*, the marginal, mentalities, structures.

History's dialogue with other sciences continued and became deeper, growing more focused and far-reaching at the same time. Alongside the persistence of the relations between history and economics (as shown, for example, by Jean Lhomme's *Economie et Histoire*, 1967), and between history and sociology (among other examples, the sociologist Alain Touraine declaring in *Un désir d'histoire*, p. 274: "I do not separate the task of sociology from the history of a society"), a privileged relation has been established between history and anthropology. On the anthropologists' side this was proposed by E. E. Evans-Pritchard (*Anthropology and History*), and envisaged more circumspectly by I. M. Lewis (*History and Social Anthropology*), who emphasizes the differing interests of the two sciences (history turns toward the past, anthropology toward the present, the former toward documents, the latter toward direct investigation, the former toward the explanation of events, the latter toward the general characteristics of social institutions). But a historian like E. H. Carr writes: "The more sociological history becomes, and the more historical sociology becomes, the better for both" (p. 66). And an anthropologist like Marc Augé asserts: "The object of anthropology is not to reconstitute past societies but to bring to light social logics and historical logics" (1979:170).

In this encounter between history and anthropology the historian has privileged certain areas and problems. For instance, there is the area of primitive man and everyday man,[79] or again that of the relations between learned culture and popular culture. (See Carlo Ginzburg's preface to his *The Cheese and the Worms: The World of a Sixteenth-Century Miller*, 1976, which begins this way: "In the past historians could be accused of wanting to know only about 'the great deeds of kings,' but today this is certainly no longer true.") Or again, there is the realm of oral history, where, from a very abundant literature, I shall single out three examples. First, I shall mention the special issue of *Quaderni storici, Oral History: fra antropologia e storia* (no. 35, maggio-agosto 1977), which clearly formulates the problems for different social classes and diverse civilizations. Second, there is the little book by Jean-Claude Bouvier and a team of anthropologists, historians, and linguists, *Tradition orale et identité culturelle, problèmes et méthodes* (Paris, 1980), which brings out the relations between orality and discourse on the past, defines the *ethnotexts* and a method for collecting and using them. And finally, one could read Dominique Aron-Schnapper and Danièle Hanet's *Histoire orale ou archives orales* (Paris, 1980), which deals with the establishment of oral archives for the history of social security and poses the problem of the relations between a new style of documentation and a new type of history.

From these experiments, contacts, and conquests, certain historians—and I count myself among them—hope to see a new historical discipline established that is closely linked to anthropology: historical anthropology.

In its 1980 supplement, the *Encyclopaedia Universalis* devotes a long article to "Historical Anthropology."[80] In this article André Burguière shows that this new label, born from the encounter between ethnology and history, is in fact more a rediscovery than a radically new phenomenon. It is situated within the tradition whose father is doubtless Herodotus, and which, in the French tradition, is expressed in the sixteenth century by Pasquier, La Popelinière, or Bodin, in the eighteenth century in the most important historical works of the Enlightenment, and it dominates Romantic historiography. It is "more analytical, seeking to trace the itinerary and the progress of civilization, interested in collective destinies more than in individuals, in the evolution of societies more than that of institutions, in ways of life more than in events," in contrast to another conception that is "more narrative, closer to the seats of political power," the one that goes from the great chroniclers of the Middle Ages to the scholars of the seventeenth century and on to the positivist, event-oriented history which triumphs at the end of the nineteenth century.

This new discipline thus represents a broadening of the domain of history in the spirit of the founders of the *Annales*: "at the intersection of the three principle axes which Marc Bloch and Lucien Febvre pointed out to historians: economic and social history, the history of mentalities, interdisciplinary investigations." Its model is Marc Bloch's *Les rois thaumaturges* (1924). One of its offspring is Fernand Braudel's *Civilisation matérielle et capitalisme*, in which he "describes the manner in which the great economic equilibriums and circuits of exchange create and modify the framework of biological and social life, the manner in which, for example, taste becomes habituated to a new food product." Burguière takes as his example a domain that historical anthropology seeks to conquer, that of a history of the body. The German historian Norbert Elias' 1938 book, *Über den Prozess der Zivilisation*, whose impact dates from the 1970s, provided a hypothesis explaining the evolution of the relations to the body in European civilization: "The occultation and the distancing of the body represented at the level of the individual the tendency to reshape the social body imposed by bureaucratic states; the latter would also explain the separation of age classes, the exclusion of deviants, the sequestering of the poor and the mad, as well as the decline in local solidarities" (*Encyclopaedia Universalis. Organum. Corpus.* 1:159). The four examples chosen in the *Encyclopaedia Universalis* to illustrate historical anthropology are: (1) the history of food and eating, which "seeks to find, study, and if possible, quantify everything related to this biological function essential to the maintenance of life: nutrition"; (2) the history of sexuality and of the family, which has brought historical demography into a new era with the exploration of massive sources (parish registers) and a problematics that takes mentalities into account, for example, attitudes regarding contraception; (3) the history of childhood,[81] which has shown that the attitudes with respect to children cannot be reduced to a hypothetical parental love but depend on complex cultural conditions; in the Middle Ages, for example, the child has no specific character; (4) the history of death, that is, of the attitudes with regard to death; this has revealed itself to be the most fertile field of the history of mentalities.

Thus the dialogue between history and the social sciences has a tendency to privilege the relations between history and anthropology, even though, to my mind for example, historical anthropology also includes sociology. Nevertheless, history tends to go beyond its territory in an even more audacious fashion when it moves in the direction of the natural sciences (see *L'Histoire du climat* by Emmanuel Le Roy Ladurie) or in the direction of the life sciences, and particularly biology.

First of all there is the scientists' desire to write the history of their own science, but not just any kind of history. Here is what François Jacob, a great, Nobel Prize-winning biologist, has written:

> For a biologist, there are two ways of imagining the history of his science. First, one can see in it the succession of ideas and their genealogy. In that case one is looking for the thread that has guided thought to the theories operative today. This history is written backwards, so to speak, by extrapolation from the present toward the past. In succession, one chooses the hypothesis that preceded the current one, then the one that preceded that, and so on. In this way the ideas acquire an independence. . . . There is thus an evolution of ideas sometimes subject to a process of natural selection based on a theoretical criterion of interpretation, hence of practical reusability, and sometimes solely to the teleology of reason. . . .
>
> There is another way of imagining the history of biology. That is to investigate the way objects have become available for analysis, thus permitting new domains to be constituted in the sciences. Here it is a question of defining the nature of these objects, the attitude of those who are studying them, their methods of observation, the obstacles that their culture puts in their way. . . . In this case there is no longer a more or less linear connection between ideas arising from each other. There is rather an area that thought tries to explore, in which it seeks to establish an order, in which it attempts to constitute a world of abstract relations in accordance not only with observations and techniques, but also with practices, values, and the currently accepted interpretations. (1970:18–19)

It is clear what is at issue here. It is the rejection of an idealist history in which ideas give birth to each other in a sort of parthenogenesis, of a history guided by the idea of linear progress, and of a history that interprets the past with the values of the present. On the contrary, François Jacob proposes a history which takes into account the material, social, and mental conditions of its production and which locates the stages of knowledge in all their complexity. But we must go further. Ruggiero Romano, basing his observations on J. Ruffié's suggestive and well-founded recent work, or on E. O. Wilson's more debatable work,[82] asserts that "Whereas history had sought to impose its authority on biology by using it (basely and badly) for demographic history, today biology wants to teach history something, and it can" (Romano 1978).

A. Nitschke has drawn attention to the value of collaboration between historians and specialists in ethology: "Numerous stimuli for historical research arise from an encounter with the ethology of the biologists. We must hope that this encounter between the two disciplines in the perspective of a historical ethology will become fruitful for both partners" (1981:74–97).

Any profound change in historical methodology is accompanied by a significant change in documentation. In this area our period has experienced a veritable documentary revolution: the irruption of the quantitative and the use of information theory. Necessitated by the new history's interest in the mass of people, postulated by the use of documents allowing the masses to be studied (such as parish registers in France, the basis for the new demography),[83] and required by the development of *serial* history, the computer has thus become one of the historian's tools. The quantitative appeared in history with economic history, in particular with the history of prices (an area in which Ernest Labrousse (1933), under the influence of François Simiand, was one of the great pioneers), and it has invaded both demographic and cultural history. After a period of naive enthusiasm, historians perceived both the indispensable services rendered by the computer in certain kinds of historical research and its limitations (see Furet, Shorter). Even in economic history one of the principal supporters of quantitative history, Marczewski, has written: "Quantitative history is only one of the methods of research in the field of economic history. It does not in any way exclude recourse to qualitative history; the latter complements it significantly" (p. 48). A model of innovative historical research based on intelligent use of the computer is D. Herlihy and C. Klapisch's book, *Les Toscans et leurs familles.*

The historian's examination of the history of his discipline has recently developed a new sector particularly rich in historiography: the history of history.

The Polish philosopher and historian Krysztof Pomian has made particularly acute observations on this subject. He has reminded us of the conditions under which the history of history arose, at the end of the nineteenth century, out of the critique of the reign of History: "Philosophers, sociologists, and even historians have begun to demonstrate that objectivity, facts given once and for all, laws of development, and progress, all of which are notions that had previously been regarded as evident, and that provided the foundation for history's claim to be a science, were no more than a mirage. . . . The historians . . . were shown to be, at best, naive, blinded by the illusions they had themselves produced and, at worst, charlatans" (1975:936). The history of historiography took as its motto Croce's saying: all history is contemporary history, and the historian, ceased to be the savant that he thought he was and became a forger of myths, an unconscious politician. But, Pomian adds, this challenge affected not only history, but "all of science, and particularly its center, physics." The history of the sciences developed in the same critical spirit as that of historiography. For Pomian, this kind of history is obsolete today, because it forgets the cognitive aspect of history, and of science in particular, and should become a science of all the historian's practices, and even more, a history of knowledge:

> The history of historiography has had its day. What we need now is a history of history which would place at the center of its investigation the interactions among knowledge, ideologies, the requirements of writing—in short, among the diverse and sometimes discordant aspects of the historian's work. And which, in so doing, would allow us to construct a bridge between the history of the sciences and that of philosophy, literature, and perhaps art. Or rather between a history of knowledge and that of the different uses made of it. (p. 952).

One proof of the broadening of the domain of history is the creation of new journals with a thematic focus—whereas the great movement that gave rise to nineteenth-century historical journals had a primarily national focus.

Among the new reviews, I will mention (1) those that are interested in quantitative history, such as *Computers and the Humanities*, published since 1966 by Queens College of the City University of New York; (2) those that concern oral history and ethnohistory, such as *Oral History*, The Journal of the British Oral History Society (1973), *Ethnohistory*, published by the University of Arizona since 1954, and the British *History Workshops*; (3) those that are devoted to comparative and interdisciplinary studies, such as the American *Comparative Studies in Society and History* (1958), and the bilingual (French and English) *Information sur les sciences sociales* published since 1966 by Fernand Braudel and Clemens Heller's Maison des Sciences de l'Homme in Paris; (4) those that focus on the theory and the history of history, the most important of which is *History and Theory*, begun in 1960.

There is another kind of broadening of the historical horizon that entails a veritable revolution in historical science. That is the necessity of putting an end to ethnocentrism, and of de-Europeanizing history.

The manifestations of historical ethnocentrism have been inventoried by Roy Preiswerk and Dominique Perrot (1975). They have identified ten forms of this colonization of history by Occidentals: (1) The ambiguity of the notion of civilization. Is there one or several? (2) Social evolutionism, that is, the conception of a single, linear evolution on the occidental model. In this respect, this declaration of a nineteenth-century anthropologist is typical: "Humanity being one since its origin, its career has been essentially the same, directed into different but uniform channels on all the continents, and evolving in a very similar manner in all the tribes and nations of humanity up to the same stage of development. The result is that the history and the experience of the Amerindian tribes represent more or less the history and the experience of our own distant ancestors when they were living under the same conditions" (L. H. Morgan 1877); (3) The use of literacy as a criterion for differentiating between the superior and the inferior. (4) The idea that contacts with the West are the foundation of the historicity of other cultures. (5) the affirmation of the causal role of values in history confirmed by the superiority of the occidental system of values: unity, law and order, monotheism, democracy, sedentarism, industrialism. (6) The unilateral legitimation of occidental actions (slavery, the propagation of Christianity, "necessary" interventions, etc.). (7) The intercultural transfer of occidental concepts (feudalism, democracy, revolution, class, the state, etc.). (8) The use of stereotypes such as the Barbarians, Islamic fanaticism, etc. (9) The autocentric selection of the "important" dates and events of history, imposing on the whole of world history the periodization developed for the West. (10) The choice of illustrations, and the references to race, blood, and color.

It is thus through the study of school textbooks that Marc Ferro has gone further in "challenging the traditional conception of 'universal history.' " Analyzing examples from South Africa, black Africa, the Antilles (Trinidad), the Indies, Islamic countries, Western Europe (Spain, Nazi Germany, France), the USSR, Armenia, Poland, China, Japan, the United States—with a glance at 'forbidden' history (Mexican-Americans, Australian aborigines), Ferro declares: "It is high time today to confront these representations, for with the enlargement of the world, with its economic unification but political explosion, the past of societies is more than ever one of the stakes in the conflicts between States, nations, cultures and ethnic groups. . . . Revolt is surging up among those whose history is 'forbidden' " (1981:7).

What a truly universal history will be, no one knows. Perhaps it will even be something radically different from what we call history. It must first inventory the differences, the conflicts. To reduce it to a bland, sweetly ecumenical history trying to please everyone is not to take the right path. Whence the partial failure of the five volumes of the *Histoire du développement scientifique et culturel de l'humanité*, published by UNESCO in 1969, which are full of good intentions.

Since the Second World War, history has been confronted by new challenges. I shall mention three of them.

The first is that more than ever, it must respond to the demands of the peoples, nations, and states that expect it to be more than a teacher of life, more than a mirror of their idiosyncrasy—an essential element of the individual and collective identity that they are anxiously seeking. It must respond to the demands of the former colonizers, who have lost their empires and find themselves limited to their little European space (Great Britain, France, Portugal); of ancient nations awakening from a nightmare (Germany, Italy); of the countries of Eastern Europe, where history is not in agreement with what Soviet domination would have them believe; of the Soviet Union, caught between the short history of its existence as a unified country and the long history of its nationalities; of the United States, which believed it had won for itself a history in the whole world, and finds itself hesitating between imperialism and human rights; of oppressed countries battling for their history as well as for their lives (Latin America); of new countries groping toward the construction of their own history. (For black Africa, see Assorodobraj 1967.)

Must we, or can we, choose between an objective history-as-knowledge and a militant history? Must we adopt the scientific schemas forged by the West or must we invent a historical methodology at the same time as a history?

For its part, the West has asked itself during its ordeals (the Second World War, decolonization, the shock of May 1968) whether the wisest thing to do was not to give up on history. Wasn't it one of the values that led to alienation and unhappiness?

To those who long nostalgically for a life without a past, Jean Chesneaux has replied by recalling the necessity to master a history, but he has proposed to make it "a history for the revolution." This is one of the possible results of the Marxist theory of the unity of knowledge and praxis. If, as I believe, history, with its specificity and its dangers, is a science, then it must escape identification with politics, an old dream of historiography, which is supposed to aid historical work in overcoming its conditioning by society, without which history would be the worst instrument of any power that came along.

The intellectual rejection of history that structuralism seemed to incarnate was more subtle. I want to say first that the danger seems to me to have come—and it has not entirely disappeared—mainly from a certain sociologism. Gordon Leff has rightly observed that "The attacks of Karl Popper upon what he mistermed historicism in the social sciences seem to have intimidated a generation; together with the influence of Talcott Parsons, it has left social theory, certainly in America, ahistorical to the degree where it seems often to be without relevance to the world of men" (1969:2).

It seems to me that Philip Abrams, ten years later, clearly defined the relations between sociology and history.[84] He did so by adhering to X. G. Runciman's opinion that there is no serious difference between history, sociology, and anthropology, but on the condition that they not be reduced to impoverishing points of view: either to a sort of psychology, or to a community of techniques, since the social sciences—like other sciences—must not subordinate problems to techniques.

On the other hand, I believe that only by distorting it can structuralism be made into a form of ahistoricism. This is not the place to examine in detail Claude Lévi-Strauss' reports. We know they are complex. We have to reread the great passages of *Anthropologie structurale* (I, I, pp. 3–33), *La Pensée sauvage*, *Du miel aux cendres*. It is clear that Lévi-Strauss often thought, with both the discipline of history and lived history in mind, that "We can weep over the fact that history exists,"[85] but I consider the most pertinent expression of his thought on the subject to be these lines from *Anthropologie structurale*: "They are following the same path, going in the same direction, only their orientation is different: the ethnologist walks forward seeking to attain, through a consciousness that he never forgets, ever more unconsciousness, towards which he proceeds; whereas the historian moves forward, so to speak, facing backwards, keeping his eyes fixed on concrete and particular activities, from which he never turns away except to envisage them in a new, richer and more complete perspective. A veritable Janus with two faces; in any case it is the solidarity of the two disciplines that permits us to keep the whole of the itinerary before our eyes" (1:32).

There is in any event a kind of structuralism historians can engage in dialogue: the genetic and dynamic structuralism of the Swiss epistemologist and psychologist Jean Piaget, according to whom structures are intrinsically evolutionary. But just as the linguists' diachrony is not identical with the time(s) of history, this evolution of structures is not the same thing as the movement of history. However, the historian may find, through comparison, that it throws an interesting light on his own object.

If history can overcome this challenge, it nonetheless faces serious problems today. I shall discuss two of these, one of them general, the other particular.

The great problem is that of global, general history, of the secular tendency to a history that would be not only universal and synthetic—an old enterprise that extends from ancient Christianity to the German historicism of the nineteenth century and to the countless universal histories produced by the popularization of history in the twentieth century—but also integral and complete, as La Popelinière put it, or global, total, as Lucien Febvre and Marc Bloch's *Annales* maintained.

Today there is a "panhistoricization" going on which Paul Veyne considers the second great mutation of historical thought since Antiquity. After a first mutation which, in ancient Greece, led from the history of collective myth to the search for a disinterested knowledge of pure truth, a second mutation, in the contemporary period, is occurring because historians "have gradually become aware of the fact that *everything is worthy of history*: no tribe, no matter how minuscule, no human act, no matter how insignificant it may seem, is unworthy of historical curiosity" (1968:424).

But is this omnivorous history capable of conceiving and structuring such a mass of data, from which nothing is excluded? Some think the time of fragmented history has arrived: "We are experiencing the explosion of history," Pierre Nora has written, founding in 1971 the collection "Bibliothèque *des* Histoires." It is possible to write *histories*, but not *history*. For my part, I have reflected on the legitimacy and the limits of "multiple approaches in history," and on the interest of taking totalizing objects as the themes of historical research and reflection, rather than totalities (see Le Goff and Toubert).

The particular problem is the need, felt by many people (whether producers or consumers of history), for a return to political history. I believe in the necessity of such a return, on the condition that this new political history be enriched by the new problematics of history, that it be a historical political anthropology (see Le Goff 1985:333–49).

Alain Dufour, taking as his model the works of Federico Chabod on the Milanese state in the time of Charles V, has argued "for a more modern political history," whose program would be "to understand the birth of modern States—or of the modern State—in the sixteenth and seventeenth centuries, by turning our attention from the sovereign toward the political personnel, toward the nascent class of bureaucrats, with its new kind of ethics, toward the political elites in general, whose more or less implicit aspirations are revealed in a given policy to which the name of the sovereign who is its standard-bearer is usually given" (Dufour 1966:20).

More general than the problem of a new political history is that of the role to be accorded the event in history, in both senses of the word "history." Pierre Nora has shown how the contemporary media have created a new kind of event and a new status for the event in history: this is the "return of the event."

However, this event does not escape the construction from which all historical documents result. The problems that result from this are even more serious today. In a remarkable study, Eliseo Veron has analyzed the way in which the media now "construct the event." Examining the accident at the Three Mile Island nuclear power plant (March-April 1979), he shows how in this case, and this is characteristic of the more and more numerous and important technological events, "it is difficult to construct a news event with pumps, filters, turbines, and especially radiation that cannot be seen." So the media transcribe it: "It is didactic discourse, especially on television, that is given the assignment of transcribing the language of technology into that of information [i.e., news reporting]." But the discourse of information in the various media conceals dangers that become greater and greater for the constitution of the memory which is one of the bases of history: "If the written press is the site of a multiplicity of modes of construction, radio follows the event and sets the tone, while television furnishes the images that will remain in the memory and will ensure the homogenization of the social imagination [*imaginaire*]." We rediscover here what has always been "the event" in history—from the point of view of lived and memorized history as well as from that of scientific history based on documents (among which the event as document has, I repeat, an essential place). It is the product of a construction that involves the historical destiny of societies and the validity of historical truth, the foundation of historical work: "Insofar as our everyday decisions and struggles are for the most part determined by the discourse of information, one can see that the stake is nothing less than the future of our societies" (Veron 1981:170).

Against this background of challenges and questions, a crisis has recently appeared in the world of historians. I shall take as an example of this the debate between two British historians, Lawrence Stone and Eric Hobsbawm, published in *Past and Present.* In his essay "The Revival of Narrative," Stone notes a return to narrative in history based on the failure of the determinist model of historical explanation, the disappointment with the paltry results produced by quantitative history, the disillusions resulting from structural analysis, and from the traditional, even "reactionary" character of the notion of "mentality." In a conclusion that is a triumph of ambiguity in an analysis of a notion that is itself ambiguous, Stone seems to make the "new historians" responsible for the shifts and displacements of history, which from a history of the determinist type is supposed to have returned to traditional history: "narrative history and individual biography are showing evident signs of rising again from the dead."

Hobsbawm replied that the methods, orientations, and productions of the "new" history in no way abandoned the great questions nor the search for causes in order to adhere to the principle of indeterminacy. Rather, they represent in large measure "the continuation of past historical methods by other means."

Hobsbawm has rightly emphasized that the new history's primary objectives are the broadening and deepening of scientific history. It has doubtless encountered problems, limits, and perhaps dead-ends. But it continues to broaden the field and the methods of history. Stone was particularly unable to see what is truly new, or "revolutionary," in the current trends in history: the critique of the document, the new way of considering time, the new relations between the "material" and the "spiritual," the analyses of the phenomenon of power in all its forms, and not only from a narrowly political point of view.

By proposing to consider the new trends in history as fads on their way out and abandoned even by their partisans, Stone has not only remained at the surface of the phenomenon but ended up allying himself in an ambiguous fashion with those who would like to bring history back to the thrashing about and narrow positivism of the past. That such people are raising their heads in the domain of historians and neighboring fields—that is the real problem of the crisis. It is a problem of society, a historical problem in the "objective" sense of the word "historical."

I should like to end with a credo and a paradox.

The claim made by historians—in spite of the diversity of their conceptions and practices—is at once modest and immense. They ask that every phenomenon of human activity be studied and put into practice taking into account the historical conditions in which it exists or existed. What should be understood by "historical conditions" is the shaping of the knowledge of concrete history, a knowledge whose scientific coherence is generally acknowledged by professional historians (even if they disagree about what it proves). It is in no way a matter of *explaining* the phenomenon in question *by* these historical conditions, of invoking a pure historical causality, and this must be the modesty of historical procedure. But this procedure also claims to challenge the validity of any explanation and of any practice that neglects these historical conditions. It is therefore necessary to repudiate every form of imperialist historicism, whether it represents itself as idealist, positivist, or materialist—or might be perceived as such.

It is also essential, however, forcefully to assert the necessity of the presence of historical knowledge in any scientific activity or in any praxis. In the domain of science, social action, politics, religion, or art, to mention a few essential areas, this presence of historical knowledge is indispensable. To be sure, it takes diverse forms. Each science has its own horizon of truth which history must respect; social action or politics must not have their spontaneity and freedom hobbled by history, and neither is history incompatible with the requirement of eternity and transcendence on the part of the religious, or with the drives of artistic creation. But as a science of time, history is an indispensable component of any activity in time. Rather than being so unconsciously, in the form of a manipulated or distorted memory, isn't it better that it should be so in the form of knowledge—even if fallible, imperfect, debatable, and never perfectly innocent—and that its norm of truth and the professional conditions under which it can be developed and exercised allow us to call it scientific?

In any case, this seems to me something that humanity today needs, in accordance with the diverse types of society, culture, relation to the past, and orientation toward the future that exist. Perhaps it will not be the same in a more or less distant future. Not because the need for a true science of time will have ceased to be felt, but because this knowledge could take other forms than those to which the term "history" can be properly applied. Historical knowledge is itself in history, that is to say, in the unforeseeable. This only makes it all the more real and true.

Girolamo Arnaldi, returning to one of Croce's ideas in *Storia come pensiero e come azione* (History as Thought and as Action), has affirmed his confidence in historiography as a "means of liberating the past," and in the fact that "historiography opens the way to a true and authentic liberation of history" (Arnaldi 1974). Without being as optimistic as he, I believe that it is the historian's task to transform history (*res gestae*) from a burden—as Hegel said—into a *historia rerum gestarum* which makes the knowledge of the past an instrument of liberation. I am not arguing here for any imperial role for historical knowledge. If I believe recourse to history to be indispensable to all the practices of human knowledge and to the consciousness of societies, I also believe that this knowledge must not be a religion and an abdication. We must reject "the establishmentarian cult of history" (Bourdieu 1979:124). I subscribe to the words of the great Polish historian Witold Kula: "The historian owes it to himself—paradoxically—to fight against the fetishization of history. . . . The deification of historical forces, which leads to a generalized feeling of powerlessness and indifference, becomes a genuine social danger; the historian must react, by showing that nothing is ever wholly inscribed in reality in advance, and that man can modify the conditions which are made for him" (*L'Histoire et ses interprétations*, 1961:173).

The paradox results from the contrast between the success of history in society and the crisis in the world of historians. The success is explained, I repeat, by societies' need to nourish their quest for identity, to feed on an *imaginaire* that is reality [*un imaginaire réel*], and the blandishments of the media have brought historical production into the movement of consumer society. It would be important, incidentally, to study the conditions and consequences of what Arthur Marwick has rightly called "the history industry" (1978:240–43).

The crisis in the world of historians results from the limits and uncertainties of the new history, from people's disenchantment when confronted by the painful character of lived history. Every effort to rationalize history, to make it offer a better purchase on its development, collides with the fragmentation and tragedy of events, situations, and apparent evolutions. This internal and external crisis is of course exploited by those who are nostalgic for a history and a society that are content with only a few ridiculous and illusory certainties. We must repeat what Lucien Febvre said: "Historizing history asks for little. Very little. Too little for me, and for many others besides me." It is the very nature of historical science to be closely linked with the lived history of which it is a part. But we can, indeed we must, beginning with each and every historian, work and struggle so that history, in both senses of the word, may become *different*.

ENDNOTES

PAST/PRESENT

1. For example, "I am going to Paris tomorrow," "I leave next Tuesday."

2. There is also a "historical future," e.g., "in 410 the barbarians will sack Rome."

3. For example, the aorist in ancient Greek, which is usually called the "gnomic aorist."

4. A. Miquel, *Un conte des "Mille et une nuits": Ajîb et Gharîb"* (Paris, 1977).

5. F. Brunot, *Histoire de la langue française des origines à 1900* (Paris, 1905).

6. P. Imbs, "Les propositions temporelles en Ancien Français," *La détermination du moment: Contribution à l'étude du temps grammatical français* (Strasbourg, 1956).

7. F. Héritier, "L'identité samo," in *L'Identité* (seminar conducted by Claude Lévi-Strauss, Paris, 1977).

8. Here I shall give only a brief outline of the attitudes regarding past and present. For more details, see subsequent chapters below, and the articles "Decadenza," "Scatologia," "Età mitiche," "Progresso/reazione" in Le Goff 1978, 1986.

9. J. de Romilly, *Histoire et raison chez Thucydide* (Paris, 1956).

10. M. I. Finley, "Thucydide et l'idée du progrès," in *Annali della Scuola Normale Superiore di Pisa* (1966), 35(2):143–91.

11. M. Eliade, *Histoire des croyances et des idées religieuses*. Vol. 2: *De Gautama Bouddha au triomphe du christianisme* (Paris, 1978).

12. Un punto solo m'è maggior letargo
Che venticinque secoli a la 'mpresa
Che fé Nettuno ammirar l'ombra d'Argo

Text and translation quoted from Charles Singleton's edition of Dante's *Divine Comedy*, Princeton, 1975.

13. Pero, donne gentil, giovane adorni,
Che vi state a cantare in questo loco,
Spendete lietamente i vostri giorni,
Che giovinezza passa a poco a poco . . .
Lorenzo il Magnifico, *Opere* (Bari, 1913–1914), 2:201.

14. J. Piaget, with J. Cl. Bringuier, *Conversations libres avec Piaget* (Paris, 1977), p. 181.

15. P. Abrams, "The Sense of the Past and the Origins of Sociology," *Past and Present* (1972), no. 55, pp. 18–32.

ANTIQUE (ANCIENT)/MODERN

1. Stefan Swiezawski, Antiqui und Moderni: Traditionsbewusstsein und Fortschrittsbewusstsein im späten Mittelalter. *Miscellanea Mediaevalia* (1974), no. 9.

2. E. Benveniste, *Le vocabulaire des institutions indo-européennes* (Paris, 1968), 2: 48–49.

3. Petrarch:"Manly strength will take up arms against favor, and their combat will show that neither *antique* valor nor the Italian heart is dead"; Ariosto: "Oh! the great valor of the *antique* knights!"; Vasari: "It is a very beautiful architectural work in all respects because it has so well imitated the *antique*"; Leopardi: "This dignity admired in all *antique* prose."

4. Petrarch, *Apologia contra cuiusdam anonymi Galli calumnias*, in *Opera omnia* (Basel, 1554), p. 1187.

5. Curtius, *La littérature européene et le Moyen Age latin* (Paris, 1956), p. 30.

6. J. Chailley, *Histoire musicale du moyen âge* (2d. ed.; Paris, 1969), p. 143.

7. Guerrand, *L'Art nouveau en Europe* (Paris, 1965).

8. Gruenbaum, *Dimensions du XXme siècle* (Geneva, 1965); Berque, *Langages arabes du présent*, p. 290.

9. Amadou Hampaté Ba, *Tradition et modernisme en Afrique noire*, p. 31.

10. Gino Germani, "Secularization, Modernization, and Economic Development," in Eisenstadt, *Protestant Ethic* (New York, 1968), p. 354.

11. Germani, Introduction to *La modernité: La femme moderne*, pp. 152–58.

12. G. Van Leeuw, *L'Homme primitif et la religion: Etude anthropologique* (Paris, 1940), pp. 163 ff.

13. Kende, *L'avènement de la société moderne*, p. 16.

14. K. S. Sherrill, in *Comparative Politics* (January 1969).

MEMORY

1. C. Flores, "Mémoire," in *Encyclopaedia Universalis*.

2. J. Piaget, *La mémoire*. Symposium of the Association of Scientific Psychology of the French Language (Paris, 1970).

3. H. Ey, "Les troubles de la mémoire," in *Études psychiatriques* (Paris, 1956), vol. 2, no. 9; and *Psychopathology of Memory*, Symposium, Tallard, ed. (Boston, 1967).

4. See Jacob, pp. 166–68.

5. A. Lieury, in *Encyclopaedia Universalis* (1971), p. 789.

6. Balandier, *La vie quotidienne au royaume du Kongo*, p. 15.

7. Balandier, p. 227.

8. J. Deshayes, *Les civilisations de l'Orient ancien* (Paris, 1969), pp. 587, 613; the works of E. Budge and L. W. King, *Annals of the Kings of Assyria* (London, 1902); D. D. Luckenbill, *The Annals of Sennacherib* (Chicago 1924); and the royal inscriptions published by E. Ebeling, B. Meissner, and E. Weidner, *Die Inschriften der altassyrischen Könige* (Leipzig, 1926).

9. F. Daumas, *La civilisation de l'Égypte pharaonique* (Paris, 1965).

10. Daumas, p. 579.

11. D. and V. Elisseeff, *La civilisation de la Chine classique* (Paris 1979), p. 50.

12. A. M. Gardiner, *Ancient Egyptian Onomastica* (London, 1947), p. 38.

13. "Mnemosyne," in A. F. Pauly and G. Wissowa, *Real-Encyclopädie der Classischen Altertumswissenschaft*.

14. M. Detienne, *Les Maîtres de vérité dans la Grèce archaïque* (Paris, 1967).

15. F. Yates, "The Ciceronian Art of Memory," in *Medioevo e Rinascimento: Studi in onore di Bruno Nardi* (Florence, 1955), 2:871–99.

16. C. Meier, "Vergessen, Erinnern, Gedächtnis im Gott-Mensch-Bezug," in H. Fromin, ed., *Signum et Signum*, vol. 1 (Munich, 1975), pp. 193–94.

17. Yahweh makes Miriam leprous because she had spoken against Moses.

18. Augustine, *Confessions*, X, 8, cited by F. Yates, p. 46.

19. G. R. Evans, " '*Interior homo*.' Two Great Monastic Scholars of the Soul: St. Anselm and Ailred of Rievaulx," *Studia Monastica* (1977), pp. 57–74.

20. H. Leclercq, "Memoria," in *Dictionnaire d'archéologie chrétienne et de liturgie* (Paris, 1933), 11(1):296–324.

21. W. Dürig, *Geburtstag und Namenstag, eine liturgiegeschichtliche Studie* (Munich, 1954).

22. A. M. Bautier, "Typologie des ex-votos mentionnés dans les textes antérieurs à 1200," *Actes du 99me Congrès National des Sociétés Savantes* (Paris, 1977), 1:237–82.

23. Marc Bloch, *Mélanges historiques* (Paris, 1963), 1:478.

24. R. H. Bautier, "Les archives," in C. Samaran, ed., *L'histoire et ses méthodes*, Encyclopédie de la Pléiade, vol. 9 (Paris, 1961).

25. P. Zumthor, *Essai de poétique médiévale* (Paris, 1972), p. 324.

26. Pierre Riché, *Les écoles et l'enseignement dans l'Occident chrétien de la fin du Vme siècle au milieu du XIme* (Paris, 1979), p. 218.

27. Alcuin, *De Rhetorica*, Halm ed., pp. 545–48.

28. Rhabunus Maurus, *De Universo*, in *Patrologie latine*, p. 141, col. 335.

29. Boncompagno, *Rhetorica Novissima*, A. Guadenzi, ed. (Bologna, 1841), p. 255.

30. Aquinas, *Summa Theologiae*, II, II, Questio LXVIII: De partibus Prudentia; Quaestio XLIX, *De singulis prudentiae partibus*, articulus 1: *utrum memoria sit pars prudentiae*.

31. Erasmus, *Opera*, Froben, ed. (1540), 1:466. Cf. Haijdu, *Das mnemotechnische Schriftum des Mittelalters* (Vienna, 1936).

32. Vico, *De l'antique sagesse de l'Italie*, tr. J. Michelet, in Vico, *Oeuvres complètes* (Paris, 1971), 1:410–11.

33. Bourdieu, *Un art moyen: Essais sur les usages sociaux de la photographie* (Paris, 1965), pp. 53–54.

34. Demarne and Rouquerol, *Ordinateurs électroniques* (Paris, 1959), pp. 5–6. Hereafter cited in text.

35. See the great project directed by Pierre Nora, *Les lieux de mémoire* (Paris, Gallimard). I: *La République*, 1984; II: *La nation* (3 vols.); III: *La France* (to come), which marks an important moment in French historiography.

36. But the *Britannica* continues to be updated.

37. G. Mansuelli, *Les civilisations de l'Europe ancienne* (Paris, 1967), pp. 139–40.

38. Balandier, *Anthropo-logiques*, p. 195.

HISTORY

1. E. Benveniste, *Le vocabulaire des institutions indo-européennes* (Paris, 1969), 2:173–74. See also F. Hartog, *Le miroir d'Hérodote* (1980).

2. For example, E. Le Roy Ladurie, *Histoire du climat depuis l'An Mil* (Paris, 1977).

3. Perrin, quoted by E. Labrousse, "Ordres et classes," in *Colloque d'histoire sociale, Saint-Cloud, 20–25 mai 1967* (Paris, 1973), p. 3.

4. See "The Constitution of the Historical Past," *History and Theory* (1977), supplement, no. 16.

5. Callot, *Ambiguités et antinomies de l'histoire et de sa philosophie* (Paris, 1962).

6. J. Prawer, *The Latin Kingdom of Jerusalem:European Colonialism in the Middle Ages* (London, 1972).

7. G. Falco, *La santa romana repubblica:Profilo storico del Medioevo* (Naples, 1942).

8. Debbins, *Essays in the Philosophy of History* (Austin, 1965).

9. See especially D. Junker and P. Reisinger; G. Leff, pp. 120–29; J. A. Passmore; and C. Blake.

10. Max Weber, *Gesammelte Aufsätze zu Wissenschaftslehre* (3d. ed., 1958), p. 177, quoted by W. Mommsen, p. 20.

11. V. K. Dibble, "Four Types of Inference from Documents to Events," *History and Theory*, 34:303–21.

12. W. Dray, *Laws and Explanation in History* (London, 1957); see S. H. Beer, "Causal Explanation and Imaginative Reenactment," *History and Theory* (1963), 3.

13. P. Beglar, "Historia del mundo y Reino del Dios," *Scripta Theologica* (1975), 7:285.

14. I have discussed elsewhere (Le Goff 1978, vol. 10) the rebirth, triumph, and critique of the idea of progress. Here I shall only offer a few remarks on technological progress.

15. B. Gille, *Histoire des techniques* (Paris, 1978), pp. viii ff.

16. G. Lichtheim, "Historiography: Historical and Dialectical Materialism," in *Dictionary of the History of Ideas* (New York 1980), 2:450–56.

17. W. C Runciman, *Sociology in Its Place and Other Essays* (London, 1970), p. 10.

18. J. Lecuir, "Enquête sur les héros de l'histoire de France," *L'Histoire* (April 1981), 33:102–12.

19. *Le roman historique*, special issue of *La Nouvelle Revue Française* (October 1972), no. 238.

20. F. Driver, *The Sense of History in Greek and Shakespearian Drama* (New York, 1960).

21. J. Fouquet, *Les Dossiers du département des peintures du Musée du Louvre* (Paris 1981), no. 22.

22. D. Fabre, "Mythe," in Le Goff et al. 1978.

23. M. Detienne, "Le mythe," in Le Goff and Nora 1974 3:74.

24. A. Miquel, *Un conte des "Mille et une nuits": Ajîb et Gharî* (Paris, 1977).

25. A. Christensen, "Les gestes des rois," in *The Idea of History in the Ancient Near East* (Paris, 1936).

26. On the Hittite annals, see *Saeculum* (1955), no. 6.

27. See G. Hölscher, *Die Anfänge der Hebräischen Geschichtsschreibung* (Heidelberg, 1942).

28. G. F. Chestnut, *The First Christian Histories: Eusebius, Socrates, Sozomen, Theodorit and Evagrius* (Paris, 1978), pp. 233, 241.

29. J. Gernet, "Écrit et histoire en Chine," *Journal de Psychologie* (1959), pp. 31–40.

30. A. Miquel, *L'Islam et sa civilisation, VIIe—XXe siècles* (Paris, 1968), p. 155.

31. A. Miquel, review of F. Gabrieli, *L'Islam nella storia: Saggi di storia e storiografia mussulmana*, in *Revue historique* (1967), 238:460–62.

32. G. F. Chestnut, p. 244.

33. Universal chronicle: A. D. Von den Brincken, *Studien zur lateinische Weltchronistik bis in das Zeitalter Ottos von Freising* (Düsseldorf, 1957); biblical history, see Pierre le Mangeur, *Historia scolastica*, c. 1170.

34. A. Paravicini-Bagliani, "La storiografia pontificia del secolo XIII," *Römische Historische Mitteilungen*.

35. G. Arnaldi, *Studi sui cronisti della marca trevigiana nell' età di Ezzelino da Romeno* (Rome, 1963), pp. 85–107.

36. N. Rubinstein, "The Beginnings of Political Thought in Florence," *Journal of Warburg and Courtauld Institutes* (1942), 5: 198–227; A. Del Monte, "Istoriografia fiorentina dei secoli XII-XIII," *Bellottino dell'Instituto Storico Italiano per il Medio Evo* (1950), 52:175–282.

37. G. Bali, "La storiografia genovese fino al secolo XV," *Studi sul Medioevo cristiano offerti a Raffaello Morghen* (Rome, 1974).

38. G. Martini, "Lo spirito cittadino e le origini della storiografia communale lombarda," *Nuova Rivista Storica* (1970), 54:1–22.

39. Montaigne, *Essais*, II, 10, "Des Livres," texts in J. Ehrard and G. Palmade, pp. 117–19.

40. B. Bucher, *La sauvage aux seins pendants* (Paris, 1977), pp. 227–28.

41. G. Arnaldi, "Il notaio-cronista e le cronache cittadine in Italia," in *Atti del primo congresso internazionale della Società Italiana di Storia del Diritto* (Florence, 1966), pp. 293–309.

42. Guizot, *Cours d'Histoire Moderne: Histoire de la civilisation en Europe depuis la chute de l'Empire romain jusqu'à la Révolution Française*, 1828, 7me Leçon, quoted by Ehrard and Palmade, p. 211.

43. Letter to J. Weydemayer, March 5, 1852, quoted by Ehrard and Palmade, p. 59.

44. de Tocqueville, *De la Démocratie en Amérique*, 1836–39; *L'Ancien Régime et la Révolution*, 1856.

45. Keith Hancock, quoted by Barraclough, *History in a Changing World*, p.157.

46. J. de Romilly, *Thucydide et l'impérialisme athénien* (Paris, 1947); *Histoire et raison chez Thucydide* (Paris, 1956).

47. A. Taleb, *Lettres de prison, Fresnes, 10 décembre, 1959*, Alger, ed., 1966.

48. Savigny, *Zeitschrift für Geschichtliche Rechtwissenschaft* (1815), 1:4.

49. Ranke, *Geschichte der romanischen und germanischen Völker*, 1824; rpt. 1957, p. 4.

50. A study on Vico in *Le Devenir Social*, 1896.

51. H. B. Adams, *New Methods of Study in History*, Johns Hopkins University Studies in History and Political Science (1884), no. 2.

52. F. Chabod, "Uno storico tedesco contemporaneo: Federico Meineke," *Nuova Rivista Storica* (1927), vol. 11.

53. E. Simon, "Ranke und Hegel," *Historische Zeitschrift* (1928), supplement 15.

54. On the constitution of Marx's historical thought, see Pierre Vilar's article "Marx" in Le Goff et al. 1978:370–74.

55. Antonio Gramsci, "Il materialismo storico e la filosofia di Benedetto Croce," in *Appunti di filosofia e idealismo*, p. 216.

56. L. Althusser and E. Balibar, *Lire le Capital*, 2:74.

57. G. della Volpe, *Logica come scienza storica* (Rome, 1969), p. 317.

58. M. Crubellier, in *L'Histoire et ses interprétations*, R. Aron, ed. pp. 85 ff.

59. Published in *Revue de Synthèse historique* (May/June 1901), quoted by Ehrard and Palmade, p. 322, n.1. See J. Herrick, 1954.

60. P. M. Duval, "Archéologie antique," in C. Samaran, ed., *L'Histoire et ses méthodes*, Encyclopédie de la Pléiade (Paris, 1961), p. 255.

61. A. Schnapp, *L'Archéologie aujourd'hui*, 1980; M. I. Finley, 1971.

62. J. M. Pesez, "Histoire de la culture matérielle," in Le Goff et al., 1978:130; R. Bucaille and J. M. Pesez, "Cultura materiale," in Le Goff 1978..

63. J. Bollack, *La Lettre d'Epicure*, Paris.

64. See Le Goff 1978 5:38–48; H. R. Immerwahr, " 'Ergon'—History as a Monument in Herodotus and Thucydides," *American Journal of Philology* (1960), 81:261–290.

65. "Nam quis nescit primam esse historiae legem, ne quid falsi audeat? deinde ne quid veri non audeat?" Cicero, *De oratore*, II, 62.

66. "Historia vero testis temporum, lux veritatis, vita memoriae, magistra vitae, nuntia vetustatis, qua voce alia nisi oratoris immortalitati commendatur?" Cicero, II, 36; quoted by R. Koselleck, "Historia magistra vitae: Über die Auflösung des Topos im Horizont neuzeitlich bewegter Geschichte," in *Nature und Geschichte. Festschrift für K. Löwith* (Stuttgart, 1967), pp. 196–219.

67. G. F. Chestnut, *The First Christian Histories: Eusebius, Socrates, Sozomen, Theodoret and Evagrius* (Macon, Ga.), 1978, p. 245.

68. Eusebius, *Chronicon* 426, 428, 429, 432, 439, 445, 454.

69. *Opera de temporibus*, C. Jones, ed., p. 303.

70. Hugh of St. Victor, *Fundamentum omnis doctrinae*, in *De tribus maximis circumstanciis gestorum*, W. M. Green, ed., *Speculum* (1943), p. 491.

71. D. Kelley, "*De origine feudorum*: The beginnings of an Historical Problem," *Speculum* (1964), 39:207–28.

72. Paul Hazard, *La crise de la conscience européenne, 1680–1715* (Paris, 1925), 1:66.

73. G. Tessier, "Diplomatique," in *Encyclopaedia Universalis* (1971), p. 641.

74. *Encyclopaedia Universalis* (1971), p. 432.

75. Ludovico Antonio Muratori, *Corrispondenza tra Muratori e Leibniz* (1892), M. Campori, ed.

76. Pierre Vilar, "Histoire marxiste, histoire en construction," *Annales, E.S.C.* (1973);. Guy Bois, "Marxisme et histoire nouvelle," in Le Goff et al. 1978:375–93.

77. *La Ricerca storica marxista in Italia*, Riuniti ed. (1974).

78. On the *Annales,* see "Annales"by Revel and Chartier in Le Goff et al. 1978:26–33; Allegra and Torre 1977; Cedronio et al. 1977.

79. F. Furet, *L'histoire et l' "homme sauvage"*; J. Le Goff, "L'historien et l'homme quotidien," in *L'historien entre l'ethnologue et le futurologue* (Venice, 1981), pp. 231–50; first printed in *Mélanges Fernand Braudel*, 1972.

80. *Organum. Corpus* (Paris, 1980), 1:157:70.80. Burguiére has taken up this subject again in articles in Le Goff et al. 1988;137–65, and Burguiére 1986:52–60.

81. P. Ariès, *L'enfant et la vie familiale sous l'Ancien Régime* (Paris, 1960); L. de Mause, ed., *The History of Childhood* (New York, 1974).

82. J. Ruffié, *De la biologie à la culture* (Paris, 1977); E. O. Wilson, *Sociobiology* (Cambridge, Mass., 1977).

83. See the exemplary study by P. Goubert, *Beauvais et le Beauvaisis de 1600 à 1730*, Paris; rpt. as *Cent mille provinciaux au XVIIe siècle* (1968).

84. P. Abrams, "Sociology and History," *Past and Present* (1971), no. 52, pp. 118–25; "The Sense of the Past and the Origins of Sociology," *Past and Present* (1971), no. 55, pp. 18–22; "History, Sociology, Historical Sociology," *Past and Present* (1980), no. 87, pp. 3–16.

85. C. Backes-Clement, *Claude Lévi-Strauss* ou *La Structure et le malheur* (2d ed. 1974), p. 141.USX

BIBLIOGRAPHY

Agulhon, M. 1978. La statuomanie et l'histoire. *Ethnologie Française.*

Allegra, L. and A. Torre. 1977. *La nascita della storia sociale in Francia. Dalla Comune alle.* "Annales." Turin.

Amalvi, C. 1979. *Les héros de l'histoire de France.* Paris, 1979.

Andreano, A. 1977. *La Nouvelle Histoire économique: Exposés de méthodologie.* Paris.

Andreano, A. 1980. *Archives orales, une autre histoire.* Special issue of *Annales E.S.C.,* 1980, 1.

Antoni, C. 1957. *Lo storicismo.* Turin.

Aries, Ph. 1954. *Le temps de l'histoire.* Paris, 1986.

Aries, Ph. 1977. *L'homme devant la mort.* Paris.

Aries, Ph. 1980. *Un historien du dimanche.* Paris.

Aries, Ph. and G. Duby, eds. 1985–1987. *Histoire de la vie privée.* 5 vols. Paris.

Aries, Ph. 1986. *Incontro con gli storici,* Bari, Laterza.

Arnaldi, G. 1966. Il notaio-cronista e le cronache cittadine in Italia, in *La storia del diritto nel quadro delle scienze storiche,* pp. 293–309. Atti del I Congressó internazionale della Societa italiana di storia del diritto. Florence.

Arnaldi, G. 1974, La storiografia come mezzo di liberazione dal passato. In F. L. Cavazza and S. R. Graubard, eds., *Il caso italinao, Italia anni' 70,* pp. 553–62. Milan.

Aron, R. 1938a. *Introduction à la philosophie de l'histoire: Essai sur les limites de l'objectivité historique.* Paris, new ed., 1986.

Aron, R. 1938b. *La philosophie critique de l'histoire. Essai sur une théorie allemande de l'histoire.* Paris, 1964; new ed., 1987.
Aron, R. 1961a. *Dimensions de la conscience historique.* Plon, Paris, Agora éd. 1985.
Aron, R. 1969. *Les désillusions du progrès.* Essai sur la dialectique de la modernité. Paris.
Assorodobraj, N. 1967. Le rôle de l'histoire dans la prise de conscience nationale en Afrique occidentale. *Africana Bulletin,* 1(7): 9–47.
Auge, M. 1979. *Symbole, fonction, histoire: Les interrogations de l'anthropologie.* Paris.
Aymard, M. 1972. The *Annales* and French historiography, *The Journal of European Economic History,* 1: 491–511.
Baron, H. 1932. Das Erwachen des historischen Denkens in Humanismus des Quattrocento, *Historische Zeitschrift,* 145(1): 5–20.
Barraclough, G. 1955. *History in a Changing World.* Oxford.
Barraclough, G. 1980. *Tendances actuelles de l'histoire.* Paris.
Barthes, R. 1964–65. L'ancienne rhétorique, aide-mémoire, *Communications* (1970), no. 16, 172–229.
Barthes, R. 1967. Le discours de l'histoire, *Informations sur les sciences sociales,* 4: 65–75.
Baudelaire, Ch. 1863. *Le peintre de la vie moderne, Le Figaro,* November 26 and 29, December 3.
Bazin, J. 1979. La production d'un récit historique, *Cahiers d'études africaines,* 19 (73–76), 435–83.
Benveniste, E. 1959. Les relations de temps dans le verbe français, *Bulletin de la Société de Linguistique,* 237–50; 54(1): reprinted in *Problèms de linguistique générale,* Paris, 1966.
Berdjaev, N. 1923. *Le sens de l'histoire humaine.* Paris, 1948.
Berger, G. 1964. *Phénoménologie du temps et prospective.* Paris.
Berlin, I. 1954. Historical inevitability. In *Four Essays on Liberty.* Oxford, 1969.
Berlin, I. 1960. The concept of scientific history. In *History and Theory,* vol. 1. 1960.
Berque, J. 1970. *L'Orient second.* Paris.
Berr, H. 1910. *La Synthèse en histoire: Son rapport avec la synthèse générale.* new ed. Paris, 1953.
Berveiller, M. 1971. "Modernismo." *Encyclopaedia Universalis,* 11: 138–39. Paris.
Besançon, A. 1967. *Le tsarévitch immolé,* Paris.
Besançon, A. 1974. ed. L'histoire psychanalytique: Une anthologie. Paris.
Blake, C. 1959. Can History be objective? In P. Gardiner, ed., *Theories of History.* Glencoe, Ill.
Bloch, M. 1941/42. *Apologie pour l'histoire ou métier d'historien.* Paris, 1949, 1974.
Bogart, L. 1968. *The Age of Television.* New York.
Bois, G. 1978. *Marxisme et histoire nouvelle,* in Le Goff et al. 1978: 375–93.
Bonaparte, M. 1939. L'inconscient et le temps. *Revue Française de Psychanalyse,* 11: 61–105.
Borst, A. 1969. *Geschichte an mittelalterlichen Universitäten.* Constance.
Bourdé, G. and H. Martin. 1983. *Les écoles historiques.* Paris.
Bourdé, G. and H. Martin. 1986. Braudel dans tous ses états: La vie quotidienne des

sciences sociales sous l'empire de l'histoire. Special number of *Espaces Temps,* no. 34/35.

Bourdieu, P. 1979. *La distinction: Critique sociale du judgement.* Paris.

Bousquet, G. H. 1967. Le hasard: Son rôle dans l'histoire des sociétés. *Annales, E.S.C.,* 22(1–3): 419–28.

Brassloff. 1901. Damnatio Memoriae. Pauly and Wissowa, eds., *Realencyclopädie der clasisschen Altertumswissenschaft,* 8/2, col. 2059–2062.

Braudel, F. 1949. *La Méditerranée et le monde méditerranéen à l'époque de Philippe II.* 4th ed. Paris. 1974.

Braudel, F. 1958. Histoire et sciences sociales: La longue durée. *Annales E.S.C.,* 13(4): 725–53; reprinted in *Ecrits sur l'histoire.* Paris, 1969.

Braudel, F. 1967. *Civilisation matérielle, économique et capitalisme.* 3 vols. 2d ed. Paris, 1979.

Brown, P. 1967. *La vie de saint Augustin.* Paris, 1971.

Bullock, A. 1976. *Is History Becoming a Social Science? The Case of Contemporary History.* Cambridge.

Burckhardt, J. 1949. *Considérations sur l'histoire universelle.* Genève, 1965; Paris, 1971.

Burguière, A. 1979. Histoire d'une histoire: naissance des Annales. *Annales E.S.C.,* 1979.

Burguière, A. 1980. Anthropologie historique, in *Encyclopaedia Universalis,* Organum-Corpus: 157–70. Paris.

Burguière, A. 1983. La notion de mentalités chez Marc Bloch et Lucien Febvre: deux conceptions, deux filiations. *Revue de Synthèse,* nos. 111–12.

Burguière, A., ed. 1986. *Dictionnaire des Sciences Historiques.* Paris.

Burke, P. 1969. *The Renaissance Sense of the Past.* London.

Butterfield, H. 1955. *Man on His Past: The Study of the History of Historical Writing.* Cambridge.

Butterfield, H. 1973. Historiography. In Ph. P. Wiener, ed., *Dictionary of the History of Ideas: Studies of Selected Pivotal Ideas,* 2: 464–98. New York.

Cantimori, D. 1945. *Storici e storia: Metodo, caratteristiche, significato del lavoro storiografico,* 2d ed. Rome, 1978.

Capitani, O. 1979. *Medioevo passato prossimo: Appunti storiografici: tra due guerre e molte crisi.* Bologna.

Caponigre, A. R. 1953. *Time and Idea: The Theory of History in Giambattiste Vico,* Chicago.

Carbonell, Ch.-O. 1976. *Histoire et historiens 1865–1885.* Toulouse.

Carbonell, Ch.-O. 1976. La Naissance de la *Revue historique:* Une revue de combat 1876–1885. *Revue historique* (1976), 518: 331–51.

Carbonell, Ch.-O. 1978. L'histoire dite positiviste en France. *Romantisme,* no. 21–22.

Carbonell, Ch.-O. 1981. *L'historiographie.* Paris.

Carbonell, Ch.-O. and G. Livet. 1983. *Au berceau des Annales.* Colloquy at Strasbourg, 1979. Toulouse.

Carr, E. H. 1961. *What Is History?* London.

Cedronio, M. et al. 1977. *Storiografia francese di ieri e di oggi.* Naples.

Certeau, M. de. 1970. Faire de l'histoire, *Recherches de science religieuse,* 58: 481–520.

Certeau, M. de. 1974. *L'opération historique,* in J. Le Goff and P. Nora, eds. *Faire de l'histoire,* 1: 3–41.

Certeau, M. de. 1975. *L'ecriture de l'histoire.* Paris.

Chabod, F. 1927. *Lezioni di metodo storico.* 2d ed., Bari, 1972.

Chabod, F. 1943–47. *L'idea di nazione.* 4th ed., Bari, 1974.

Changeux, J.-P. 1974. Discussion—J.-P. Changeux—A. Danchin, *Apprendre par stabilisation sélective de synapses en cours de développement.* In Morin and Piattelli Palmarini, pp. 351–57.

Charbonnier, J. 1980. *L'interprétation de l'histoire en Chine contemporaine.* Thesis, University of Lille.

Chatelet, F. 1962. *La naissance de l'histoire: La formation de la pensée historienne en Grèce.* Paris.

Chaunu, P. 1974. La durée, l'espace et l'homme à l'époque moderne, *L'histoire sciene sociale.*

Chaunu, P. 1978. Histoire quantitative, histoire sérielle. *Cahier des Annales,* no. 37.

Chesneaux, J. 1976. *Du passé faisons table rase? A propos de l'histoire et des historiens.* Paris.

Childe, V. G. 1953. *What Is History?* New York.

Childs, B. S. 1962. *Memory and Tradition in Israel.* London.

Clanchy, M. T. 1979. *From Memory to Written Record: England 1066–1307.* London.

Cohen, G. A. 1978. *Karl Marx's Theory of History.* Oxford.

Collingwood, R. G. 1932. *The Idea of History.* Oxford, 1946.

Condominas, G. 1965. *L'exotique est quotidien.* Paris.

Conze, W., ed. 1972, *Theorie der Geschichtswissenschaft und Praxis des Geschichtsunterrichts.* Stuttgart.

Cordoliani, A. 1961. Comput, chronologie, calendriers. In Ch. Samaran, ed., L'histoire et ses méthodes, in *Encyclopédie de la Pléiade,* 11: pp. 37–51.

Coutau-Bégarie, 1983. *Le phénomène "Nouvelle Histoire": Stratégie et idéologie des nouveaux historiens.* Paris.

Croce, B. 1915. *Théorie et histoire de l'historiographie.* Paris, 1978.

Croce, B. 1938. *L'histoire comme pensée et comme action.* Geneva, 1968.

Croce, B. 1983. *La philosophie comme histoire de la liberté, contre le positivisme.* Paris, 1983.

Dahl, N. A. 1948. Anamnesis: Mémoire et commémoration dans le christianisme primitif. *Studia Theologica,* 1(4): 69–95.

Dainville, F. de. 1954. L'enseignement de l'histoire et de la géographie et la "ratio studiorum." *Studi sulla Chiesa antica e sull' Umanesimo: Analecta gregoriana,* 70: 427–54.

Del Treppo, M. 1976. La liberta della memoria. *Clio* (July-September 1976), 12: 189–233.

Den Boer, Pim. 1987. *Geschiedenis als Beroep,* en néerlandais (le métier d'historien, la professionnalisation de l'histoire en France 1818–1914), Nimègue, SUN.

Dentan, R. C., ed. *The Idea of History in the Ancient Near East.* New Haven, 1969.

De Rosa, G. 1987. *Tempo religioso e tempo storico.* Saggie e note di storia sociale e religiosa del Medioevo all'età contemporanea. Rome.

Diaz, F. 1958. *Voltaire storico.* Turin.

Dosse, F. 1987. *L'histoire en miettes: Des "Annales" a la "nouvelle histoire"* Paris.

Dray, W. H. 1957. *Law and Explanation in History.* London.

Duby, G. 1967. *Remarques sur la littérature généalogique en France des XIe et XIIe* siècles. In *Hommes et structures du Moyen Âge*. Paris, 1979.

Duby, G. 1973, *Le dimanche de Bouvines, 27 juillet 1214*.Paris.

Duby, G. and G. Lardreau. 1980. *Dialogues*. Paris.

Dufour, A. 1966. *Histoire politique et psychologie historique*. Geneva.

Dumont, L. 1964. *La Civilisation indienne et nous*. 2d ed., Paris, 1975.

Dupront, A. 1972. *Du sentiment national*. In M. François, ed., *La France et les Français*. Paris.

Ehrard, J. and G. Palmarde. 1964. *L'histoire*. Paris.

Eickelmann, D. F. 1978. The art of memory: Islamic education and its social reproduction. *Comparative Studies in Society and History*, 20: 485–516.

Eisenstadt, S. N., ed. 1968. *The Protestant Ethic and Modernization: A Comparative View*. New York.

Eisenstein, E. L. 1966. Clio and Chronos: An essay on the making and breaking of history-book time. *History and Theory: Studies in the Philosophy of History*. V, suppl. 6 (History and the Concept of Time), pp. 36–64.

Elias, N. 1939. *Uber den Prozess der Zivilisation*. Vol. 1: *La civilisation des mœurs;* vol. 2: *La dynamique de l'Occident*. Paris, 1973, 1975.

Erdmann, K. D. 1964. Die Zukunft als Kategorie der Geschichte. *Historische Zeitschrift*, 198(1): 44–61.

Erikson, E. H. 1962. *Young Man Luther: A Study in Psychoanalysis and History*. New York.

Erikson, E. H. 1975. Forces productives et problèmes de transition. In *Ethnology and History*. Paris.

Evans-Pritchard, E. E. 1940. *Les Nuer: Description des modes de vies et des institutions politiques d'un peuple nilotique*. Paris, 1968.

Evans-Pritchard, E. E. 1961. *Anthropology and History*. Manchester. *Anthropologie et histoire* in *Les anthropologues face à l'histoire et à la religion*. Paris, 1971.

Faber, K. G. 1978. The use of history in political debate. *History and Theory: Studies in the Philosophy of History*, XVII, 4, suppl. 17 (*Historical Consciousness and Political Action*), pp. 19–35.

Favier, J. 1958. *Les archives*. Paris.

Febvre, L. 1933. *Combats pour l'histoire*. Paris.

Ferro, M. 1977. *Cinéma et histoire*. Paris.

Ferro, M. 1980. *Cinéma et histoire*. Paris.

Ferro, M. 1981. *Comment on raconte l'histoire aux enfants à travers le monde entier*. Paris. *Film et histoire*. Paris, 1984.

Ferro, M. 1985. *L'histoire sous surveillance*. Paris.

Finley, M. I. 1971. Archaeology and History. *Daedalus*, 100(1): 168–86.

Finley, M. I. 1981. *Mythe, Mémoire, Histoire*, Paris.

Finley, M. I. 1985. *Sur l'histoire ancienne: La matière, la forme et la méthode*. Paris. 1986.

Fogel, R. W. and G. R. Elton. 1983. *Which Road to the Past? Two Views of History*. New Haven.

Fossier, F. 1977. La charge d'historiographe du XVIe aux XIXe siècle. *Revue Historique*, 258: 73–92.

Foucault, M. 1966. *Les mots et les choses: Une archéologie des sciences humaines*. Paris.

Foucault, M. 1969. *L'archéologie du savoir.* Paris.
Fraisse, P. 1967. *Psychologie du temps.* Paris.
Friedlander, S. 1975. *Histoire et Psychanalyse: Essai sur les possibilités et les limites de la psychohistoire.* Paris.
Folz, R. 1950. *Le souvenir et la légende de Charlemagne dans l'Empire germanique médiéval.* Paris.
Freud, S. 1899. *L'interprétation des rêves.* Paris, 1967.
Fueter, E. 1911. *Geschichte der neueren Historiographie.* Münich-Berlin.
Furet, F. 1971. L'histoire quantitative et la construction du fait historique. *Annales E.S.C.,* 26(1): 63–75.
Furet, F. 1982. *L'atelier de l'histoire.* Paris.
Fustel de Coulanges, N. D. 1862. Leçon faite à l'Université de Strasbourg, in Une leçon d'ouverture et quelques fragments inédits. *Revue de synthèse historique* (1901), 2/3(6), 241–63.
Gabrieli, F. 1966. *L'Islam nella storia: Saggi di storia e storiografia musulmana.* Bari.
Gadamer, H. G. 1963. *Le problème de la conscience historique.* Louvain.
Gadoffre, G., ed. 1987. *Certitudes et incertitudes de l'histoire.* Paris.
Gaeta, F. 1955. *Lorenzo Valla: Filologia e storia nell'Umanesimo italiano.* Naples.
Gallie, W. B. 1963. The historical understanding. In *History and Theory: Studies in the Philosophy of History,* 3(2): 149–202.
Gardiner, P. 1952. *The Nature of Historical Explanation.* London.
Gardner, C. S. 1938. *Chinese Traditional Historiography.* Cambridge, Mass.
Garin, E. 1951. Il concetto della storia nel pensiero del Rinascimento. *Rivista critica di storia della filosofia,* 6(2): 108–18.
Gauchet, M. 1985. *Le désenchantement du monde: Une histoire politique de la religion.* Paris.
Geis, R. R. 1955. Das Geschichtsbild des Talmud. *Saeculum,* 6(2): 119–24.
Genicot, L. 1975. *Les généalogies.* Paris.
Genicot, L. 1980. Simples observations sur la façon d'écrire l'histoire. *Travaux de la Faculté de Philosophie et Lettres de l'Université catholique de Louvain,* 23:4.
Gernet, A. H. 1947. *Anthropologie de la Grèce antique.* Paris.
Gibert, P. 1979. *La Bible à la naissance de l'histoire.* Paris.
Gilbert, F. 1965. *Machiavelli and Guicciardini: Politics and History in Sixteenth-Century Florence.* Princeton, N.J.
Gilbert, F. and St. R. Graubard. 1971. *Historical Studies Today.* New York.
Ginzburg, C. 1976. *Le fromage et les vers: l'univers d'un meunier au XVI*e *siècle.*Paris, 1980.
Glasser, R. 1936. *Studien zur Geschichte des französischen Zeitbegriffs.* Munich.
Glenisson, J. 1965. L'historiographie française contemporaine: Tendances et réalisations. *Vingt-cinq ans de recherche historique en France (1940–1965),* pp. ix-lxiv. Paris.
Goody, J. R. 1977a. Mémoire et apprentissage dans les sociétés avec et sans écriture: la transmission du Bagre. *L'Homme,* 17: 29–52.
Goody, J. R. 1977b. *La raison graphique: La domestication de la pensée sauvage.* Paris, 1979.
Goy, J. 1978. Orale (Histoire), in J. Le Goff et al., *La Nouvelle Histoire.*
Graf, A. 1915. *Roma nella memoria e nelle immaginazioni del Medio Evo.* Turin.

Gramsci, A. 1931–32. *Appunti di filosofia: Materialismo e indealismo,* pp. 1040–93. Turin.

Gramsci, A. 1931–35. *Cahiers de prison,* vols. 2 and 3. Paris, 1983, 1978.

Graus, F. 1975. *Lebendige Vergangenheit: Uberlieferung im Mittelalter und in den Vorstellungen vom Mittelalter.* Cologne, Vienna.

Grossi, P., ed. 1986. *Storia sociale e dimensione giuridica.* Milan.

Grundmann, H. 1965. *Geschichtsschreibung im Mittelalter. Gattungen—Epochen—Eigenart.* Göttingen.

Grunebaum, G. von 1962. *L'identité culturelle de l'Islam.* Paris, 1973.

Guenée, B. 1976–77. Temps de l'histoire et temps de la mémoire au Moyen Âge. *Bulletin de la Société de l'Histoire de France,* no. 487, pp. 25–36.

Guenée, B. 1978. Les généalogies entre l'histoire et la politique: la fierté d'être Capétien, en France, au Moyen Âge, in *Annales E.S.C.,* 33(3):450–77.

Guenée, B. 1980. *Histoire et culture historique dans l'Occident médiéval.* Paris.

Guenée, B. 1987. Introduction (Biographie et biographies) à *Entre l'Eglise et l'Etat: Quatre vies de prélats français à la fin du Moyen Âge,* pp. 7–16. Paris.

Guenée, B., ed. 1977. *Le métier d'historien au Moyen Âge: Etudes sur l'historiographie médiévale.* Paris.

Guerrand, R. H. 1965. *L'Art nouveau en Europe.* Paris.

Guerreau, A. 1980. *Le féodalisme, un horizon théorique.* Paris.

Guillaume, G. 1929. *Temps et verbe: Théorie des aspects, des modes et des temps.* Paris.

Guizot, F. P. G. 1829. *Cours d'histoire moderne I. Histoire générale de la civilisation en Europe.* Paris.

Gumbrecht, H. U., U. Ling-Heer, and P. M. Spangenberg, eds. 1987. *Grundriss der romanischen Literaturen.* Vol. 11(1), *La littérature historiographique des origines à 1500.* Heidelberg.

Halbwachs, M. 1925. *Les cadres sociaux de la mémoire.* Paris.

Halbwachs, M. 1950. *Mémoires collectives.* Paris.

Halevy, D. 1948. *Essai sur l'accélération de l'historie.* Paris.

Halkin, L. E. 1963. *Initiation à la critique historique.* 3d ed. Paris.

Harsin, P. 1963. *Comment on écrit l'histoire.* 7th ed. Liège.

Hartog, F. 1980. *Le miroir d'Hérodote: Essai sur la représentation de l'autre.* Paris.

Haskell, F. 1971. The manufacture of the past in XIXth century painting. *Past and Présent,* no. 53, pp. 109–20.

Hauser, H. 1930. *La modernité du XVIe siècle.* Paris.

Hegel, G. W. F. 1822–30. *La Raison dans l'histoire.* Paris, 1965.

Hegel, G. W. F. 1830–31. *Leçon sur la philosophie de l'histoire.* Paris, 1963.

Hempel, C. G. 1942. *The Function of General Laws in History.* London.

Herlihy, D. and Ch. Klapisch. 1978. *Les Toscans et leurs familles: Une étude du catasto florentin de 1427.* Paris.

Herrick, J. 1954. *The Historical Thought of Fustel de Coulanges.* Washington, D.C.

Hexter, J. H. 1962. *Reappraisals in History.* New York.

Hexter, J. H. 1985. *Histoire sociale, sensibilités collectives et mentalités: Mélanges Robert Mandrou.* Paris, 1985.

Hincker, F. and A. Casanova, eds. 1974. *Aujourd'hui l'histoire.* Paris.

L'Histoire, science humaine du temps présent. Revue de Synthèse, vol. 85. Paris, 1965.

L'Histoire Sociale: Sources et Méthodes: Colloque de l'Ecole Normale Supérieure de Saint-Cloud, 1965. Paris, 1967.

L'Historien entre l'ethnologue et le futurologue. International Seminar in Venice, 1971. Paris, 1972.

Hobsbawm, E. J. 1972. The social function of the past: Some questions. *Past and Present,* 55:3–17.

Hobsbawm, E. J. 1980. The revival of narrative: Some comments. *Past and Present,* no. 86, pp. 3–8.

Hollinger, D. A. 1973. T. S. Kuhn's theory of science and its implications for history. *American Historical Review,* 78: 370–93.

Huizinga, J. 1919. *Le déclin du Moyen Âge.* Paris, 1932.

Huizinga, J. *L'automne du Moyen Âge.* Paris, 1975.

Huizinga, J. 1936. A defintion of the Concept of History. In R. Klibansky and H. J. Platon, eds., *Philosophy and History: Essays Presented to Ernst Cassirer.* Oxford.

Huppert, G. 1968. Naissance de l'histoire de France: Les Recherches d'Estienne Pasquier. *Annales E.S.C.,* pp. 69–105.

Huppert, G. 1970. *L'idée de l'histoire parfaite.* Paris, 1973.

Huyghebaert, H. 1972. *Les documents nécrologiques.* Paris.

Ibn Khaldun. *Al-Muqqaddima: Discours sur l'histoire universelle.* 3 vols. Beyreuth, 1967–1968.

Iggers, G. G. 1971. *Deutsche Geschichtswissenschaft: Eine Kritik der traditionnellen Geschichtsauffassung von Herder bis zur Gegenwart.* Munich.

Iggers, G. G. 1973. "Historicism." In Ph. P. Wiener, ed., *Dictionary of the History of Ideas: Studies of Selected Pivotal Ideas,* 2: 456–64.

Iggers, G. G. 1974. Die "Annales" und ihre Kritiker: Probleme modernen französischer Sozialgeschichte. Historische Zeitschrift, 219: 578–608.

Iggers, G. G. 1978. *Neue Geschichtswissenschaft: Vom Historismus zur historischen Sozialwissenschaft.* Stuttgart.

Iggers, G. G. 1980. Introduction: The transformation of historical studies in Historical Perspective. In Iggers and Parker, *International Handbook of Historical Studies,* pp. 1–14.

Iggers, G. G. 1987. *Images et Histoire,* nos. 9–10. Paris.

Iggers, G. G. and H. T. Parker, eds., 1979. *International Handbook of Historical Studies: Contemporary Research and History.* Westport, Conn.

Jacob, F. 1970. *La logique du vivant: Une histoire de l'hérédité.* Paris.

Jauss, H. R. 1955. *Zeit und Erinnerung in Marcel Proust, "A la recherche du temps perdu."* Heidelberg.

Jockel, S. 1985. *"Nouvelle histoire" und Literaturwissenschaft.* 2 vols. Rheinfelden, 1985.

Jockel, S. 1983. Histoire des Sciences et Mentalités. *Revue de Synthèse* (July-December), special number 111–112.

Joutard, P. 1977. *La légende des Camisards: Une sensibilité au passé.* Paris.

Joutard, P. 1983. *Ces voix qui nous veinnent du passé.* Paris.

Junker, D. and P. Reisinger. 1974. Was kann Objektivität in der Geschichtswissenschaft heissen und wie ist sie möglich? In Th. Schieder, ed., *Methodenprobleme der Geschichtswissenschaft,* in *Historische Zeitschrist,* 3:1–46.

Kelley, D. R. 1970. *Foundations of Modern Historical Scholarship: Language, Law, and History in the French Renaissance.* New York.
Keuck, K. 1934. *Historia; Geschichte des Wortes und seiner Bedeutung in der Antike und in den romanischen Sprachen.* Emsdetten.
Keylor, W. 1975. *Academy and Community: The Foundation of the French Historical Profession.* New York.
Koselleck, R. 1979. *Vergangene Zukunft. Zur Semantik geschichtlicher Zeiten.* Frankfort.
Kosselleck, R. and W. D. Stempel, eds. 1973. *Geschichte, Ereignis, und Erzählung.* Munich.
Kracauer, S. 1966. "Time and History." *History and Theory: Studies in the Philosophy of History.* V, suppl. 6 (*History and the Concept of Time*), pp. 65–78.
Kruger, K. H. 1976. *Die Universalchroniken.* Paris.
Kuhn, Th. S. 1957. *La révolution copernicienne.* Paris, 1973.
Kula, W. 1958. *Réflexions sur l'histoire.*
Kula, W. 1961. L'objectivité historique et les valeurs. In R. Aron, ed., *L'histoire et ses interprétations: Entretiens autour d'Arnold Toynbee,* pp. 172–74. Paris.
Kula, W. 1985. *L'Acte historique et son sujet. Mi-Dit,* special number 10–11.
Labrousse, E. 1933. *Esquisse du mouvement des prix et des revenus en France au XVIIIe siècle.* Paris.
Labrousse, E., ed. 1967. *Ordres et classes. Colloque d'histoire sociale,* Saint-Cloud, May 1867. Paris, 1973.
Lacoste, Y. 1966. *Ibn Khaldoun: Naissance de l'histoire, passé du Tiers Monde.* Paris.
Lacouture, J. 1978. *L'histoire immédiate.* In Le Goff et al. 1978: 270–93.
Lacroix, B. 1971. *L'historien au Moyan Âge.* Paris.
Lammers, W. ed. 1965. *Geschichtsdenken und Geschichsbild im Mittelalter.* Darmstadt.
Landfester, R. 1972. *Historia magistra vitae: Untersuchungen zur humanistischen Geschichtstheorie des 14. bis 16. Jahrhunderts.* Geneva.
Langlois, Ch. V. and Ch. Seignobos. 1898. *Introduction aux études historiques.* 3d ed. Paris, 1902.
Lefebvre, H. 1962. *Introduction à la modernité.* Paris.
Lefebvre, H. 1970. *La fin de l'histoire.* Paris.
Lefebvre, G. 1945–46. *La naissance de l'historiographie moderne.* Paris, 1971.
Leff, G. 1969. *History and Social Theory.* London.
Lefort, C. 1952. Société "sans histoire." *Cahiers internationaux de sociologie,* **XII**. *Les formes de l'histoire, essai d'anthropologie politique.* Paris, 1978.
Le Goff, J. 1971. Is politics still the backbone of history? In F. Gilbert and S. R. Graubard, eds., *Historical Studies Today,* pp. 337–58. New York. French version: L'histoire politique est-elle toujours l'épine dorsale de l'histiore? In J. Le Goff, *L'imaginaire médiéval,* pp. 335–49.
Le Goff, J. 1974. Il peso del passata nella coscienza colletiva degli italiani. In F. L. Cavaza and S. R. Graubard, eds., *Il casa italiana, Italia anni '70,* pp. 344–52. Milan.
Le Goff, J. 1978. L'histoire nouvelle. In Le Goff, Chartier, and Revel, *La nouvelle histoire,* pp. 210–41. Paris.
Le Goff, J. 1982. *Intervista sulla storia.* Bari.
Le Goff, J. 1985. *L'imaginaire médiévale.* Paris.
Le Goff, J. 1986. *Storia e Memoria.* Paris.

Le Goff and P. Toubert. 1975. Une histoire totale du Moyen Age est-elle possible? Actes du 100th Congres Nationale des Sociétiés savantes, Paris, 1975. 1: *Tendances, perspectives, et methodes de l'histoire medievale,* pp. 31–34. Paris, 1977.

Le Goff and P. Nora, eds. 1974. *Faire de l'histoire.* 2d ed., Paris 1986.

Le Goff, J., R. Chartier, and J. Revel. eds. 1978. *La nouvelle histoire.* Paris; new complete edition, Brussels, 1988.

Leroi-Gourhan, A. 1964–65. *Le geste et la parole.* Vol. 2: *La mémoire et les rythmes.* Paris.

Leroi-Gourhan, A. 1974. Les voies de l'histoire avant l'écriture. In Le Goff and Nora, eds. *Faire de l'histoire,* 1: 93–105.

Le Roy Ladurie, E. 1967. *Histoire du climat depuis l'an mil.* 2d ed., Paris, 1983.

Le Roy Ladurie, E. 1973, 1978. *Le territoire de l'historien.* 2 vols. Paris.

Lévi-Strauss, C. 1962. *La pensée sauvage.* Paris.

Lévi-Strauss, C., M. Auge, and M. Godelier,1975. Anthropologie, histoire, idéologie. *L'Homme,* 15(3–4): 177–88.

Lewis, I. M. 1968. *History and Social Anthropology.* London-New York.

Lhomme, J. 1967. *Economies et histoire.* Geneva.

Loraux, N. 1980a. L'oubli dans la cité. *Le temps de la réflexion,* 1: 213–242.

Loraux, N. 1980b. Thucydide n'est pas un collègue. *Quaderni di Storia* (July-December), 12: 55–81.

Loraux, N. and P. Vidal Naquet. 1979. *La formation de l'Athènes bourgeoise: Essai d'historiographie 1750–1850.* In R. R. Bolgar, ed., *Classical Influences on Western Thought,* pp. 162–222.London.

Lubasz, H., ed. 1964. Symposium: Uses of Theory in the Study of History (Harvard, 1961), in *History and Theory,* 3/1.

Lubbe, H. 1977. *Geschichtsbegriff und Geschichtsinteresse: Analytik und Pragmatik der Historie.* Bâle.

Lukacs, G. 1923. *Histoire et conscience de classe.* Paris, 1960.

Lyons, J. 1968. *Introduction to Theoretical Linguistics.* London.

McLennan, G. 1981. *Marxism and the Methodologies of History.* London.

McLuhan, M. 1962. *La galaxie Gutenberg.* Paris, 1967.

Mairet, G. 1974. *Le discours et l'historique: Essai sur la représentation historienne du temps.* Paris.

Malrieu, Ph. 1953. *Les origines de la conscience du temps: Les attitudes temporelles de l'enfant.* Paris.

Mandelbaum, M. 1971. *History, Man, and Reason: A Study in Nineteenth Century Thought.* Baltimore.

Mandelbaum, M. 1977. *The Anatomy of Historical Knowledge.* Baltimore.

Mandrou, R. Art. Histoire. Histoire des mentalités. *Encyclopaedia Universalis,* 8: 436–38.

Marczewski, J. V. 1965. *Introduction à l'histoire quantitative.* Geneva, Paris.

Marin, L. 1978. *Le récit est un piège.* Paris.

Marin, L. 1979. Pouvoir du récit et récit du pouvoir. *Actes de la recherche en sciences sociales,* no. 25, pp. 23–43.

Marrou, H. I. 1950. *L'ambivalence du temps de l'histoire chez saint Augustin.* Institut d'études médiévales, Montreal.

Marrou, H. I. 1961. Qu'est-ce que l'histoire? In Ch. Samaran, *L'histoire et ses méthodes,* 11: 1–23.
Marrou, H. I. 1968. *Théologie de l'histoire.* Paris.
Marwick, A. 1970. *The Nature of History.* London.
Marx, K. 1857–58. *Grundrisse der Kritik der politischen Ökonomie.* Berlin,1953.
Marx, K. 1867. *Le Capital.* 2 vols. Paris, 1971.
Massicotte, G. 1981. *L'histoire problème: La méthode de Lucien Febvre.* Paris.
Mazzarino, S. 1966. *Il pensiero storico classico.* 3 vols. Bari.
Meinecke, F. 1936. *Die Entstehung des Historismus.* Munich-Berlin.
Mélanges René Van Santbergen. 1984. Special number of *Cahiers de Clio.*
Meyerson, J. 1956. Le temps la mémoire, l'histoire. *Journal de psychologie,* 53: 333–54.
Mitre Fernandez, E. 1982. *Historiografia y mentalidades historicas en la Europa medieval.* Madrid.
Momigliano, A. 1977. *Essays in Ancient and Modern Historiography.* Oxford.
Momigliano, A. 1986. *Problèmes d'historiographie ancienne et moderne.* Paris.
Mommsen, W. J. 1978. Social conditioning and social relevance in historical judgments. *History and Theory: Studies in the Philosophy of History,* 17(4): 19–35.
Moniot, H. 1974. L'histoire des peuples sans histoire. In J. Le Goff and P. Nora, 1986: 106–23.
Moniot, H. 1983. *Enseigner l'histoire: Des manuels à la mémoire.* Paris.
Moraze, Ch. 1968. L'Histoire et l'unité des sciences de l'homme. *Annales E.S.C.,* pp. 233–40.
Moraze, Ch. 1967, *La logique de l'histoire.* Paris.
Morgan, J. S. 1966. Le temps et l'intemporel dans le décor mural de deux églises romanes. *Mélanges offerts à René Crozet,* 1:531–48.
Morgan, L. H. 1877. *Ancient Society: or Research in the Lines of Human Progress from Savagery through Barbarism to Civilization.* Chicago.
Morin, E. 1975. *L'esprit du temps: Une mythologie moderne.* Paris.
Morin, E. and M. Piattelli Palmarini, eds. 1974. *L'unité de l'homme: Invariants biologiques et universaux culturels.* Paris.
Nadel, G. H., ed. *Studies in the Philosophy of History.* New York, 1965.
Namer, G. 1983. *Batailles pour la mémoire, la commémoration en France, de 1945 à nos jours.* Paris.
Namer, G. 1987. *Mémoire et Société.* Paris.
Nitschke, A. 1981. *Historische Verhaltensforschung.* Stuttgart.
Nora, P. 1962. Ernest Lavisse: Son rôle dans la formation du sentiment national. *Revue historique,* 228: 73–106.
Nora, P. 1966. Le "fardeau de l'histoire" aux Etats-Unis. In *Mélanges Pierre Renouvin: Etudes d'Histoire des Relations Internationales,* pp. 51–74. Paris.
Nora, P. 1974. Le retour de l'événement. In J. Le Goff and P. Nora, 1974: 210–28. Paris.
Nora, P. 1978. Mémoire collective. In Le Goff et al. 1978. Paris.
Nora, P. 1978. Présent. In J. Le Goff et al. 1978: 467–72. Paris.
Nora, P., ed. 1984. *Les lieux de mémoire.* I: *La République,* Paris.
Nora, P. 1986. *Les lieux de mémoire.* II: *La Nation,* 3 vols. Paris.

Notopoulos, J. A. 1938. Mnemosyne in Oral Literature. *Transactions and Proceedings of the American Philological Association,* 69: 465–93.
Oexle, O. G. 1976. Memoria und Memorialüberlieferung im früheren Mittelalter. *Frühmittelalterliche Studien,* 10: 70–95.
Orsi, P. L. 1983. La storia delle mentalità. In Bloch and Febvre, *Rivista di storia contemporanea,* pp. 370–395.
Ozouf, M. 1976. *La Fête révolutinonaire: 1789–1799.* Paris.
Passmore, J. A. 1958. The objectivity of history. *Philosophy,* 33: 97–110.
Pedech, P. 1964. *La méthodé historique de Polybe.* Paris.
Perelman, Ch. 1969. *Les catégories en histoire.* Brussels.
Périodisation en Histoire des Sciences et de la Philosophie. 1987. Special number of the *Reveue de Synthèse,* no.3–4.
Pertusi, A., ed. 1970. *La storiografic veneziana fino al secolo* XVI. Florence.
Les philosophies de l'histoire. Paris, 1980.
Piaget, J. 1946. *Le développement de la notion de temps chez l'enfant.* Paris.
Piaget, J. and B. Inhelder. 1968. *Mémoire et intelligence.* Paris.
Pillorget, R. 1982. La biographie comme genre historique: Sa situation actuelle en France. *Revue d'histoire diplomatique* (January-June).
Plumb, J. H. 1969. *The Death of the Past.* London.
Pomian, K. 1975. L'histoire de la science et l'historie de l'historie. *Annales, E.S.C.,* 30(5): 935–52.
Pomian, K. 1984. *L'ordre du temps.* Paris.
Popper, K. R. 1960. *Misère de l'historicisme.* Paris, 1956.
Posner, E. 1972. *Archives in the Ancient World.* Cambridge, Mass.
Poulat, E. 1971. "Modernisme." In *Encyclopaedia Universalis,* 11: 135–37. Paris.
Poulet, G. 1950. *Etudes sur le temps humain.* Paris.
Preiswerk, R. and D. Perrot. 1975. *Ethnocentrisme et histoire: L'Afrique, l'Amérique indienne et l'Asie dans les manuels occidentaux.* Paris.
Problèmes et méthodes de la biographie. Paris, 1985. (Actes du Colloque Sorbonne, mai 1985).
Pulleyblank, E. G. 1955. *Chinese History and World History.* London.
Rabb, T. K. and R. I. Rotbarg. 1982. *The New History: The 1980s and Beyond.* Princeton, N.J.
Ranger, T. O. 1977. Memorie personali ed esperienza popolare nell'Africa centro-orientale. *Quaderni Storici,* 12(35): 359–402.
Ranke, L. von, 1973. *Theory and Practice of History.* Indianapolis.
Reappraisals. 1968. A new look at history: The social sciences and history. *Journal of Contemporary History,* 3: 2.
Redondi, P., ed. 1987. *Science: The Renaissance of a History.* Special number of *History and Technology,* 4: 1–4.
Revel, J. 1979. Histoire et sciences sociales: Le paradigme des Annales. *Annales, E.S.C.* (1979).
Revel, J. and R. Chartier. 1978. *"Annales."* In Le Goff et al. 1978: 26–33.
Ricœur, P. 1955. *Histoire et vérité.* 2d ed., Paris, 1955.
Ricœur, P. 1961. Histoire de la philosophie et historicité. In R. Aron, ed., *L'histoire et*

ses interprétations: Entretiens antour d'Arnold Toynbee, pp. 217–27. Paris.
Ricœur, P. 1983. *Temps et récit.* Paris.
Romano, R. 1978. *La storiografia italiana oggi.* Milan.
Rosenberg, H. 1959. *The Tradition of the New.* New York.
Rosenthal, F. 1952. *A History of Muslim Historiography.* Leyde.
Rossi, P. 1956. *Lo storicismo tedesco contemporaneo.* 3d ed., Turin, 1979.
Rossi, P., ed. 1983. *La Storia della storiografia oggi.* Milan.
Rousset, P. 1951. La conception de l'historie à l'époque féodale. In *Mélanges d'histoire du Moyen Âge, dédiés à la mémoire de Louis Halphen,* pp. 623–33. Paris.
Rousset, P. 1966. Un problème de méthodê: l'événement et sa perception. *Mélanges R. Crozet,* pp. 315–21. Paris.
Roy, B. and P. Zumthor. 1985. *Jeux de mémoire: Aspects de la mnémotechnie médiévale.* Paris.
Russen, J. and H. Sussmith. 1980. *Theorien in der Geschichtswissenschaft.* Düsseldorf.
Salmon, P. 1969. *Histoire et critique.* 2d ed., Brussels, 1976.
Samaran, Ch. éd. 1961. *L'histoire et ses méthodes,* in *Encyclopédie de la Pléiade,* XI, Paris, Gallimard.
Sanson, R. 1976. *Le 14 juillet (1789–1975). Fête et conscience nationale.* Paris.
Saussure, F. de 1906–11. *Cours de linguistique générale,* Lausanne-Paris, 1916.
Schaff, A. 1970. trad. du polonais, *Histoire et vérité. Essai sur l'objectivité de la connaissance historique.* Paris, 1971.
Schieder, Th. 1978. The role of historical consciousness in political action, in *History and Theory, Studies in the Philosophy of history,* XVII, 4, suppl. 17 (*Historical Consciousness and Political Action*), pp. 1–18.
Schmid, K. and J. Wollasch, eds. 1984. *Memoria. Der geschichtliche Zeugniswert des liturgischen Gedenkens im Mittelalter.* Munich.
Schmidt, R. 1955–1956. Aetates Mundi. Die Weltalter als Gliederungsprinzip der Geschichte. *Zeitschriftfür Kirchengeschichte,* 67:288–317.
Schonen, S. de 1974. *La mémoire: connaissance active du passé.* Paris.
Schulin, E. 1973. *Die Frage nach der Zukunft in Geschichte heute. Positionen, Tendenzen und Probleme.* Göttingen.
Seckler, M. 1967. *Le salut et l'histoire. La pensée de saint Thomas d'Aquin sur la théologie de l'historie.* Paris.
Shorter, E. 1971. *The Historian and the Computer. A Practical Guide.* Englewood Cliffs, N.J.
Silvestre, H. 1965. "Quanto iuniores, tanto perspicaciores". Antécedents à la querelle des anciens et des modernes, in *Publications de l'Université Lovanium de Kinshasa. Recueil commémoratif du Xe Anniversaire de la Faculté de Philosophie et Lettres,* pp. 231, 255. Paris.
Simmel, G. 1984. *Les problèmes de la philosophie de l'histoire,* (préface de R. Boudon), Paris.
Simon, E. 1928. Ranke und Hegel, in *Historische Zeitschrift,* suppl. 15.
Sirinelli, J. 1961. *Les vues historiques d'Eusèbe de Césarée durant la période pérnicéenne.* Dakar.
Sous l'histoire la mémoire. 1980. no. 30.

Spengler, O. 1918–22. *Le déclin de l'Occident,* 2 vols. Paris, 1948.
Spuler, B. 1955. Islamische und abendländische Geschichtsschreibung. In *Saeculum,* 6(2):125–37.
Stadler, P. 1789–1871. *Geschichtsschreibung und historisches Denken in Frankreich.* Zurich, 1958.
Starr, G. C. 1966. Historical and philosophical time, in *History and Theory. Studies in the Philosophy of History,* V, suppl. 6 (*History and the Concept of Time*), pp. 24–35.
Stelling-Michaud, J. 1959. Quelques problèmes du temps au Moyen Âge, in *Etudes suisses d'histoire générale,* XVII.
Stern, F., ed. 1956. *The Varieties of History: Voltaire to the Present.* Cleveland.
Stoianovich, T. 1976. *French Historical Method: The Annales Paradigm.* Ithaca.
Stone, L. 1979. Retour au récit ou réflexions sur une nouvelle vieille histoire, in *Le débat,* Sept. 1980, pp. 116–142.
Stone, L. 1981. *The Past and the Present.* Boston.
Struever, N. S. 1970. *The Langauge of History in the Renaissance: Rhetoric and Historical Consciousness in Florentine Humanism.* Princeton.
Svenbro, J. 1976. *La parole et le marbre. Aux origines de la poétique grecque.* Lund.
Tagliacozzo, G., ed. 1969. *Giambattista Vico. An International Symposium.* Baltimore.
Temps, mémoire, tradition au Moyen Âge. 1982. Aix-en-Provence.
Tenenti, A. 1957. *Sens de la mort et amour de la vie à la Renaissance en Italie et en France.* L'Harmattan, 1983.
Tenenti, A. 1963. La storiografia in Europa dal Quattro al Seicento, in *Nuove Questioni di storia Moderna.* Milan.
Thomas, L. 1963. History and Anthropology, in *Past and Present* (April), no. 24.
Thompson, J. Westfall. 1942. *A History of Historical Writing.* 2 vols. New York.
Thomson, P. 1978. *The Voice of the Past: Oral History.* Oxford University Press.
Thuillier, G. and J. Tulard. 1986. *La méthode en histoire.* Paris.
Tilly, Ch. 1984. The old new social history and the new old social history, in *Review,* 7:363–406.
Topolski, J. 1973. *Methodology of History.* Boston, 1976.
Touraine, A. 1977. *Un désir d'histoire.* Paris.
Toynbee, A. J. 1934–39. *L'histoire. Un essai d'interprétation.* Paris, 1951.
Toynbee, A. J. 1961. *L'Histoire et ses interprétations. Entretiens autour d'Arnold Toynbee.* Paris.
Trigger, B. J. 1968. Major Concepts of Archeology in Historical Perspective, *Man,* 3.
Triuizi, A. 1977. Storia dell'Africa e fonti orali, in *Quaderni Storici,* 12(35):470–80.
Troeltsch, E. 1924. *Der Historismus und seine Überwindung.* Berlin.
Tulard, J. 1971. *Le mythe de Napoléon.* Paris.
Valery, P. 1931. *Regard sur le monde actuel.* Paris.
Vedrine, H. 1975. *Les philosophies de l'histoire. Déclin ou crise?* Paris.
Vendryes, J. 1921. *Le langage, introduction linguistique à l'histoire.* Paris, 1968.
Vendryes, P. 1952. *De la probabilité en histoire. L'exemple de l'expédition d'Egypte.* Paris.
Vernant, J.-P. 1965, *Mythe et pensée chez les Grecs. Etudes de psychologie historique.* Paris, 1985.
Vernant, J.-P. and P. Vidal Naquet. 1972. *Mythe et tragédie en Grèce ancienne.* Paris, 1986.

Veron, E. 1981. *Construire l'événement. Les médias et l'accident de Three Miles Island.* Paris.

Veyne, P. 1968. *Histoire,* in *Enciclopedia Universalis,* 8:423–24. Paris.

Veyne, P. 1971. *Comment on écrit l'histoire. Essai d'épistémologie.* Paris.

Veyne, P. 1973. *Le pain et le cirque.* Paris.

Veyne, P. 1976. *L'inventaire des différences.* Paris.

Vidal-Naquet, P. 1960, Temps des dieux et temps des hommes, in *Revue d'histoire des religions,* 157:55–80.

Vidal-Naquet, P. 1987. *Les assassins de la mémoire.* Paris.

Vierhaus, R. 1972. Was ist Geschichte? In G. Alföldy, ed., *Probleme der Geschichtswissenschaft.* Düsseldorf.

Vilar, P. 1973. Histoire marxiste, histoire en construction. Essai de dialogue avec Althusser, in *Annales E.S.C.,* 27(1):165–98.

Vilar, P. 1982. *Une histoire en construction. Approche marxiste et problématiques conjoncturelles.* Paris.

Violante, C., ed. 1982. *La storia locale. Temi, fonti e metodi della ricerca.* Bologne.

Vivanti, C. 1962. Alle origini dell'idea di civiltà: le scoperte geografiche e gli scritti di Henri de la Popelinière, in *Rivista storica italiana,* 79:1–25.

Vovelle, M., ed. 1974. *Mourir autrefois. Attitudes collectives devant la mort aux* XVIIe *et* XVIIIe *siècles.* Paris.

Vovelle, M., ed. 1978. L'histoire et la longue durée, in le Goff, *Chartier et Revel,* pp. 316–43. Paris.

Wachtel, N. 1971. *La vision des vaincus, les Indiens du Pérou devant la conquête espagnole.* Paris.

Ward-Perkins, J. B. 1965. Memoria, Martyr's Tomb and Martyr's Church, in *Internationalen Kongresses für christliche Archäologie.* Vatican City, 1969.

Weber, M. 1922. *Essai sur la théorie de la science.* Paris, 1965.

Weinrich, H. 1971. *Le Temps: le récit et le commentaire.* Paris, 1973.

White, H. V. 1966. The Burden of History. In *History and Theory,* 5:111–134.

White, H. V. 1973. *Metahistory, the Historical Imagination in Nineteenth Century Europe.* Baltimore.

Wilcox, D. J. 1969. *The Development of Florentine Humanist Historiography.* Cambridge, Mass.

Wolman, B. B., ed. 1971. *The Psychoanalytic Interpretation of History.* New York.

Yardeni, M. 1964. La conception de l'histoire dans l'œuvre de La Popeliniere. In *Revue d'histoire moderne et contemporaine,* 11:109–26.

Yates, F. A. 1966. *L'art de la Mémoire.* Paris, 1975.

Yavetz, Z. 1976. Why Rome? Zeitgeist and ancient historian in early 19th century Germany, in *American Journal of Philology,* 97(3)276–96.

Yerushalmi, Y. H. 1982. *Zakhor, histoire juive et mémoire juive.* Paris, 1984.

Zimmermann, A., ed. 1974. *Antiqui und Moderni Traditionsbewasstgein und Fortschrittsbewusstsein im späten Mittelalter.* Berlin-New York.

Zonabend, F. 1980. *La mémoire longue. Temps et histoires au village,* Paris.

A NOTE ON THE AUTHOR

Jacques Le Goff was born in Toulon, France, in 1924. He was trained at the École normale supérieure in Paris and is a former member of the École Française de Rome. He also studied at the University of Prague and at the University of Oxford (Lincoln College). He held positions at the University of Lille and at the Centre national de la recherche scientifique; since 1960 he has been at the École pratique des hautes études (since 1975 known as the École des hautes études en sciences sociales), where he succeeded Fernand Braudel as president and where he is director of studies.

Le Goff has published numerous works, all of which have been translated into several foreign languages. Among them are *Medieval Callings, The Medieval Imagination, Time, Work, and Culture in the Middle Ages, The Birth of Purgatory, Your Money or Your Life: Economy and Religion in the Middle Ages,* and *Constructing the Past: Essays in Historical Method.* In the tradition of the *Annales* school (he is codirector of the journal), he remains faithful to the idea of a total history. He is a pioneer in the domain of historical anthropology and the history of mentalities. He has taken an interest in historical methodology and has coedited, with Pierre Nora,

Faire de l'histoire (3 vols., 1974; rpt. Folio, 1986), and with Roger Chartier and Jacques Revel, *L'histoire nouvelle* (Retz, 1978).

From 1983 to 1985 Le Goff presided over the Commission nationale pour la rénovation de l'enseignement de l'histoire et de la géographie. Since 1968 he has been the moderator of the radio program "Les lundis de l'histoire," and in 1986 he received the Diderot-Universalis prize. He continues to work as a consultant for the *Encyclopaedia Brittanica.* In 1987 he was awarded the Grand Prix national de l'histoire.

INDEX